Science and Belief in the Nuclear Age

Books by Peter E. Hodgson

Physics

The Optical Model of Elastic Scattering. Oxford: Clarendon Press, 1963.

Nuclear Reactions and Nuclear Structure. Oxford: Clarendon Press, 1971.

Nuclear Heavy-Ion Reactions. Oxford University Press, 1978.

Growth Points in Nuclear Physics. Vol. 1. Oxford: Pergamon Press, 1980.

Growth Points in Nuclear Physics. Vol. 2. Oxford: Pergamon Press, 1980.

Growth Points in Nuclear Physics. Vol. 3. Oxford: Pergamon Press, 1981.

Nucleon Momentum and Density Distributions in Nuclei (with A. N. Antonov and I. Zh. Petkov. Oxford: Clarendon Press, 1988.

Spacetime and Electromagnetism (with J. R. Lucas). Oxford: Clarendon Press, 1990.

Pre-Equilibrium Nuclear Reactions (with E. Gadioli). Oxford: Clarendon Press, 1991.

Nucleon Correlations in Nuclei (with A. N. Antonov and I. Zh. Petkov) Berlin: Springer-Verlag, 1993.

The Nucleon Optical Potential. Singapore: World Scientific, 1994.

Introductory Nuclear Physics (with E. Gadioli and E. Gadioli-Erba). Oxford University Press, 1996.

Nuclear Physics (with S. A. Sofianos). Pretoria: University of South Africa, 1997.

Physics and Society

Nuclear Physics in Peace and War. London: Burns and Oates, 1961.

Our Nuclear Future? Belfast: Christian Journals Ltd., 1983.

Science and Christianity. Tokyo: Kinseido, 1992.

Energy and Environment. Tokyo: Kinseido, 1995.

Energy and Environment. London: Bowerdean, 1997.

Science, Technology and Society. Tokyo: Kinseido, 1999.

Nuclear Power, Energy and the Environment. London: Imperial College Press, 1999.

Christianity and Science. Johannesburg: St. Augustine College, 2002.

The Roots of Science and its Fruits. London: The Saint Austin Press, 2003.

Science and Belief in the Nuclear Age. Naples: Sapientia Press, 2005.

Theology and Modern Physics. Aldershot: Ashgate Publishing, 2005.

Science and Belief in the Nuclear Age

PETER E. HODGSON

Sapientia Press
of Ave Maria University

Requests for permission to make copies of any part of the work should be directed to:

Sapientia Press
of Ave Maria University
24 Frank Lloyd Wright Drive
Ann Arbor, MI 48106
888-343-8607

Cover Design: Eloise Anagnost

Printed in the United States of America.

Library of Congress Control Number: 2005900803

ISBN 1-932589-20-1

Table of Contents

Preface

THE EXPLOSIVE GROWTH of science during the last hundred years has made possible a vast range of technological applications that have transformed our lives. For the first time in history the world is united by easy communication and travel; the shops are full of new products that make our lives easier than ever before. All this has been made possible by the deeper understanding of the natural world that has been revealed by the work of generations of scientists.

These developments raise urgent moral problems, and we are faced by many critical choices that will affect our future for good or for ill. The Church has given a strong lead, but much remains to be done.

Some of these problems are discussed in the articles collected here. Most of them were written in response to particular needs, and inevitably there is some repetition. They include short articles written for newspapers and other periodicals and longer and more detailed treatments of particular subjects.

The principal theme is that when considering these urgent problems it is first of all necessary to establish the truth. The first section is therefore devoted to the problems of science and belief, beginning with a summary of some of the teachings of Pope John Paul II. Science itself, on which all these new developments depend, first attained its modern form in the Christian civilisation of the High Middle Ages, as described in the second article. The lives of Newman and Chesterton provide examples of men who devoted their lives to a search for the truth, whatever the personal cost. Two articles follow on the relation between science and belief. Finally there is a reflection on the connection between Physics and the Catholic faith.

The second section is devoted to philosophical studies of science from several points of view beginning with reviews of books by Mariano Artigas and Stanley Jaki, followed by one by Mary Midgley. Then there are brief notes on the similarities between science and religion, fraud, beauty, chance and time.

The most important advances due to modern physics have come from studies of the atomic and nuclear worlds. First of all Einstein extended Newtonian dynamics to the domain of very high energies by his theory of relativity. This has been widely believed to have theological implications, and these merit detailed discussion. In order to study the atomic and nuclear worlds scientists developed quantum mechanics. This is a very successful theory, and enables a wide range of phenomena to be calculated, often to high accuracy. It is however difficult to understand, and raises many problems of interpretation that are discussed in the remainder of the third section. Quantum mechanics has been interpreted as showing that the world is inherently indeterminate, and if so it can provide a possible explanation of how God can act on the world without overriding the laws of physics. However it is an essentially statistical theory that applies to ensembles of similar systems, but not to particular events. There are other interpretations of quantum mechanics that are consistent with a deterministic world.

One of the most important applications of nuclear physics is the possibility that it can provide the energy on which our civilisation depends. This raises many moral problems, which have been addressed by the Pontifical Academy of Sciences, as described in the fourth section. To decide on the best source of the needed energy, it is essential to consider the capacity, cost, safety, reliability and effects on the environment of all possible sources. Many aspects of nuclear power, including nuclear waste, climate change and global warming, are considered in the subsequent articles in this section.

The final section is devoted to general considerations of the place of science in our society and the optimum conditions for its proper use, including the contribution of scientists to the life of the Church.

These essays can do no more than serve as introductions to vast subjects, and further information can be obtained in the references cited and in the my book *The Roots of Science and its Fruits* published in 2003 by the Saint Austin Press.   ⚛

Peter E. Hodgson
Oxford, 2004

Acknowledgments

I AM PARTICULARLY GRATEFUL to the Ashgate Press for permitting me to reproduce several sections from my book Theology and Modern Physics. I also thank the editors and publishers of the following journals for permission to reprint articles and book reviews: *The Catholic Herald* (11, 12); *The Chesterton Review* (4); *Contemporary Physics* (8, 9, 19, 22); *Convergence* (26); *The Fellowship of Catholic Scholars Quarterly* (7, 20); *History and Philosophy of the Life Sciences* (10); *The Month* (23); *Sapientia* (3); *The St. Austin Review* (1, 5, 6, 14, 15); *Second Spring* (13); and *Zygon* (16, 18).

PART I
Theology

CHAPTER 1

Pope John Paul II and Science*

THROUGHOUT his pontificate, Pope John Paul II has repeatedly shown his interest in science and its applications. During his period as Cardinal Archbishop of Cracow he held discussion meetings with university-wide professors on a range of subjects of current interest. The secretary of these meetings was Dr. Josef Zycinski, professor of the philosophy of science at the Pontifical Academy in Cracow, subsequently Bishop of Tarnow and now Archbishop of Lublin and Grand Chancellor of the Catholic university there.

The Pope strongly supports the Pontifical Academy of Sciences, which holds meetings in Rome devoted to specialised studies of a wide range of scientific problems and publishes the results in a series of reports. The subjects of papal addresses to these meetings have included energy and humanity, the nuclei of galaxies, biological experimentation, the protection of the environment, the responsibilities of scientists, the impact of space experimentation on mankind, cosmic rays in interplanetary space, science for peace, chemical reactions and the environment, tropical forests and the conservation of species, science for development, and resources and population.

The Vatican Observatory continues at Castel Gandolpho near Rome, though most of the scientific observations are now made from an observatory in Arizona.

---

* Reprinted with permission from *St. Austin Review* (October 2002): 26.

The subjects of the Pope's other addresses range from fundamental questions such as the freedom and the responsibility of scientists to seek the truth, through general scientific problems such as cosmology to the practical questions concerning the environment and the science of medicine.

In his encyclical letter *Fides et Ratio* the Pope speaks directly to scientists: "In expressing my admiration and in offering encouragement to these brave pioneers of scientific research, to whom humanity owes much of its current development, I would urge them to continue their efforts without ever abandoning the horizon within which scientific and technical achievements are wedded to the philosophical and ethical values which are the distinctive and indelible mark of the human person. Scientists are well aware that the search for truth, even when it concerns a finite reality of the world of man, is never-ending, but always points beyond to something higher than the immediate object of study, to the questions which give access to Mystery."[1]

In an address to university professors the Pope once again strongly encouraged scientists in their work, and urged them to "make universities 'cultural laboratories,' in which theology, philosophy, human sciences and natural sciences may engage in constructive dialogue, looking to the moral law as an intrinsic requirement of research and a condition for its full value in seeking out the truth." Indeed, "a culture without truth does not safeguard freedom but places it at risk. The demands of truth and morality neither degrade nor abolish our freedom, but on the contrary enable freedom to exist and liberate it from its own inherent threats. In this sense, the words of Christ remain decisive: 'The truth will set you free.'"

"Rooted in the perspective of truth, Christian humanism implies first of all an openness to the Transcendent. It is here that we find the truth and grandeur of the human person, the only person in the visible world capable of self-awareness and recognising that he is surrounded by that supreme Mystery which both reason and faith call God. What is needed is a humanism in which the perspectives of

---

[1] *Fides et Ratio*, paragraph 106.

science and faith no longer seem to be in conflict. Yet we cannot be satisfied with an ambiguous reconciliation of the kind favoured by a culture which doubts the very ability of reason to arrive at the truth. This path runs the risk of misconstruing faith by reducing it to a feeling, to emotion, to art: in the end stripping faith of all critical foundation. But this would not be Christian faith, which demands instead a reasonable and responsible acceptance of all that God has revealed in Christ. *Faith does not sprout from the ashes of reason!* I strongly encourage all of you to spare no effort in rebuilding that aspect of learning which is open to Truth and the Absolute."[2]

The task of the scientists is thus to search for truth, and so "basic research must be free with regard to political and economic authorities, which must cooperate in its development, without hampering its creativity or harnessing it to serve their own purposes. Like any other truth, scientific truth is answerable only to itself and to the supreme Truth, God, the creator of man and of all things."[3]

The creation of all things by God has important consequences: "From the very circumstance of their having been created, all things are endowed with their own stability. Truth, goodness, proper laws and order—man must respect these as he isolates them by the appropriate methods of individual sciences or arts. . . . Indeed whoever labours to penetrate the secrets of reality with a humble and steady mind is even unawares being led by the hand of God, who holds all things in existence. . . . For without the creator the creature would not exist. For their part, all believers of whatever religion have always heard his revealing voice in the discourse of creatures. For when God is forgotten, the creature itself grows unintelligible."[4]

"The legitimate autonomy of earthly things is linked with today's deeply felt problem of ecology, that is the concern for the protection and preservation of the natural environment. The ecological destruction, which always presupposes a form of selfishness opposed to community well-being, arises from an arbitrary—and in the last analysis

---

[2] From the address to university professors on 9 September during the Holy Year 2000.

[3] From a discourse to the Pontifical Academy of Sciences, 10 November 1979.

[4] Ibid.

harmful—use of creatures, whose laws and natural order are violated by ignoring or disregarding the finality immanent in the work of creation. This mode of behaviour derives from a false interpretation of the autonomy of earthly things—man uses these things 'without reference to the Creator,' to quote the words of the Council, he also does incalculable harm to himself. The solution of the problem of the ecological threat is in strict relationship with the principles of the legitimate autonomy of earthly things—in the final analysis, with the truth about creation and about the Creator of the world."[5]

In an address to the United Nations in 1990, the Pope reiterated his concern for the environment: "The topic you have been studying is of immense importance. It is to the undeniable credit of scientists that the value of the biodiversity of tropical ecosystems is coming to be more understood and appreciated. However, the extent of the depletion of the earth's biodiversity is, indeed, a very serious problem. It threatens countless other forms of life. Even the quality of human life, because of its dynamic interaction with other species, is being impoverished. Tropical forests deserve our attention, study and protection. As well as making an essential contribution to the regulation of the earth's climatic conditions, they possess some of the richest varieties of the earth's species, the beauty of which merits our profound aesthetic appreciation. Moreover, some plants and micro-organisms of the forest are capable of synthesising unlimited numbers of complex substances of great potential to the manufacture of medicines and antibiotics. Other plants possess value as sources of food or as a means of genetically improving strains of edible plants."

"Unfortunately the rate at which these forests are being destroyed or altered is depleting their biodiversity so quickly that many species may never be catalogued or studied for their possible value to human beings. If an unjustified search for profit is sometimes responsible for deforestation of tropical ecosystems and the loss of their biodiversity, it is also true that a desperate fight against poverty threatens to deplete these important resources of the planet. An

[5] From an address to a general audience in 1986.

intense programme of information and education is needed. In particular your study and research can contribute to fostering an enlightened and urgent moral commitment."

"In this way the present ecological crisis will become an occasion for a renewed consciousness of man's place in this world and of his relationship to the environment. The created universe has been given to mankind, not for selfish misuse, but for the glory of God which consists, as St. Irenaeus said many centuries ago, in 'the living man.'"[6]

In his message for the 1990 World Day of Peace, the Pope "emphasizes the fundamentally moral character of the ecological crisis and its close relationship to the search for genuine and lasting world peace. In calling attention to the ethical principles, which are essential for an adequate and lasting solution to that crisis, I lay particular emphasis on the value and respect for life and for the integrity of the created order."

"Since the ecological crisis is fundamentally a moral issue, it requires that all people respond in solidarity to what is a common threat. Uncontrolled exploitation of the natural environment not only menaces the survival of the human race, it also threatens the natural order in which mankind is meant to receive and to hand on God's gift of life with dignity and freedom. Today responsible men and women are increasingly aware that we must pay attention to what the earth and its atmosphere are telling us: namely, that there is an order in the universe which must be respected, and that the human person, endowed with the capability of choosing freely, has a grave responsibility to preserve this order for the well-being of future generations. As you know in the recent message for the World Day of Peace, I called to the attention of every person of goodwill a serious issue—the problems of ecology—recalling that in finding a solution, we must direct the efforts and mobilise the will of citizens. An issue like this cannot be neglected—for it is vital to human survival—nor can it be reduced to a merely political problem or issue. It has, in fact, a moral dimension which touches everyone and thus, no one can be indifferent to it."

---

[6] From the address to UNESCO and the United Nations, 1990.

"At this brief time in this century, humanity is called to establish a new relation of attentiveness and respect toward the environment. Humanity must protect its delicate balance, keeping in mind the extraordinary possibilities but, also, the formidable threats inherent in certain types of experimentation, scientific research and industrial activity—and that must be done if humanity does not want to threaten its very development or draw from it unimaginable consequences. . . . Ecological problems enter into everyone's homes, they are discussed in the family circle and people wonder what tomorrow will be like."

"We must, therefore, mobilise every effort so that each person assumes his or her own responsibility and creates the basis of a lifestyle of solidarity and brotherhood. All have to commit themselves to the equal distribution of this earth's goods, to respect for the life of the neighbour in trouble or on the fringe, to development of volunteer agencies which today can undertake an important role in the support and co-ordination in these areas."[7]

This concern for the well-being of every person extends to research into the human body. In an address on biological experimentation the Pope reminded his hearers that: "Science and Wisdom, which in their truest and most varied expressions constitute a most precious heritage of humanity, are *at the service of* man. The Church is called, in her essential vocation, to foster the progress of man, since, as I wrote in my first Encyclical: '. . . man is the primary route that the Church must travel in fulfilling her mission: *he is the primary and fundamental way for the Church*, the way traced out by Christ Himself.' Man is also for you the ultimate term of scientific research, the whole man, spirit and body, even if the immediate object of the sciences that you profess is the body with all its organs and tissues. The human body is not independent of the spirit, just as the spirit is not independent of the body, because of the deep unity and mutual connection that exists between one and the other."

"The substantial unity between spirit and body, and indirectly with the cosmos, is so essential that every human activity, even the

---

7 From an address to the Regional Council of Lazio, 1991.

most spiritual one, is in some way permeated and coloured by the bodily condition: at the same time the body must in turn be directed and guided to its final end by the spirit. There is no doubt that the spiritual activities of the human person proceed from the personal centre of the individual, who is predisposed by the body to which the spirit is substantially united. Hence the great importance, for the life of the spirit of the sciences that promote the knowledge of corporeal reality and activity."

"Consequently, I have no reason to be apprehensive for those *experiments in biology* that are performed by scientists who, like you, have profound respect for the human person, since I am sure that they will contribute to the *integral well-being of man*. On the other hand, I condemn, in the most explicit and formal way, experimental manipulations of the human embryo; since; the human being, from conception to death, cannot be exploited for any purpose whatsoever. Indeed, as the Second Vatican Council teaches, man is 'the only creature on earth God willed for itself.' Worthy of esteem is the initiative of those scientists who have expressed their disapproval of experiments that violate human freedom, and I praise those who have endeavoured to establish, with full respect for man's dignity and freedom, guidelines and limits for experiments concerning man."[8]

Throughout the ages people have looked at the night sky with wonder and awe, and the psalmist proclaimed that the heavens show forth the Glory of the Lord. The Vatican observatory testifies to the Church's continuing interest in astronomical studies, and the Pontifical Academy of Sciences frequently holds conferences to study the latest advances. In an address to one of these, the Pope remarked that "cosmogony and cosmology have always aroused great interest among people and religions. The Bible itself speaks to us of the origin of the universe and its make-up, not in order to provide us with a scientific treatise, but in order to state the correct relationship of man with God and the universe. Sacred Scripture wishes simply to declare that the world was created by God, and in order to teach this truth it expresses itself in terms of the cosmology

---

[8] From an address to a study week audience in 1982.

in use at the time of the writer. The sacred Book likewise wishes to tell men that the world was not created as the seat of the gods, as was taught by other cosmogonies and cosmologies, but was rather created for the service of man and the glory of God. Any other teaching about the origin and makeup of the universe is alien to the intentions the Bible, which does not wish to teach how heaven was made but how one goes to heaven."[9]

This last remark is an echo of a remark by Cardinal Baronius that was used by Galileo when he had to defend himself against the Aristotelians who accused him of holding scientific views contrary to the Bible. "If Scripture cannot err," he wrote to Benedetto Castelli, "some of its interpreters and commentators can, and in many ways." It is therefore necessary to clarify the relations between different ways of knowing, so the Pope goes on to say: "If contemporary culture is marked by a tendency to scientism, the cultural vision of the age of Galileo was unitary and bore the imprint of a particular philosophical formation. This unitary character of culture, which is in itself positive and still desirable today, was one of the causes of the condemnation of Galileo. The majority of theologians did not perceive *the formal distinction between Holy Scripture and its interpretation*, which led them to the improper transposition of a question of scientific fact into the realm of doctrine and faith."[10]

The recognition of the autonomy of religion and science, and the relation between them, was emphasized by the Pope in his discourse to the Pontifical Academy when it commemorated Einstein: "The collaboration between religion and science is to the advantage of both, without violating their respective autonomy in any way. Just as religion demands religious freedom, so science rightly claims freedom of research. The Second Vatican Council, after reaffirming, with the First Vatican Council, the rightful freedom of the arts and of human disciplines in the field of their own principles and their

---

[9] From the discourse to the participants in the study week on "Cosmology and Fundamental Particles" on 3 October 1981.

[10] From the address to the Pontifical Academy of Sciences, 31 October 1992. In *Après Galilée: Science et Foi: nouveau dialogue*, under the direction of Cardinal Paul Poupard (Paris: Desclée de Brouwer, 1994), 99.

own method, solemnly recognises 'the legitimate autonomy of culture and especially of the sciences.' On the occasion of this solemn commemoration of Einstein, I would like to confirm again the declarations of the Council on the autonomy of science in its function of research on the truth inscribed in creation by the finger of God."

"The Church, filled with admiration for the genius of the great scientist in whom the imprint of the creative spirit is revealed, without intervening in any way with a judgment which it does not fall upon her to pass on the doctrine concerning the great systems of the universe, proposes the latter, however, to the reflection of theologians to discover the harmony existing between scientific truth and revealed truth."[11]   ⚛

---

[11] From the address to university professors on 9 September during the Holy Year 2000.

CHAPTER 2

The Judeo-Christian Origin
of Modern Science*

Introduction

WE ARE SO FAMILIAR with the presence of science in our lives and the multitude of its technological applications that we easily forget that this is a unique feature of our civilisation. Nothing remotely similar is found in any of the great civilisations of antiquity. We find in them, of course, highly developed social structures, great cities, men and women of high culture, great works of architecture, metalwork, ceramics, as well as philosophy, drama, and literature—but no science as we know it now.

Here it is necessary to specify in more detail just what we mean by modern science. In ancient civilisation we often find great skill in practical things, and also profound thinkers who tried to understand the working of the world. One thinks especially of the ancient Greeks with their great contributions to mathematics and to practical astronomy. Democritus, for example, speculated about the possibility that the world is made of atoms, small hard ultimate particles that cannot be further subdivided. But he had no idea about how to see if this is indeed the case, or, if it is, how we could find out how

---

* An Italian translation of this article was published in *Dizionario Interdisciplinaire di Scienza e Fede*, vol. 2, ed. Giuseppe Tanzella-Nitti and Alberto Strumia (Rome: Urbana University Press, 2002), 1262–72. Some sections are also in the corresponding chapter in *Theology and Modern Physics* (Aldershot: Ashgate Press, 2005).

big they are and what is their structure. These and many other questions have only been answered in the last century.

The Greeks sought to understand the world by intuiting the essences of things and from this deducing their behaviour. They saw a purposeful world in which everything seeks its natural place. This was overambitious and mistaken: we cannot intuit the essences of things. It was Galileo, building on the work of his medieval predecessors, who realised that a much more modest and painstaking approach was needed. Physical phenomena must not only be observed, they must be measured as accurately as possible, and the measurements correlated by mathematics. This was already understood by Grosseteste in the thirteenth century, who applied geometrical rules to understand optical phenomena. Galileo went beyond this and studied the motion of falling bodies by measuring the time taken to fall a measured distance, and correlating the results by mathematical equations. By emphasizing that science is quantitative, not qualitative, and that it is based on exact measurements, Galileo stands at the threshold of modern science. By his insight into the method of science, by his painstaking observations and measurements and by his vision of the future he did more than any other to destroy Aristotelian physics and open the way to modern science.

The Scriptures often use expressions from everyday speech without intending to endorse any particular scientific theories. It is thus important to distinguish between theological and scientific discussions, which both have their distinct methods and criteria of truth. In Galileo's time the debate was tragically confused by the opposition of the Aristotelians to his discoveries and by the failure to understand that genuine scientific discoveries show forth the works of the Creator. Furthermore, if we examine the origin of modern science, we find that it is rooted in the Christian beliefs on the nature of the material world.

By modern science I mean the detailed quantitative understanding of the material world expressed in the form of differential equations. This was first achieved by Newton when he formulated his three laws and showed how they can be used to calculate the motions of the planets and the fall of an apple. Likewise Maxwell showed how his equations enable us to understand all electric and magnetic phenomena. In the microworld of atoms and nuclei, quantum mechanics, usually in the form of Schrödinger's equation, performs the same function. The pattern is always the same: if we know the initial conditions, we can compute the subsequent course of the system in great and quantitative detail.

This detailed knowledge of the world is the essential basis of all modern technology. Without it there would be no aeroplanes, no television, no power stations. We may, of course, say that we would be better off in some respects without modern technology, and it is evident that the knowledge that we have gained is frequently put to evil use. We may also reflect that if it were not for modern science most of us would not be here at all, and most of the remainder would be living in squalor.

We are thus led to ask why it is that in all the civilisations of the world, only in our civilisation, that has flourished in Europe during the second millennium, has science developed in its modern form? This can be answered by seeing what is unique in our civilisation, and by connecting that with the origin of science.

The Conditions for the Birth of Science

All the great civilisations are characterised by an advanced social structure that enables some people to spend their time thinking about the world without worrying where the next meal is coming from. Most of them also have some system of writing, so that thoughts can be recorded, and some mathematics.

There are also present the practical skills necessary to make any instruments that may be required. These are what may be called the material conditions for the emergence of science, and their universality implies that the answer to our question must be sought elsewhere.

Perhaps what is important is the attitude of mind toward the material world. Clearly if we believe that the world is evil and not worthy of attention, then we are not likely to study it in any detail.

For science to begin, the world must be regarded as in some sense good, or at the very least neutral.

We must also believe that the world is rational and orderly, so that what we find out one day is still true the next day, and in other places. This order must be of a very special kind. If we believe that the order in the world is a necessary order, that it could not be otherwise, then we might well hope to find that order just by thinking about it, as we do in mathematics. If on the other hand the order in the world is a dependent or contingent order, so that it could be otherwise, then the only way to find out about it is by looking at the world as it is, and by making experiments on it.

Scientific research is a frustrating business, and things go wrong all too often. It is easy to give up. Often the only way to succeed is by heroic persistence, and this can only come if there is a firm belief that there is an order, and that the order can be found. So we must also believe that the order in nature is open to the human mind, that the whole enterprise is practicable.

Scientific knowledge can only be gained by the cooperative endeavour of very many men and women over many years. This will only happen if the knowledge that any one gains is not treated as a secret, but is freely shared.

As soon as it is found that scientific knowledge gives us some control over the working of the world, this provides another strong motive for scientific research. It also encourages the other members of society to regard the scientist not as a harmless eccentric indulging in his own interests, but as one whose work can be of inestimable value to society. The society will then support the scientist by providing the equipment and helpers that he needs. Of course there is a danger in this, that society will start to tell the scientist what the has to do, and there is no surer way of destroying all hope of fruitful research.

These are some of the beliefs about the material world that we can see by introspection that are necessary before science can begin. They are beliefs that must be held and indeed taken for granted by the ordinary members of society.

They may seem to us to be rather obvious beliefs, but they are a very special set of beliefs that has only been found together once in human history. If we look at the beliefs about the material world that are found in other civilisations we find something quite different. Matter is regarded as evil, or controlled by capricious demons. In such soil it is impossible for science to develop.

A very general belief in ancient civilisations is that of a cyclic universe. This is sometimes called the doctrine of the Great Year, the belief that after a very long time everything is repeated. There is nothing new; everything that happens has already happened an infinite number of times in the past and will be repeated an infinite number of times in the future. Such a belief is intensely debilitating: if we are in the grip of an inexorable fate, what is the point of trying to do something new?

So now we are faced with the question how it was that the very special set of beliefs that is necessary for the rise of science was first imprinted on the European mind. As we have seen, modern science really took off with Newton, but its roots can be traced back through the work of Galileo and many others in the preceding centuries. We are thus led to look for the roots of science in the Middle Ages. The origin of science can be traced even further back, to the early Christian centuries, so we begin there.

The Early Christian Centuries

During the centuries following the foundation of Christianity, the Christians were one small persecuted sect among many others. The bitter struggle against pagan ideas made them suspicious of Greek science and philosophy. Nevertheless, there is inherent in Christian teaching a set of beliefs about the natural world that eventually led to the first viable birth of science in the High Middle Ages, and to its subsequent flowering in the Renaissance. The foundations of these beliefs were revealed to the Israelites, in particular the belief in the rationality of the world.

The Old Testament beliefs on creation were reinforced and extended by the teaching of Christ. The Christian belief concerning creation emphasizes not only that the universe was created by God out of nothing and in time, but also that the universe is totally dependent on God and totally distinct from God. The universe at any instant is sustained in being by God, and without this sustaining power it would immediately lapse into nothingness.

In the early Christian centuries there were passionate debates about the nature of Christ, and heresies abounded. To define the true nature of Christ was the task of a series of Councils of the Church, and of these the Council of Nicea formulated the creed that is widely held today:

"Credo in unum Deum. Pattern omnipotentum, factorem coeli et terrae, visibilium omnium et invisibilium. Et in unum Dominum Jesum Christum, Filium Dei unigenitum. Et ex Patre natum ante omnia saecula. Deum de Deo, lumen de luminae, Deum verum de Deum vero. Genitum, non factum, consubstantialem Patri; per quem omnia facta sunt. . . ."

It is easy to recite those hallowed phrases without fully realising their impact, and still more their importance for science. The beginning of the Nicene creed asserts the creation of the universe by God: "Factorem coeli et terrae." One of the early heresies was pantheism that failed to distinguish between God and His creation, holding that it is in some way part of God. In the Greco–Roman world the universe was thought of as an emanation from a divine principle that is not distinguished from the universe. Pantheism is explicitly excluded by the Nicene creed when it says that Christ is the only-begotten Son of God. Christ is begotten, not made. Only Christ was begotten and thus shared in the substance of God; the universe was made, not begotten. ("Et in unum Dominum Jesum Christum, Filium Dei unigenitum. Genitum, non factum.") Since pantheism was one of the beliefs preventing the rise of science in all ancient cultures, the Nicene creed prepared the way for the one viable birth of science in human history

Many ancient cosmologies held that the world is a battleground between the spirits of good and evil. This dualism in inimical to science because it makes the world unpredictable. Dualism is excluded by the Nicene creed when it says that all creation takes place through Christ ("per quem omnia facta sunt").

Inherent in the Christian doctrine of creation is the belief that God freely chose to create the universe. He was not in any way constrained either to create or not to create it in the way that He did. It is therefore not a necessary universe in the sense that it has to be created or could have been created otherwise. There is therefore no possibility of finding out about the universe by pure thought or by a priori reasoning. We can only hope to understand it by studying it and by making experiments. Thus the Christian doctrine of creation encouraged the experimental method, essential for the development of science.

All ancient cultures held a cyclic view of the world, and this was one of the beliefs that hindered the development of science. This cyclic pessimism was decisively broken by the belief in the unique Incarnation of Christ; thereafter time and history became linear, with a beginning and an end.

The theological disputes of the early Christian centuries seem a long way away, but they were of decisive importance for subsequent history. Who now has heard of the Valentinians, the Marcosians, the Nicolaitans, the Encratites, the Borbonians, the Ophites, or the Sethians, to list but a few? More have heard of the Arians, a heresy still prevalent today. Arius and his followers were prepared to accept only-begotten, but consubstantial was unacceptable because it is not to be found in Scripture. If the young deacon Athanasius had not prevailed against them, Christianity would have been completely destroyed.

In his epistle to the Colossians, St. Paul says that in Christ all things took their being, and were all created through him and in him. He stressed Christ as the divine logos and the consequence that the creation must be fully logical and orderly.

In the early Christian centuries the attitude of theologians ranged from those of Tertullian (ca. 160–ca. 240), who mistrusted philosophers, to those like Justin Martyr and Clement of Alexandria (ca. 150–ca. 215), who regarded Greek learning as a useful aid to theology but not worthy of study for its own sake. Even St. Augustine of Hippo

(354–430), who in his early days supported the liberal arts that included geometry and astronomy, came to regard them in his later years as of little value. Nevertheless, his theology encouraged the systematic study of the natural world, since he believed that its sacramental nature is symbolic of spiritual truths. He was a compulsive observer of a wide range of natural phenomena, always on the lookout for anything that gave even a fleeting glimpse of the Reason that he believed lie behind all things. He was interested in nature primarily because it revealed God to the attentive observer. His philosophical reflections on the nature of time are still quoted as among the most profound ever written.

In the early sixth century John Philoponus, a Christian Platonist who lived in Alexandria, wrote extensively on the material world, showing the influence of Christian beliefs on those of the surrounding pagan world, particularly those derived from ancient Greece. He commented extensively on Aristotle, whom he greatly admired, but when the teaching of Aristotle was contrary to Christian belief he did not hesitate to differ from it. This was particularly important in his commentary on Aristotle's physics where he said, contrary to Aristotle, that all bodies would fall in a vacuum at the same speed, irrespective of their weight, and that projectiles move through the air not due to the motion of the air but because they were initially given a certain quantity of motion. This is a remarkable anticipation of ideas normally associated with Galileo, and shows a decisive break with Aristotelian physics. He was not the first writer in antiquity to break with Aristotle, but he did so more clearly and decisively.

The connection between his rejection of Aristotelian ideas and his Christian beliefs is to be found in the doctrine of creation. Addressing the question of motion, he asked "could not the sun, moon and the stars be not given by God, their Creator, a certain kinetic force, in the same way as heavy and light things were given their trend to move?" He also believed that the stars are not made of the ether but of ordinary matter, thus rejecting Aristotle's distinction between celestial and terrestrial matter.

This shows very clearly that the Christian beliefs about the world are incompatible with the Aristotelian views on the divinity of celestial matter and the eternity of motion. It was thus inevitable that the spread of Christianity should lead eventually to the destruction of Aristotelian physics, thus opening the way to modern science.

Philoponus was also the first to say that Genesis was written for spiritual and not for scientific instruction, a wise statement that was too far in advance of its time to be congenial to contemporary theologians. This theological boldness perhaps explains why Philoponus's ideas did not lead to further scientific developments. To be fruitful, ideas have not only to be right, they need to fall on fertile ground, in this case a society sufficiently developed to make full use of them. This was lacking for Philoponus, but not in the High Middle Ages.

The Middle Ages

The Middle Ages is often neglected and derided, but an objective analysis shows that it was one of the most outstandingly creative periods in human history. It is convenient to define it as the period between 800 and 1450, the later years from 1200 to 1450 being the High Middle Ages. That period saw in Western Europe the foundation of universities; unprecedented technological developments that raised the standard of living to new heights; the organisation of an extensive financial system; and, most important of all, the birth of modern science.

Underlying all this was a new attitude to the material world, a new confidence, dynamism, and sense of purpose. It was a time of intellectual ferment. Universities were being founded all over Europe, and the writings of the ancient Greeks were becoming available in translation. Christian theology was being rethought using their unfamiliar but powerful concepts. The writings of Augustine and of others like Philoponus were already forming new attitudes to the natural world.

In the early twelfth century, Adelard of Bath wrote his *Quaestionta Naturales*, which marks the dawn of medieval science. His nephew believed that the spontaneous appearance of life in a dish of dried soil was miraculous. At a time when there was a strong devotion to miracles, it would have been easy for Adelard to agree. Instead he drew a firm distinction between the action of the Creator and the natural workings of His creation: "It is the will of the Creator that herbs should sprout from the earth. But the same is not without a reason either." When his nephew persisted and pointed out that a natural explanation from the doctrine of the four elements was inadequate, he stuck to his point: "Whatever there is, is from Him and through Him. But the realm of being is not a confused one, nor is it lacking in disposition which, so far as human knowledge can go, should be consulted." In other words, we should persist in seeking a natural explanation, and avoid attributing anything that we do not understand to the direct action of God. This advice, that is still worth heeding today, contains the essential attitude to the natural world that lies at the basis of science.

The two characteristics of the Western intellectual tradition that make science possible are the insistence on logical coherence and experimental verification. These are already present in a qualitative way among the Greeks, and the vital contribution of the Middle Ages was to refine these conditions into a more effective union. This was done principally by insisting on the quantitative precision that can be attained by using mathematics in the formulation of the theories, and then verifying them not by observation alone, but by precise measurements. This transition was achieved in the twelfth century, principally by Robert Grosseteste, who is regarded as the founder of experimental science.

Grosseteste was a widely read man who made extensive contributions to many areas of human knowledge. He was one of the first chancellors of the University of Oxford and did much to establish the nascent university. He was also Bishop of Lincoln, the diocese in which Oxford used to be situated.

His work on experimental science owed much to Plato, who taught that the pure forms behind the appearances of things are mathematical in nature, and so if we are to show this our theories must themselves be mathematical and the results of our measurements must be expressed in numbers.

Grosseteste elaborated his theory of the scientific method in some detail, though he did not himself carry out many experiments. He recommended the method of analysis and synthesis; namely that the problem is first resolved into its simplest parts and, when these are understood, the results can be combined to give the explanation of the whole. The observations and experiments may themselves suggest hypotheses and then theories, and these in turn may be verified or disproved by comparison with further observations and measurements.

He first applied his method to the phenomena of light. He believed that light is the most fundamental form, the first principle of motion, so that the laws of light must lie at the basis of scientific explanation. God created light, and from that all things came. Light itself follows geometrical rules, in the way it is propagated, reflected, and refracted, and is the means whereby higher bodies act on lower. Motion is therefore also geometrical. He studied the rainbow and his criticisms of the explanations of Aristotle and Seneca were useful steps along the road to an adequate explanation.

Implicit in his work is the insistence on quantitative measurement, and this in turn comes from the biblical insistence on the rationality of the Creator, who disposed everything in number, weight, and measure.

It should not be thought that these examples are typical of medieval thought about the world. They are in fact rather untypical of an age characterised by a baffling mixture of keen insights and naive credulity, of sound reasoning and fantastic superstitions, of critical analysis and magical incantations.

Nevertheless, in spite of this confusion, there did exist the insistence on rational thought, on mathematical formulation and quantitative verification, that was eventually to lead to modern science. At first it may have been but a flicker in the darkness, but that flicker grew steadily stronger until modern science was born. Essential to that birth was the insistence on quantitative precision, and this was made possible by the immense technological growth in the Middle Ages, which must now be considered.

At the beginning of the Middle Ages the monasteries were the centres of technological innovation. They were primarily houses of prayer, but the need to be largely self-supporting, often in rather remote and underdeveloped areas, forced them to develop a wide range of skills, including building and architecture, farming, cloth-making, clock-making, metallurgy, and printing.

First and most obviously the monastery itself was an integrated complex of buildings housing the monks and laybrothers and their various activities, with the church at its centre. Often the abbey church also served as the cathedral of a city, and we still have visible reminders of the magnitude of the achievements of those generally anonymous medieval builders. Visitors to Canterbury and York, Salisbury and Winchester, Durham and Lincoln, to name but a few English cities, go first to their medieval cathedrals. These were constructed when the population was but a small fraction of today's number, and there were no steel cranes or electric saws to facilitate their construction, and yet we can now barely afford to keep them in repair. They bear silent witness to the extraordinary technical skill, tenacity of purpose, and self-sacrifice of their builders.

In the countryside, the monasteries mainly supported themselves by farming. They often owned large areas of land, sometimes in more remote areas hacked out of the wilderness by the monks themselves. The actual farm work in the larger monasteries was done by laybrothers. The medieval centuries saw many advances in agricultural techniques, such as the modern plough, which turns the earth over as well as opening it up. Horses were made more efficient by providing them with nailed horseshoes, and the breast harness enabled them to pull loads four times heavier than before. Horses were harnessed one in front of another, and the stirrup gave horse riders much greater control.

Monasteries were often built near a river, so that the water could drive machinery as well as clean the buildings. Fishponds provided the monks with fish, and frequently there was a water mill to grind the corn, and fulling machines to make cloth. The latter made use of the cam, another medieval invention, to transform rotational to linear motion. The cam also made possible mechanical saws that enabled wood for building to be prepared much more easily. Windmills were known quite widely; in Tibet they drove prayer wheels, but in Europe they ground corn.

Monasteries were strictly regulated by a rule, for the Benedictine monasteries that of St. Benedict. This prescribed the hours of prayer, of work, eating and sleeping, and all had to be aware of the time, even those working in distant fields. The bells of the monasteries chimed the hours and regulated all the activities throughout the day and night. Clocks were thus essential to the smooth functioning of the monasteries. The early sand and water clocks, accurate to a few minutes, might well have been sufficient, but this did not satisfy the monks, and they developed the earliest clocks. A very early example (1386), showing a sophisticated double feedback mechanism, is to be seen in the nave of Salisbury cathedral. Clocks were soon installed on towers in the city centres, where they regulated commerce. Extremely complicated clocks were made, such at that in Strasbourg cathedral, which gives not only the time but a whole range of astronomical information.

The manufacture of bells and clocks required enhanced metallurgical skills, and here again the monks were among the leaders. Brass was first made in Tintern Abbey, now an imposing ruin in the narrow valley of the river Wye.

In the early Middle Ages, manuscripts were laboriously copied by the monks, and so were very rare. Woodblock printing was introduced from the East, followed by moveable type in the early fifteenth century. The improved methods soon allowed books to be produced in ever-increasing numbers. This was an invention that has transformed our society more than any other. Although many of these technological developments started in the monasteries, they were eagerly taken up by others, and soon became generally available.

Another important industry was the manufacture of glass, which made possible both the stained glass windows and, around 1280, the first spectacles. Mining became a key industry as it provided so many of the minerals needed by the growing manufacturing industries, as well as the coal that was rapidly replacing the increasingly scarce wood.

From the thirteenth century onward, universities were founded in many cities such as Bologna, Padua, Paris, Oxford, and Prague, and soon became very active centres of learning. Students studied a wide range of subjects, including grammar, dialectic, rhetoric, music, natural philosophy, arithmetic, and geometry, bringing together the liberal and the mechanical arts. In medieval times the university was true to its name in providing a universal education, and one that contained a large scientific and technological component.

All this activity stimulated the growth of international trade, as commodities were exported from one country to another in ever-increasing quantities. This required a reliable monetary system, including a coinage and an international banking organisation. Great merchant banks such as the Medici in Florence were founded and controlled trade over all Europe. This led to greatly increased standards of living, although progress was sometimes interrupted by famines, plagues, and wars.

Science and Christian Belief

The Middle Ages saw the flourishing of a Christian civilisation for the first time in history. Christian ideas gradually permeated the European mind and formed the prevailing view of the world. We are thus led to enquire, what is the Christian concept of the material world, and how is it connected with the beliefs that we have seen are necessary for the rise of science?

The Christian believes that the world is good: we read in the first chapter of Genesis that God looked upon all that He had made, and saw that it was "very good." Matter was further ennobled by the Incarnation, when "the Word was made flesh and He dwelt amongst us."

Matter is ordered and rational because it was created by a rational God. We read in the Book of Wisdom that the Creator ordered everything in measure, number, and weight, which was the most often quoted biblical phrase in medieval times. The order of the material world is freely chosen by God. He could have made the world in many different ways, but chose to make it the way He did. This shows very clearly the importance of our theological beliefs on our view of the material world. We believe that God is both rational and free. If we stress His rationality at the expense of His freedom, we have a necessary world, and no possibility of science. But conversely, if we stress his freedom at the expense of His rationality we have an unpredictable world, and again no science. This is the reason for the failure of science to develop in Muslim lands.

Christians believe that the order in nature is open to the human mind, that it is possible to learn about the world because God commanded man to subdue the earth: "Be fruitful, multiply, fill the earth and conquer it. Be masters of the fish of the sea, the birds of heaven and all living animals on the earth."

Christian beliefs also provide the motivation to study the world, because by learning about it we can learn more about God. In the parable of the talents Christ urged us to make full use of all our abilities, and this includes learning more about the world by observation and experiment.

The remaining condition for the development of science, the belief that knowledge must be freely shared, is enjoined by the Book of Wisdom: "What I have learned without self-interest, I pass on without reserve; I do not intend to hide her riches. For she is an inexhaustible treasure to men, and those who acquire it win God's friendship."

We thus find that during the critical centuries before the birth of science, the collective mind of Europe was inspired by a system of beliefs that included just those special elements that are necessary for the development of science. It is thus very plausible to say that there is thus a living, organic continuity between Christian revelation and modern science. Christianity provided just those beliefs that made possible the birth of modern science, and the moral climate that encouraged its growth.

It might however be said that this is just historical coincidence; how can we be sure that there is a real causal influence operating? This can indeed be found if we examine the work of some of the philosophers of the High Middle Ages.

At that time the prevailing ideas of the nature of the world were derived from the Greek philosopher Aristotle. He believed in the eternity of the world, in a cyclic universe, and in a world of purpose, even in material things. He also believed that celestial matter, the world of the stars and planets, is incorruptible, unlike terrestrial matter that can undergo change. These beliefs in effect prevented the development of science for two thousand years. Their stranglehold had to be broken before science could develop into its modern form.

So great was the prestige of Aristotle that the philosophers of the medieval schools taught by commenting on his texts. Some of Aristotle's teaching, however, was inconsistent with the Christian faith, and the philosophers did not hesitate to differ from Aristotle when it seemed necessary. There was intense discussion on a variety of topics, notably concerning the creation of the world and the motion of bodies. In 1277 the Bishop of Paris, Etienne Tempier, found it necessary to condemn 219 philosophical propositions as contrary to the Christian belief in creation out of nothing. This was a turning point in the history of thought, as it channelled philosophical speculations about motion in a direction that led eventually to the destruction of Aristotelian physics, thus opening the way to modern science.

One of these philosophers, John Buridan, was particularly interested in the nature of motion. This is the most fundamental problem of physics, and so if science is to begin it must begin here. In full consistency with his belief in creation, he wrote that "God, when He created the world, moved each of the celestial orbs as he pleased, and in moving them He impressed upon them impetuses which moved them without Him having to move them any more except by the method of general influence whereby He concurs as co-agent in all things which take place."

This shows a clear break with Aristotle, who required the continuing action of the mover throughout the motion. What Buridan called impetus was later refined into the concept of momentum, and the idea in the above passage became Newton's first law of motion. Buridan's works were widely published and his ideas became known throughout Europe, and in particular to Leonardo da Vinci and hence to the scientists of Renaissance times.

The Christian belief in the creation of the world by God also undermined Aristotle's sharp distinction between celestial and terrestrial matter. Since they are both created, why should they be different? This made it possible for Newton to see that the same force that pulls an apple to the ground also keeps the moon in its orbit.

A vital component in the rise of science is the belief in the order of the world, that is the idea that every event is the precise result of preceding events. This implies that whatever measurements we make should correspond exactly, that is within the uncertainties of measurement, with our theories. A corollary to this is that if we want to test out theories we should make the most accurate measurements we can. This insistence on precision is essential for the progress of science. An illustration of this is the work of Kepler on the orbit of the planet Mars. Some very accurate measurements had been made of its position by Tycho Brahe, probably the most accurate that could be made before the invention of the telescope. Kepler resolved to find the orbit. He believed, following Aristotle, that the orbit was circular, as befits incorruptible celestial matter. He found that indeed it is very nearly a circle, but however hard he worked, he could not make it fit Tycho's measurements. He could find a circular orbit that agreed with the measurements to about ten minutes of arc, but not to two, which was the accuracy of the measurements. Many people would have said that this was good enough, and gone on to do something else. But it was not good enough for Kepler, who believed that the fit must be exact, within the uncertainties of the measurements. So he toiled on and on for years, until he finally realised that he could never get the circle to fit. Then he tried an ellipse, and now the orbit could be fitted. This was a breakthrough that made possible Newton's work on the planetary orbits, when he showed from his theory of celestial dynamics that they must indeed be ellipses.

This vital stage in the development of science was made possible by the strong belief in the order of nature. This is what led Whitehead to say, in his Lowell lectures in 1925 on "Science and the Modern World" that "the Middle Ages formed one long training of the intellect of Western Europe in the sense of order. This by itself is not enough." He went on: "I do not think that I have even yet brought out the greatest contribution of medievalism to the formation of the scientific movement. I mean the inexpugnable belief that every detailed occurrence can be correlated with its antecedents in a perfectly definite manner, exemplifying general principles. Without this belief the incredible labours of scientists would be without hope. It is this instinctive conviction, vividly poised before the imagination,· which is the motive power of research: that there is a secret, a secret which can be unveiled." He went on to ask how was this conviction so vividly implanted in the European mind, and concluded: "My explanation is that the faith in the possibility of science, generated antecedently to the development of modern scientific theory, is an unconscious derivative from medieval theology."

One might indeed query whether unconscious is the right word, for many of the medievals explicitly saw their work as showing forth the works of the Creator. Furthermore, explicitly Christian beliefs played a decisive part in making modern science possible. Thus the debilitating belief in a cyclic universe was decisively broken by the Christian belief in the uniqueness of the Incarnation. Henceforth history was no longer an infinite series of dreary cycles, but a linear story with a beginning and an end.

Galileo

The Aristotelian philosophers regarded the universe as a living organism suffused by purpose, and they analysed it in terms of essences and causes. Galileo, following Euclid and Archimedes, saw it as made of objects moving according to mathematical laws that could be discovered by experiment. He therefore studied the problem of motion in a new way, not by asking its causes, but by seeking simple mathematical descriptions of the ways things move.

Galileo had to overcome the general belief that the Greeks had attained supreme mastery of every art and science, so that every question can be studied by appeal to their authority. The idea of the progressive increase in knowledge, so familiar today, was conspicuously absent. Nature has spoken through the mouth of Aristotle, and our task is to listen and interpret. Galileo, however, believed that the book of nature is written in the language of mathematics and that we can read from the book of nature by making observations and experiments

Kepler had already realised the importance of numerical accuracy in observing the heavens, and established the laws of planetary motion. Galileo did the same for motions on the surface of the earth. He studied how balls roll down an inclined plane, and how projectiles move through the air, and was able to express his results in simple laws connecting positions, velocities, and times.

The fundamental ideas of dynamics were established qualitatively by Buridan and his successors, and subsequently there was much discussion about the motions of falling bodies and of projectiles, in particular about the relationship between the distance fallen and the time, and the trajectories of projectiles. Concepts such as momentum and energy were only refined to their present precision by centuries of effort.

Galileo realised the importance of accurate measurements, but was in a more difficult situation than Kepler. Long times, such as the periods of rotation of the planets, can be measured quite accurately by primitive means, but it is much more difficult to measure accurately the much shorter time taken by a body to fall a measured distance. According to a probably apocryphal story, Galileo used his own pulse to measure the period of swing of the lamp in the cathedral of Pisa, and found that it is independent of the amplitude. For a falling body a more accurate measure is needed, and he used a thin jet of water coming from a large jar, weighing the amount that came out during the fall. He further increased the accuracy by allowing the ball to roll down an inclined plane instead of falling freely, for then the time is much longer and so easier to measure.

By such measurements he showed that the distance traversed is proportional to the square of the time taken. This applies also to free fall, and he obtained a rough estimate of what we now call the acceleration due to gravity. He also studied the motion of projectiles, and found that the range is a maximum when the angle of elevation of the gun is 45°. The famous story of his dropping two weights from the top of the leaning tower of Pisa is probably apocryphal, but he did show that the time of fall is independent of the mass, contrary to Aristotle.

As we saw with Kepler, the advance of science often depends on the precision of the measurements. Those of Brahe were as accurate as possible by direct sighting. The next step, the invention of the telescope, was due mainly to Galileo. Lenses had been used in spectacles for centuries, Kepler already understood the magnifying power of lenses, and early telescopes magnifying three or four times were made in Holland and France. Galileo heard of this work and succeeded in making a telescope that magnified thirty times, and was thus much superior to any other existing at that time. After extensive observation of objects on the earth convinced him that it gave real knowledge, he turned his telescope to the sky and immediately made a series of critical discoveries. He saw the sunspots and the mountains on the moon, imperfections unexpected in perfect Aristotelian spheres. He discovered several of the satellites of the planet Jupiter, and found that they revolved around it. This was just like a miniature solar system, and gave support to the Copernican idea of the solar system.

The work of Galileo was of decisive importance in several respects. It replaced the qualitative and unverifiable speculations of the Aristotelians with quantitative mathematical reasoning supported by accurate experimental verification. He showed how scientific instruments like the telescope can be used to extend the powers of our senses in a reliable way. He criticised the use of ill-defined and unverifiable concepts like "absolute perfection" and showed that they have no place in science. He replaced the imprecise terms of everyday speech with a new scientific terminology where every concept is given a precise mathematical and measurable meaning. The spirit of the new science was optimistic. It was confident that old misunderstandings and prejudices could be overcome, the secrets of nature revealed, and the world transformed.

In this way Galileo completed the destruction of Aristotelian physics began so many years previously. The Aristotelian philosophers did not give in easily. They made many plausible objections to Galileo's work, but gradually these were shown to be false or unsupportable. Some of Galileo's arguments for the motion of the earth round the sun were indeed incorrect, and he was vindicated only centuries later. He realised the central importance of the Copernican theory and succeeded in removing most of the arguments used against it on the basis of common sense. This made possible the subsequent scientific developments that were eventually to provide the definitive proof of the Copernican theory.

Galileo saw very clearly that if the new science was to prevail, it must have the support of the Church. He had many friends in high ecclesiastic circles who were very sympathetic to his work. However, his Aristotelian opponents were able to point to passages in Scripture that seemed to be inconsistent with the heliocentric system. Galileo believed that Scripture often uses the language of ordinary speech, without thereby endorsing scientific theories. At this critical moment for the development of science the debate concerning the nature and method of science and the validity of its conclusions in the context of the teaching of the Church assumed central importance, and this continues to be the case today.

The Discovery of the Christian Origin of Science

These Christian roots of modern science are not generally known. The man primarily responsible for uncovering the evidence for the Christian origin of science was the French physicist Pierre Duhem. He was a theoretical physicist working mainly in the field of thermodynamics, but he had always been interested in the history of physics. He was asked to write a series of articles on the history of mechanics, and easily wrote the first one on the ideas of ancient Greeks. Like most historians of science, he expected to pass rapidly over the Middle Ages to the giants of the Renaissance. But he was a careful man, not content to rely on secondhand sources. He found obscure references to earlier work, and following them up, primarily in the archives in Paris, discovered the work of Buridan and his pupil Oresme, and of many other medievals who contributed to the origin of science.

Duhem wrote two volumes on the history of mechanics, three on Leonardo da Vinci, and then embarked on his greatest work, the *Systeme du Monde.* The first volume, devoted to the Greeks, was published in 1913, and was highly praised by George Sarton, the founder and editor of the journal *Isis,* who said that he looked forward eagerly to the second volume. When he read the second volume, however, he realised that what Duhem had found was highly uncongenial to his secularist beliefs. Duhem left him in no doubt whatever. Writing on the doctrine of the Great Year, he said: "To the construction of that system all disciples of Hellenic philosophy—Peripatetics, Stoics, Neo-Platonist—contributed; to that system Abu Masar offered the homage of the Arabs; most illustrious rabbis, from Philo of Alexandria to Maimonides, have accepted it. To condemn it and to throw it overboard as a monstrous superstition, Christianity had to come."

Sarton did not try to refute Duhem; that would have been impossible. Instead he used the one remaining weapon, that of silence. None of the following volumes were reviewed in *Isis,* and the name of Duhem was thereafter hardly ever mentioned. In Sarton's own vast volumes on the history of science Duhem receives but a few mentions, whereas quite minor figures receive extensive discussion.

Tragically, Duhem died in 1916 when only the first five volumes of his *Systeme du Monde* had been published. Duhem left the text of the remaining five volumes in manuscript, and the publisher was bound by the terms of the contract to publish them in successive years. The secularist establishment however was bitterly opposed to their publication, and succeeded in preventing this for forty years. Only the death of his most determined opponent, and the threat of legal action, finally forced the publishers to act.

It is not surprising that the secularists should be so determined to prevent the publication of books of massive scholarship that completely undermine their view of the development of science, and show that science as we know it is built on Christian foundations. What is surprising is that Christians have been so slow to recognise and publish his work. Even now, after many decades of scholarly work on medieval science, the name of Duhem is hardly known outside specialist circles. It deserves to be familiar to Christians, particularly to those concerned with the education of the young, who are still taught that there is a fundamental opposition between science and the Christian faith.

CHAPTER 3

Newman and Science*

Introduction

JOHN HENRY NEWMAN (1801–1890) was one of the outstanding religious thinkers of the nineteenth century. He foresaw many of the religious troubles and laboured incessantly to prepare the Church to face them, and had a dominating influence on the Second Vatican Council.

He was born in London and went to Trinity College, Oxford, for his undergraduate studies. After graduation he was elected a Fellow of Oriel College, took Anglican Orders, and was appointed Vicar of the University Church of St. Mary the Virgin. Sunday after Sunday he preached to the university, recalling his hearers back to the beliefs of the early Church. He was a leader of the Oxford Movement that tried to establish a *Via Media* between the Church of England and what he then believed to be the decadent Roman Church. Eventually, after intense spiritual struggles, he saw that this was a chimera, that it is the Roman Church that has unbroken continuity with the Church of the Fathers, and that the Church of England is but a manmade national church. He recognised that he could not remain an Anglican and save his soul, and so was received into what he called the One True Fold in 1845. In so doing, he abandoned the secure and well-endowed life of an Oxford don for the uncertainties and privations of life as a Catholic in Victorian

* Reprinted with permission from *Sapientia*. LIV(1999): 395.

England. In spite of many trials, he never looked back nor regretted his conversion, affirming that the Hand of God was most wonderfully over him.

Soon after his reception, he was ordained to the priesthood and established the Oratory of St. Philip Neri in Birmingham. There he continued his preaching and writing, largely in obscurity. This was changed when an Anglican vicar, the Rev. Charles Kingsley, accused him of advocating lying. To clear his name, Newman wrote his *Apologia pro Vita Sua*, giving the full story of his spiritual journey.

This re-established him in the eyes of his countrymen, and the seal was set on his life's work by his elevation to the cardinalate in 1879.

Newman is well known as a theologian and preacher through his many writings and by his extensive correspondence, now published in thirty-one volumes. He made important contributions to philosophy, notably in his *Essay in Aid of a Grammar of Assent*, a sensitive and subtle account of what it is to believe. He is recognised as a master of English prose and as the author of *The Dream of Gerontius*. Much less well-known is his keen interest in science and mathematics and this, together with his work on logic, accounts for the clarity and cogency of his writings.

To Newman, material phenomena were remote compared with his vivid apprehension of the abiding presence of Almighty God. His religious experiences at the age of 15 confirmed him in his "mistrust of the reality of material phenomena" and made him "rest in the thought of two and only two supreme and luminously self evident beings, myself and my Creator."[1]

Yet in spite of this there are seminal aspects of his thought and work that are related to science. Mathematics and physics had a large place in his early undergraduate studies, and he had a keen understanding and considerable knowledge of the science of his time. This awareness helped to give his writings the concreteness and force that has enabled them to transcend the accidents of his

---

[1] J. H. Newman, *Apologia pro Vita Sua* (Oxford: Oxford University Press, 1913), 108.

era and to carry their message to succeeding generations. Indeed, so perceptive was his insight into science that a philosopher of science would find his writings worthy of study while anyone concerned with the perennial tensions between the beliefs of the Christian and the speculations of the agnostic would find that, over a century ago, he cogently outlined the Christian's reply to the many of the problems raised by modern science.

Oxford

When Newman went up to Oxford, toward the end of the second decade of the nineteenth century, experimental science as we understand it now was virtually unknown. But mathematics flourished, and it was through its study that Newman developed his clear and logical mind, and came to know the power and elegance and generality of those methods of thought that science, as it comes to maturity, increasingly absorbs into its very being.

Newman read for Honours in both Mathematics and Classics and, as a young freshman, he was astonished that his mathematical tutor, Mr. Short, began his lectures at the Asses' Bridge, which the young Newman had long left behind at school. It was the tutor's turn to be astonished, when, on enquiring whether Newman had done any Euclid before, was told that he had been through five books. So impressed, indeed, was Mr. Short by Newman's mathematical ability that he urged him to sit for the newly opened Trinity Scholarship; Newman did so and was successful.

For his final examination he offered, in addition to Euclid, Bridge's *Algebra* and *Trigonometry*, Newton's *Principia* (how many scientists today have ever opened his classic work?), Robertson's *Conic Sections*, Vince's *Fluxions, Hydrostatics and Astronomy*, and Wood's *Mechanics and Opthics*.

In the following year he considerably broadened his interests, attending lectures in Anatomy and Mineralogy. Commenting acutely on Buckland's lectures on Geology, he remarked that:

> [T]he science is so in its infancy, that no regular system is formed. Hence the lectures are rather an enumeration of facts from which

probabilities are deduced, than a consistent and luminous theory
of certainties illustrated by occasional examples.[2]

At the same time he continued his mathematical studies and
wrote an essay on how the mysteries of mathematics prepare the
mind to receive the mysteries of religion, thus foreshadowing his
later work on the analogy between scientific and religious assent.

In 1822 he conceived the audacious plan of standing for the
Oriel Fellowship. Writing to his father he admitted that:

> [F]ew have attained the facility and comprehension which I have
> arrived at from the regularity and constancy of my reading and the
> laborious and nerve-bracing and fancy-repressing study of mathe-
> matics, which has been my principal subject.[3]

And later: "I lay great strength on the attention I have given
to Mathematics on account of the general strength it imparts to
the mind."[4]

As a Fellow of Oriel, he was increasingly drawn into the theological issues of the day and his time was absorbed by his duties as
tutor and curate. But he still took a lively interest in the affairs of
his contemporaries. His constant friend and companion, Froude,
wrote of his catholicity of interests:

> He was interested in everything that was going on in science, in
> politics, in literature. Nothing was too large for him, nothing too
> small, if it threw light on the central question, what man really
> was, and what was his destiny.[5]

In 1827 he began a course of study in advanced mathematics,
wishing to learn "analytics and differentials." In the summer he
worked on trigonometry and Hamilton's *Conics* and the following

[2] J. H. Newman, *Letters & Diaries* (Oxford: Oxford University Press, 1978), Vol.
1, 109.
[3] Ibid., 125.
[4] Ibid., 126.
[5] J. A. Froude, "The Oxford Counter-Reformation," in *Short Studies on Great
Subjects*, 4th series (New York: Charles Scribner's Sons, 1910).

January he began the *Principia* in earnest. But this noble resolve was soon forgotten as things of even greater moment began increasingly to occupy his mind and soul. In March he began his *Arians of the Fourth Century*, and was soon swept into that tide of prayer and study that was, seventeen years later, to carry him into the Catholic Church.

In the midst of his winter of trials and sufferings, he had little thought for science; yet the knowledge he gained at Oxford was never lost, and it was destined to flower again in the coldness of the coming spring.

The Catholic University in Ireland

On 9 May 1845, a bill was introduced into Parliament establishing three "Queen's Colleges" in Ireland to provide higher education of a strictly non-sectarian character. The Irish bishops considered them to be unsuitable for Catholic young men and were therefore faced with the task of providing alternative means of higher education for the few students desiring it. The advice of Rome was sought, and the bishops were urged to establish a Catholic university, taking Louvain as their model.

Thus it was that on 18 July 1851, Dr. Cullen, Archbishop of Armagh and Primate of Ireland, visited Newman in Birmingham and invited him to become Rector of the proposed new Catholic University in Dublin. After seeking the advice of his friends, Newman accepted this invitation, and set to work on the immense and complex task of building a university.

In ordinary circumstances, this task would have been hard enough, but several ideological, political, and educational factors conspired to make Newman's work of exceptional difficulty.

The middle of the nineteenth century was a period of unprecedented scientific and intellectual advance, and many believed that science would soon be able to solve all human and sociological problems, thus making religion a superfluous relic of a bygone age. Perhaps understandably, Catholics tended on the whole to react against this exaggerated view of science by looking with extreme suspicion on the new advances. Thus Newman had the delicate task of asserting on the one hand the immutable doctrines of the Church and protecting his university against the rising tide of materialism and, on the other, that of preventing his university from becoming just a seminary for the laity, subject to such strict ecclesiastical control as to prevent all independence and originality of thought.

Politically Ireland was, as ever, in turmoil, with party contending against party and all parties united only by their aversion to the English. Newman, an Englishman himself, had to overcome their suspicion that the proposed university was but another instrument of subjugation and had to try to win their support for his new venture.

This task was made doubly difficult by his lack of knowledge concerning the intricacies of Irish politics, as well as the personalities involved.

Educationally Ireland was at a low ebb. It was just after the potato famine when large numbers of the population had died of starvation or had emigrated, and most of those who remained were too preoccupied with the task of survival to care much for higher education. Heroic but sporadic efforts to organise primary and secondary education were being made, but, on the whole, there was hardly any demand for education at a university level, and experienced observers warned Newman that this lack of interest would be one of his most serious difficulties. They were right.

One of Newman's first acts was to seek to arouse interest in and support for the proposed university by a series of discourses on the nature and scope of university education, afterward published as *The Idea of a University*. In these discourses he emphasized the unit of knowledge and laid down that a university "teaches all knowledge by teaching all branches of knowledge."[6] Hence, contrary to the demands of the materialists, theology must be included in the curriculum. Science, also, in all its complexity, must be included. He went on to discuss the relation between this scientific knowledge and the Catholic Faith that pervades and inspires the whole university.

---

6 F. McGrath, *Newman's University: Ideal and Reality* (London: Longmans Green, 1971), 135.

It was proposed that the university should be divided into four faculties: Arts, Medicine, Law, and Theology. The Arts Faculty was founded at once, with Medicine soon after. Law and Theology were to follow when practicable. The Faculty of Arts was subdivided into Letters and Science. Letters comprised Latin, Greek, Semitic, and Modern Languages; History (ancient and modern); Archaeology; and English Literature and Criticism. Science comprised Logic, Metaphysics, Ethics (including Economy and Politics), Philosophy of Religion, Mathematics, Natural Philosophy, Chemistry, Natural History, Mineralogy, Geology, and so on. As a subsidiary to the Faculty of Arts, there was to be a School of Engineering. It is clear from this list that the word "science" was used in a rather broader sense than is usual today.

The course of studies lasted five years: for the first two years all students followed the same lectures on liberal and cultural subjects, and in the final three they devoted themselves to more specialised professional studies. They were thus "educated" according to Newman's ideal, and also trained for the professions that they aspired to enter.

Newman built a university Church to be the centre of the life of the university and he expressed the hope that it would "maintain and symbolise that great principle in which we glory as our characteristic, the union of Science with Religion."[7] It was not until 18 May 1854 that a Synodal Meeting of the Irish Episcopate formally announced their decision to erect a university, and laid down the essentials of its Constitution. On 5 June 1854, Newman was installed as Rector, Cardinal Cullen publicly charging him to: "Teach the young committed to your care to cultivate every branch of learning. To scan the depths of every science, and explore the mysteries of every art."[8]

Undeterred by the inadequacy of his resources, Newman announced that:

It is proposed to open the classical and mathematical schools of the university on the Feast of St. Malachi next Friday November

---

[7] Ibid., 277.
[8] Ibid., 314.

3rd. The schools of Medicine, of civil engineering and of other material and physical sciences will be opened at the same time, or as soon after as possible.[9]

It will be noticed how large a part of Newman's infant university was devoted to the sciences.

Among the names that he submitted provisionally to the Archbishops on 3 October 1854 were those of Edward Butler as Professor of Mathematics and Terence Flanagan as Professor of Civil Engineering. Later, in 1856, William K. Sullivan, Professor of Theoretical and Practical Chemistry in the School of Science of the Museum of Irish Industry in Dublin, was appointed Professor of Chemistry. He was later to become Professor of Theoretical Chemistry in the Royal College of Science, Dublin, and President of Queen's College, Cork. The following year the mathematical physicist Henry Hennessy, FRS, was appointed to the Chair of Natural Philosophy. He later became the Professor of Applied Mathematics at the Royal College of Science.

Newman was fortunate in obtaining fully equipped premises for this medical school. The school opened in October 1855 and flourished right up to its incorporation into the National University of Ireland in 1908. "Did our efforts toward the foundation of a Catholic University," he wrote, "issue in nothing beyond the establishment of a first-rate Catholic School of Medicine in the Metropolis, as it has already done, they would have met with sufficient reward."[10]

In his Report to the Bishops on 31 October 1857, Newman recorded that the medical school had 43 students and a chemical laboratory "in state of completeness that may safely challenge comparison with anything of a similar kind in these islands."[11] It was modeled on German lines, and provided facilities for medical students and also for pure research and the needs of those studying the application of chemistry to industrial processes.

Newman was particularly anxious to establish the Faculty of Science. "The establishment of a good School of Science," he wrote,

[9] Ibid., 316.
[10] Ibid., 369.
[11] Ibid., 420.

"was one of the foremost objects which I kept in view."[12] Writing to J. M. Capes on 1 February 1857, he discussed possible ways in which English gentlemen might help the university: "Or let them do a thing which must be good, whatever comes of the university, for example, set up a School of Physical Science, or make us a present of instruments and apparatus."[13]

In spite of his efforts, the faculty of science was never fully established in his time. His report in 1858 urged the immediate establishment of chairs of Botany and Zoology and of Geology and Mineralogy, and the expenditure of £20,000 on scientific laboratories. He referred also the urgent recommendations that he had received from "persons of the highest consideration in Rome,"[14] to further the study of physical science at the university.

He also wanted the university to include a school of useful arts, comprising professorships of engineering, mining, and agriculture in order to develop and to apply the natural resources of Ireland. A century ago this was a bold and farsighted innovation.

The School of Engineering was opened in 1855 and provided a five-year course. In 1858 a new periodical *The Atlantis* was started. It had a markedly scientific character in order to justify the faculty of science to the public. Newman also tried to set up astronomical and meteorological observatories, but he was unable to do so for lack of funds.

To Newman, a university was primarily a teaching institution, and research took second place. He considered that teaching and research abilities were not usually found combined in the same person, and that the university teacher had neither the time nor the solitude necessary for research. Nevertheless, he desired that his professors undertake some research, in order that they become better teachers through contact with the latest advances. Newman also envisaged a series of research institutes for the single-minded purpose of original investigations. It is interesting that this idea is now

[12] Ibid., 330.
[13] Ibid., 435.
[14] Ibid., 372.

being increasingly followed in the national research centres of pure science and in many industrial laboratories.

Newman remained Rector of the university for seven years. Throughout this time he was also the Superior of the Oratory in Birmingham, and the strain of the double responsibility bore heavily on his health. He had ever considered that his task in Ireland was simply to establish the university, and that it would be the work of others to develop and extend it. These and other considerations led to his resignation on 12 November 1858.

Theological and Scientific Knowledge

In the course of his lectures on the "Scope and Nature of University Education," later published in book form under the title *The Idea of a University*, and in addresses on other occasions, Newman developed in some detail his view of the relation between theological and scientific knowledge. This is worth recalling, not only because of the intrinsic interest attaching to his masterly handling of so difficult a theme, but also because mistaken views of the relation are still prevalent today.

In his discourses, Newman had to steer a delicate course between two erroneous views. On the one hand, the rising tide of materialistic humanism proclaimed that scientific knowledge alone was worth having, and that consequently theology could be disregarded as either false and superseded or as the private affair of the individual. On the other hand, he had to avoid making science so subservient to theology that its natural growth and development would be made impossible.

He began his lectures by showing that theology constitutes genuine knowledge, and thus cannot be excluded from the curriculum of a university. Likewise, because of the unity of knowledge, theology and science cannot be kept in watertight compartments; that is, a relation exists between these two types of knowledge. Furthermore, the scientist must be a man of faith and the theologian aware of contemporary science.

From the unity of knowledge it follows that there is no intrinsic antagonism between religion and science, since truth cannot contradict truth. There is thus a relation between theological and scientific knowledge: they cannot be divorced from each other. This relation, however, is rather a subtle one, and in Newman's view may conveniently be approached by first considering an erroneous conception of it. According to this view, science and theology must ever advance hand in hand, each advance of one being reflected by an advance of the other. No scientific discovery must be made that does not immediately appear to confirm and illustrate theology not only as it is contained in the defined doctrines of the Church, but also in the popular imagination of the time. Likewise, nothing must be found likely to dissipate even the most naïve pious fancies of the faithful. The scientist must ever be anxiously looking over his shoulder, so to speak, to see the effect of his work on the beliefs of the multitude. Even his research programme must be planned in advance in order to provide results to confirm *this* doctrine or refute *that* argument that is currently being urged against the Church.

It is clear that, according to this view, science becomes a mere slave to theology, simply existing to provide useful illustration of revealed truth, but with no life or freedom of its own. That view is decisively rejected by Newman: The scientist, he writes:

> is not bound, in conducting his researches to be at every moment adjusting his course by the maxims of the scholars or by popular traditions . . . or to be determined to be edifying or to be ever answering heretics and unbelievers.[15]
>
> Unless he is at liberty to investigate on the basis, and according to the peculiarities of his science, he cannot investigate at all.[16]
>
> Great minds need elbow room, not indeed in the domain of Faith, but of thought.[17]
>
> If you insist that in their speculations, researches, or conclusions in their particular science, it is not enough that they should submit to the Church generally, and acknowledge its dogmas, but that they must get up all that divines have said or the multitude

[15] J. H. Newman, *The Idea of a University* (London: Longmans Green, 1947), 348–49.
[16] Ibid., 349.
[17] Ibid., 350.

believed upon religious matters, you simply crush and stamp out the flame within them, and they can do nothing at all.[18]

I say, then, that it is a matter of primary importance in the cultivation of those sciences, in which truth is discoverable by the human intellect, that the investigator should be free, independent, unshackled in his movements; that he should be allowed and enabled, without impediment, to fix his mind intently, nay, exclusively, on his special objects, without the risk of being distracted every other minute in the process and progress of his enquiry, by charges of temerariousness, or by warning against extravagance or scandal.[19]

The essential harmony between religion and science thus means that each can be followed using the appropriate methods, without constantly worrying about their exact concordance at every stage. In the end, when our knowledge is complete, they will appear in perfect agreement, but this is not necessarily the case for all our partial and provisional views evolved in the course of discovery. While it is true that truth cannot contradict truth, it is frequently the case that one truth seems contrary to another, and thus "we must be patient with such appearances, and not be hasty to pronounce them to be really of a more formidable character."[20]

Newman pointed out that there are many inexplicable truths and contradictions in other departments of knowledge, so we should not be surprised to find some apparent antagonisms between religious beliefs on the one hand, and contemporary scientific speculations on the other. We confidently expect that in the former case these difficulties will be dissipated by the advance of knowledge, so it is reasonable to expect the same in the latter.

The freedom of the scientist naturally demands responsible exercise. Apparent disagreements should not be published in a sensational manner that could scandalise those unacquainted with the difficulty of attaining truth. Newman would be horrified by the

---

[18] Ibid., 351.
[19] Ibid., 346.
[20] Ibid., 338.

mass media of today, ever ready to exploit the wildest scientific speculations to the detriment of religion.

Newman was being rather optimistic when he asked:

> religious writers, jurists, economists, physiologists, chemists, geolo-
> gists and historians to go on quietly, and in a neighbourly way, in
> then-respective lines of speculation, research and experiment, with
> full faith in the consistency of that multiform truth.[21]

He believed that the Catholic is not:

> a nervous creature who startles at every sound, and is fluttered by
> every strange or novel appearance that meets his eyes. He has no
> sort of apprehension, he laughs at the idea that anything can be dis-
> covered by any other scientific method which can contradict any of
> the dogmas of religion.[22]

A deeper insight into the relation between science and theology
may be obtained by comparing their respective subject matter and
methods of enquiry. This Newman does in his essay on "Christianity
and Physical Science," and he is here more concerned to point out the
differences than to emphasize the similarities. He begins by observing
that, broadly speaking, we may divide knowledge into the natural and
the supernatural, science being concerned with the former and theology with the latter. The most detailed knowledge of either of these
worlds does not by itself give us any knowledge of the other.

He allows that the two worlds do sometimes intersect:

> as far as supernatural knowledge includes truths and facts of the
> natural world, and as far as truth and facts of the natural world are
> on the other hand data for inference about the supernatural. But
> on the whole, Theology and Science, whether in their respective
> ideas, or again in their own actual fields, on the whole, are incom-
> municable, incapable of collision, and needing at most to be con-
> nected, never to be reconciled.[23]

---

[21] Ibid., 341.
[22] Ibid., 342.
[23] Ibid., 310.

This separation is even more marked when we compare theology with physics. The physicist is concerned to understand the measurable aspects of phenomena in terms of laws and first principles. Physics begins with matter and ends with matter. It is of no concern to the physicist, as such, to ask how the universe is sustained, how it came to be, or whether it can cease to be. He cannot say whether the laws of nature are immutable or can be suspended, or what is the nature of time or causality. Theology, on the other hand, does not deal with matter at all. It is concerned with just those questions that are beyond the sphere of the physicist.

> Theology contemplates the world, not of matter, but of mind; the Supreme Intelligence; souls and their destiny; conscience and duty; the past, present and future dealings of the Creator with the creature.[24]

As a result, the physicist and the theologian regard phenomena from different points of view. The physicist is concerned with the behaviour of matter, not with its origin and purpose. This is a methodological limitation, a definition of the subject matter. In this sense it is atheistic, and this is why the exclusive purpose of science can tend to indifference or scepticism concerning theological questions.

Having thus described the respective spheres of theology and science, and shown that they but rarely impinge on each other from the very nature of their subject matter, Newman goes on to contrast their respective methods. Theology, he points out, is deductive, whereas physics is inductive. Theology is based on the truths of revelation, and nothing further can be added. Physics lacks such known principles and has to find them through a detailed analysis of diverse phenomena. Thus theology relies on tradition, physics on experiment; theology looks to the past, physics to the future.

These distinctions between theology and physics need to be qualified in several respects, and Newman did so in his other writings. In his day, theology was unduly systematised, and uneasily fitted into a strict deductive mould, while science as we know it now,

---

[24] Ibid., 313.

with the vast interlocking structure of theoretical physics, was barely glimpsed. It is indeed possible to draw several instructive parallels between the methods of theology and science, thus modifying the sharp antithesis painted by Newman. In a certain sense theology also is progressive and inductive, as Newman himself showed in his *Essay on the Development of Christian Doctrine*. Deduction, on the other hand, plays a central part in modern science in drawing out the numerous consequences of its general principles.

The inadequacy of the simple antithesis between induction and deduction to characterise the respective methods of science and theology was shown by Newman in his later work on a *Grammar of Assent*, where he shows the similarity between assent in religion and in science. Newman was concerned to justify the certainty with which Catholics hold the faith, even though they may be unable to provide a rational justification.

He began by distinguishing between notional and real assent. If we are shown a geometrical proof, for example, and are unable to see any flaw, we accept it notionally. It does not engage us deeply, we would not die for it, as we know very well that there may be a hidden flaw. If, however, we are provided with the demonstration of a result that is embedded in a web of arguments, all pointing to the same conclusion, our assent is much stronger and can be called real. An example is provided by the many arguments, from a wide variety of premises, that support the Lorentz transformation in special relativity.

It is a common experience in scientific research that assent to the reality of a certain phenomenon grows gradually as many separate indications coalesce and fall into place. It is rather like forming a friendship. At first one is unsure, but gradually the various impressions join together to reveal a real person. Once the real assent is attained, it is possible to predict the likely behaviour of the phenomenon, or of the friend, in circumstances not yet experienced. In such cases:

> the warrant for our certitude about them is not mere common sense, but the true healthy action of our ratiocinative powers, an

action more subtle and more comprehensive than the mere appreciation of a syllogistic argument.[25]

Many other examples can be adduced from experimental science and from our everyday experiences. We believe that the planets rotate around the sun, that the stars are very far away, and that the earth rotates on its axis, each on the basis of a large number of probable arguments. Newman gives many examples of such assents, all showing how it is possible for many individual arguments, each probable, to fuse together to give certainty. Newman called this the illative sense. This way to belief is found in everyday affairs, in science and also in religion. It is indeed fitting that our religious beliefs should engage the whole person and not just our minds for "man is not a reasoning animal; he is a seeing, feeling, contemplating, active animal."

It might well be objected that sometimes we are quite certain about some belief, and afterward find that we are mistaken. In such cases, however, it is possible to find an underlying continuity between the new belief and the old, so that the one can be seen as a natural development of the other. In physics this is found, for example, in the transition from Newtonian to Einsteinian dynamics, where the latter is a development of the former. Similarly, in theology, we find an organic growth through the years, as described by Newman in his *Essay on the Development of Christian Doctrine.*

Newman emphasizes both the apparently paradoxical aspects of the relation between theology and science. On the one hand, since all knowledge is ultimately one, they are intimately linked together, yet, on the other, this link is such as to permit each to develop in full freedom in accord with its own inner life.

Such a relationship has many parallels, both in the material works and in human affairs. The nucleus in the atom, the atom in the molecule, the molecule in the cell, the cell in the body, the individual in the family and the family in society each has a distinct life of its own and yet is bound to the higher organism of which it is a part.

---

[25] J. H. Newman, *An Essay in Aid of a Grammar of Assent* (London: Longmans Green, 1947), 241.

This relationship Newman expresses in the terminology of scholastic philosophy by calling theology the external form of the sciences. In saying this he maintains that Christianity, "where it has been laid as the first stone (of education) and acknowledged as the governing spirit, it will take up into itself, assimilate, and give a character to literature and science."[26] But this is not done by dictating any of the specific methods or results of science, as it would be if theology were the internal form of science. In making this distinction Newman rejects the notion "that Theology stands to other knowledge as the soul to the body; or that the sciences are but its instruments or appendages. Theology is the highest, and the widest, but it does not interfere with the real freedom of any secular science in is own secular department."[27]

Evolution

In an entry in his *Philosophical Notebook*, dated 9 December 1863, Newman reflects:

> There is as much want of simplicity in the idea of the creation of distinct species as in that of the creation of trees in full growth, whose seed is in themselves, or of rocks with fossils in them. I mean that it is as strange that monkeys should be so like men with no historical connection between them, as the notion that there should be no course of history by which fossil bones got into rocks.[28]

In this passage, Newman is not concerned to consider the detailed scientific arguments for and against the theory of evolution. He does not see it as his duty to argue for or against the theory. Instead, he simply remarks that in its overall sweep it is far more plausible than the belief in special creation a few thousand years ago, a view that is still vigorously propagated. Such creationists, having rejected the authority of the Church as the Divine interpreter of Scripture, are trapped by the superficial meaning of the

---

[26] J. H. Newman, *The Idea of a University,* 319–20.

[27] Ibid.

[28] Cf. *The Philosophical Notebook of John Henry Newman*, ed. by E. Sillem (Louvain: Nauwelaerts Publishing House, 1969), Vol. 2, 158.

words, which inevitably leads them to a position that is antithetical both to theology and to science.

Newman believed that the Creator lets His work develop through secondary causes, which have imparted "certain laws to matter millions of ages ago, which have surely and precisely worked out, in the course of these long ages, those effects which He from the first proposed."[29] In a letter to Pusey, he addresses the same question: "If second causes are conceivable at all, an Almighty Agent being supposed, I don't see why the series should not last for millions of years as for thousands."[30] Thus, "Mr. Darwin's theory *need* not be atheistical, be it true or not; it may simply be suggesting a large idea of Divine Prescience and Skill."[31]

This is not, of course, to say that Newman concurred with all of Darwin's views. By 1871 Darwin had been a rank materialist for over thirty years, although he concealed it to avoid controversy. In particular, Newman was clear about what should be behind talk about chance as the causative agent in evolution. In a letter to Mivart he emphasized that *chance is not a cause*, because "what seems chance must be the result of existing laws as yet undiscovered."[32] In another letter he expressed his view that the "atheist did not necessarily have to hold that 'the *accidental* evolution to living beings is inconsistent with divine design,'" adding that "it is accidental to us, not to God."

Newman was not much interested in meetings of the British Association for the Advancement of Science and kept well clear of them. He deplored the habit of scientists, on the occasion of these meetings, to air their views on theological matters.

In a letter written in 1874 to the Rev. David Brown, a Free Kirk minister, he remarked:

> Doubtless theologians have meddled with science, and now scientific men are paying them off by meddling with theology. With

---

[29] J. H. Newman, Letter to Canon J. Walker, *Letters & Diaries* (Oxford: Oxford University Press, 1973), 24.77.
[30] Letter to Pusey, ibid., 25.137.
[31] Ibid.
[32] Letter to Mivart, ibid., 26.384.

you, I see nothing in the theory of evolution inconsistent with an Almighty Creator and Protector: but these men assume, assume with an abundant scorn of us and superciliousness, that religion and science are on this point contradictory, and on this audacious assumption they proceed dogmatically to conclude that there is no truth in religion. It is dreadful to think of the number of souls that will suffer while the epidemic lasts; but the truth is too powerful not in the end to get the upper hand.[33]

One can only remark that the epidemic has lasted a rather long time.

Science and Man

When Newman was in his prime, the high tide of scientific humanism was in full flood. Enthusiastic and loquacious orators vied with one another to introduce the masses to the marvels of the new worlds opened up by science. Museums were founded, libraries and reading rooms established, and evening classes started for the instruction of all.

On the occasion of the opening of the library and reading room at Tamworth, no less a person than Sir Robert Peel excelled himself in enthusiastically praising the benefits of the new learning:

> Let me earnestly entreat you not to neglect the opportunity which we are now willing to afford you! It will not be our fault if the ample page of knowledge, rich with the spoils of time, is not unrolled to you. . . . Not only will this spread new knowledge, but man in becoming wiser will become better. He will rise at once in the scale of intellectual and moral existence, and by being accustomed to such contemplations, he will feel the *moral dignity of his nature exalted*. Not only is physical knowledge the means of useful knowledge and rational recreation, but its pleasures supersede the indulgence of sensual appetites. Thus it will contribute to the intellectual and *moral improvement* of the community.[34]

---

[33] Letter to Rev. David Brown, ibid., 27.43.

[34] Sir Robert Peel, Lecture on the Occasion of the Opening of the Tamworth Reading Room. 19 January 1841, published in *The Times*, London, and subsequently as a pamphlet.

Newman enquires: "*how* these wonderful moral effects are to be wrought under the instrumentality of the physical sciences. . . . Does Sir Robert Peel mean to say that . . . you have but to drench the popular mind with physics and moral and religious advancement follows?" He points out that "to know is one thing, to do is another; the two things are altogether distinct." Newman immediately puts his finger on the error lying behind this—the view "that true excellence comes not from within, but from without; not wrought out through personal struggles and sufferings, but following upon a passive exposure to influences over which we have no control."[35]

After some further exposures of the total inadequacy of the new method of elevating people's morals by diffusing scientific knowledge, he releases upon it the full force of his withering scorn:

> It does not require many words, then, to determine that, taking nature as it is actually found, and assuming that there is an Art of life, to say that it consists, or in any essential manner is placed, in the cultivation of Knowledge, that the mind is changed by a discovery, or saved by a diversion, and can thus be amused into immortality—that grief, anger, cowardice, self-conceit, pride or passion, can be subdued by an examination of shells and grasses, or inhaling of gases, or chipping of rocks, or calculating the longitude, is the veriest of pretences which sophist or mountebank ever professed to a gaping auditory. If virtue be a mastery over the mind, if its end be action, if its perfection be inward order, harmony and peace, we must seek it in graver and holier places than in libraries and reading rooms.[36]

This insistence on interior formation rather than on exterior organisation as the means of improvement, Newman applied also to human society as a whole. He was not impressed by the optimism of those who sought to ensure the happiness of mankind by the devising of a perfect political system.

---

35 J. H. Newman, *Discussions and Arguments on Various Subjects* (London: Longmans Green, 1947), 261.
36 Ibid., 294.

"Men see that those parts of the national system," he observed, "which really depend on personal and private virtue, do not work well—and, not seeing where the deficiency lies, viz., in want of personal virtue, they imagine that they can put things right by applying their scientific knowledge to the improvement of the existing system. . . . I will state a principle," he continues, "which seems to me most important and most neglected—that the difference between this or that system is *as nothing* compared with the effects of human will upon them, that till the will be changed from evil to good, the difference of the results between the two systems will be imperceptible."

Conclusion

Newman was notable for his holiness, long-suffering, sensitivity, and courage. He was ever conscious of the presence of God, and devoted his life to His service. During the first half of his life he served God in the Church of England, and conscientiously carried out his duties to his students and parishioners. Then, as he reflected on contemporary events, he gradually came to the agonising realisation that the Church of England, which he had loved so ardently and served so faithfully, is a house divided against itself, a manmade sham.[37] As he studied ever more deeply the early history of the Church and the writings of the Fathers he saw that it is the Church of Rome that has maintained the true faith throughout the ages. Once convinced, he did not hesitate to abandon the security of a well-endowed Oxford don to join the despised remnant of the Catholic Church in England where he was treated with suspicion and incomprehension. He was always absolutely obedient to his superiors, although bitter experience taught him that he could never trust them. He was always unconditionally loyal to the papacy.

In his writings he showed a keen insight into the psychology of belief, and illustrated his discourses on its nature by examples from the whole realm of human experience from mathematics and physical science to history and theology. His early studies of mathematics

---

[37] S. L. Jaki, *The Church of England as Viewed by Newman* (Port Huron, MI: Real View Books, 2004).

and physics, and his later work on logic, gave his writings a clarity and cogency that place them far above those of his contemporaries.

His courage was not only spiritual and intellectual. When cholera was raging he was asked to send two priests to replace those who had died. Newman went himself, accompanied by the ever faithful Ambrose St. John.

Although he always put truth above friendship, he nevertheless retained the affection of his Anglican friends and won for himself a unique place in the esteem of Englishmen and indeed of people everywhere, from his own times until the present day.   ✣

References

Culler, A. D. 1955. *The Imperial Intellect.* New Haven: Yale University Press.

Froude, J. A. "The Oxford Counter-Reformation," in *Short Studies on Great Subjects*, 4th series (New York: Charles Scribner's Sons, 1910).

Jaki, S. L. 2004. *The Church of England as Viewed by Newman.* Port Huron: Real View Books.

———. 1998. *The One True Fold: Newman and his Converts.* Royal Oak: Real View Books.

———. 1991. Newman and Evolution, *Downside Review.* January 1991.

Ker, I. 1988. *John Henry Newman: A Bibliography.* Oxford: Oxford University Press.

Kitcher, P. 1983. *Abusing Science: The Case Against Creationism.* Milton Keynes, England: Open University.

Lucas, J. R., and P. E. Hodgson. 1990. *Spacetime and Electromagnetism.* Oxford: Oxford University Press.

McGrath, F. 1971. *Newman's University: Ideal and Reality.* London: Longmans Green.

Newman, J. H. 1978. *Letters & Diaries.* Oxford: Oxford University Press.

———. 1960. *An Essay on the Development of Christian Doctrine.* London: Sheed & Ward.

———. 1947. *An Essay in Aid of a Grammar of Assent.* London: Longmans Green.

———. 1947. *Discussions and Arguments on Various Subjects.* Longmans Green.

———. 1947. *The Idea of a University.* London: Longmans Green.

———. 1913. *Apologia pro Vita Sua.* Oxford: Oxford University Press.

Peel, Sir Robert, 1841. "Lecture on the occasion of the opening of the Tamworth Reading Room." London, *The Times*.

Sillem, E., ed. 1969. *The Philosophical Notebook of John Henry.*

———. *Newman*. Louvain: Nauwelaerts Publishing House, 2 volumes.

CHAPTER 4

Chesterton and Science[*]

I WAS SOMEWHAT ASTONISHED on receiving the invitation to give the Annual Chesterton Lecture on September 17, 1991. This is very likely the first time that a scientist, let alone a nuclear physicist, has been invited to talk about Chesterton. My astonishment is probably equalled by that of the reader as he begins to read this printed version of my talk. Whatever he was, Chesterton was certainly not a scientist. The very idea of finding him in a scientific laboratory stretches the imagination. He would have considered my title richly paradoxical. Indeed, a superficial reading of Chesterton could lead one to suppose that he was anti-scientific. Time and again he pokes fun at, and even ridicules, the solemn pronouncements of scientists on a wide range of subjects that have little to do with science. He visited the Crystal Palace; and, as he tells us, found about it

> something negative . . . arching over all our heads, a roof as remote as the sky . . . impartial and impersonal. . . . Our attention was fixed on the exhibits, which were all carefully ticketed and arranged in rows; for it was the age of science.[1]

---

[*] The Eleventh Annual Chesterton Lecture London, 17 September 1991. *The Chesterton Review* XX (November 1994). Reprinted with permission.

[1] G. K. Chesterton, *The Catholic Church and Conversion* (New York: The Macmillan Company, 1926), 77.

He seems to regard science as an impersonal and somewhat dull affair, concerned with classifying, arranging, and labelling.

It would however be a mistake to suppose that Chesterton was opposed to real science, for which indeed he had a healthy respect.[2] What he opposed with all his might was the pretentious folly of "scientism," the claim that only the scientific method can yield valid knowledge and reliable value judgments.[3] The last two decades of the nineteenth century were filled with optimism about the future development of mankind, when peace and plenty and even virtue were to be ushered in by the ever-increasing application of science. Popular writers such as Peel, Huxley, Bradlaugh, Spencer, and Wells waxed lyrical about the dawning of a new age, which they contrasted with the poverty, ignorance, and superstition of the religious ages of the past.

Chesterton, like Newman, faced an age increasingly and pervasively dominated by science. Neither of them doubted for an instant the value of genuine science; what appalled them, and drew forth the full force of their invective, was the tendency to make it a religion, to imagine that science has superseded Christianity, and can now provide the answer to all man's deepest needs, moral and spiritual. This they denounced as shallow sophistry.

Likewise, both were faced by a widespread scepticism about the very possibility of attaining objective truth. Not for nothing was Newman called the "Pillar of the Cloud." Always careful with words, he defined liberalism in religion as:

> the doctrine that there is no positive truth in religion, but that one creed is as good as another. . . . it is inconsistent with any recognition of religion as true . . . revealed religion is not a truth but a sentiment and a taste; not objective fact, not miraculous,

---

[2] Cecil Chesterton, *GKC: A Criticism* (New York: John Lane, 1909), 124–25. See also G. K. Chesterton, *The Defendant* (New York: Dodd, Mead, 1902), 75, and G. K. Chesterton, *The Club of Queer Trades* (London: Harper & Brothers, 1905), 236.

[3] Charles Bradlaugh, *A Plea for Atheism* (London: Freethought Publishing Company, 1877), 10.

and it is the right of each individual to make it say just what strikes his fancy.[4]

The very same belief faced Chesterton when he distinguished the philosophy of the tree and of the cloud:

> When a tree grows a branch at the top, it does not break away from the roots at the bottom; on the contrary it needs to hold more strongly by its roots the higher it rises with its branches. That is the true image of the vigorous and healthy progress of a man, a city, or a whole species. By contrast, when the evolutionists I speak of talk to us about change . . . they mean something that changes completely and entirely in every part, at every minute, like a cloud.[5]

True revolutions respect the element of continuity through the change, a continuity rooted in the underlying reality. It is to Chesterton's credit that no one has argued more persuasively on behalf of objective reality as a safeguard of sanity, including the sanity of science.

As John Coates points out, the evolutionary cults of the late nineteenth century "take as the starting point the denial of an objective, know-able, external world and of an identifiable human nature."[6] And he continues: "The varying and superficially conflicting creeds of 1890 to 1914 all involved, at some stage, a denial of the physical reality of individual objects, of the distinction between truth and falsehood, and even the very identity of the individual."[7] Among the proponents of these evolutionary cults, Haeckel

> promised a vast, uniform, uninterrupted and eternal process of development, linking organic and inorganic, matter and spirit, life

---

[4] J. H. Newman, "Biglietto Speech," April 27, 1879, quoted by I. Ker in his book, *Newman* (Oxford: Oxford University Press, 1988), 271.

[5] G. K. Chesterton, "Of Sentimentalism and the Head and the Heart," *The Church Socialist Quarterly* (January 1909): 12–15.

[6] John Coates, "Chesterton and the Modern Cultural Context," *Chesterton Review* (February–May 1989): 65.

[7] Ibid., 59.

and art. Again, the individual was an evanescent and momentary phenomenon in the flow of unending development.[8]

It found more sophisticated expression in the writings of T. H. Green, whose philosophy set itself "to overthrow the view that reality exists as a fact, given to us in experience. The simple data of sense can never be real. The best we can have are the relations the mind makes, and, therefore, the 'real world' must be through and through the world made by the mind."[9] As a young man, Chesterton had fathomed that abyss:

> I also dreamed that I had dreamed the whole creation. I had been behind and at the beginning of all things; and that without me no thing was made that was made. Anybody who has been in that centre of the cosmos knows what it is to be in hell.[10]

Against this debilitating solipsism, Chesterton stood like a rock of common sense. In answer to those who, like Hamlet, ask "To be or not to be, that is the question?" Chesterton conjures up Aquinas to answer, with a voice like thunder: "To BE, that is the answer." Or, even more succinctly, "There is an IS."[11] The importance of this assertion of reality can hardly be overestimated. Although an opponent of materialism, Chesterton knew that it was a far lesser evil than solipsism or idealism. One of the characters in his books expresses this conviction with emphasis:

> Materialists are all right; they are at least near enough to heaven to accept the earth and not imagine they made it. The dreadful doubts are not the doubts of the materialist. The dreadful doubts, the deadly and damnable doubts, are the doubts of the idealist.[12]

---

[8] Ibid., 60.
[9] Ibid.
[10] G. K. Chesterton, *The Poet and the Lunatics* (New York: Dodd, Mead, 1929), 125.
[11] G. K. Chesterton, *St. Thomas Aquinas* (New York: Sheed & Ward, 1933), 204 and 206.
[12] G. K. Chesterton, *The Poet and the Lunatics,* 124.

The original priest of the Father Brown stories, Father John O'Connor, recalled how Chesterton suffered the pains of subjectivism, but finally "emerged into the liberty of glory which philosophers class as Moderate Realism."[13] And Father O'Connor continues:

> His whole History of Mind is, could we see it clearly, a commentary on the Universe, seen and unseen. When philosophy begins, it is faced with a dilemma. Do I begin from thought within myself, or from reality outside my thought? If I choose my thought as the measure of reality, I am free to perish in the wilderness, if such freedom boots at all. If I choose reality as the measure of my thoughts, I am not so free for empty speculation, but my philosophising will be fruitful because rooted in the soil, and I carry ballast, and do not capsize in a gale.[14]

Attending Chesterton's lectures in Toronto, Gilson was astonished at his instinctive ability to anchor his starting point invariably and with unfailing ease in the intellectually perceived reality.[15] This is the opposite to the procedure of most philosophers since Descartes and Kant, who begin with ideas and never get to reality—with devastating results.

Chesterton followed closely the contemporary debates, heavily influenced as they were by "the apostles of scientism." Although he had no scientific training, he had an acute insight into science, and was able to put his finger with uncanny accuracy on the philosophical errors underlying their writings. This is why, although it may come as a surprise to some, an extract from Chapter 4 of *Orthodoxy* on "The Ethics of Elfland" was reprinted in a book titled *Great Essays in Science*. Indeed, it has been described as "one of the most penetrating discourses on the nature of scientific reasoning that has been so far produced."[16]

---

[13] Father J. O'Connor, *Father Brown on Chesterton* (London: F. Muller, 1938), 154.

[14] Ibid., 155.

[15] Etienne Gilson, "Letter to Reverend Kevin Scannell, January 7, 1966," as quoted in Stanley L. Jaki, *Chesterton, A Seer of Science* (Urbana: University of Illinois Press, 1986), 127.

[16] S. L. Jaki, *Chesterton, A Seer of Science,* 13.

To explain what Chesterton said in this passage and why it is much more important than might appear at first sight, some digression into the philosophical ideas underlying science is needed. It might even appear strange that there are such ideas, and most scientists would be hard put to list them. But science does not exist in a vacuum; it rests on certain definite philosophical beliefs about the nature of the material world. Without those beliefs strongly held, it would never have started; and now that those beliefs are weakening, science is itself in danger. The origin of these beliefs will be considered later; now we are concerned with what they are. Science is based on observations and experiments made at many places and times. We find that if due care is taken, the same results are obtained for an experiment wherever and whenever it is performed. From these regularities we generalise and formulate laws. But what is the justification for this procedure? If we have observed a certain sequence of events a thousand times, how can we be sure that the same thing will happen the next time? This is the old problem of induction.

Various responses are possible, depending on our beliefs about the material world. We could believe that the world is a strictly determined world, so that every event is fixed by its antecedents; that there is a logical necessity built into the very structure of the world. This indeed could provide the basis of science, but at the cost of turning everything into a great machine that moves inexorably forward. This belief has been described as "a deep and sincere faith in the incurable routine of the cosmos."[17] In the context of such a belief, it is difficult to accommodate free will, and hence the very activity of science itself. If what I write and say is strictly determined by various configurations of atoms, then can it have any meaning? To believe so is nothing less than the destruction of man. Another possibility is to suppose that everything in the universe is the result of chance at the deepest atomic level. The regularities we see are then statistical regularities; necessity arises out of chance. Unfortunately the proponents of such ideas never specify just what they mean by chance.[18]

---

[17] G. K. Chesterton, *Orthodoxy* (London: John Lane, 1921), 126.
[18] S. L. Jaki, *Chesterton, A Seer of Science,* 27.

Chesterton emphasized that logic belongs to mathematics and not to things. Stanley Jaki explains Chesterton's view point in the following way: "A law implies that we know the nature of generalisation and enactment; not merely that we have noticed some of the effects." By law, Chesterton means strict necessity, whereas "All the terms used in the scientific books—law, necessity, order, tendency, and so on—are really unintellectual because they assume an inner synthesis which we do not possess."[19] There is, thus, a "sharp distinction between the science of mental relations, in which there really are laws, and the science of physical facts, in which there are no laws, but only weird repetitions."[20] Furthermore, it is the specificity of things that is the principal means to restore sensitivity to the real, and such an all-embracing specificity is the result of a choice transcending the cosmos, which is, therefore, the sole privilege of the Creator.

Having thus exposed the ontological emptiness of the notion of scientific law, and achieved a realist's grasp of existence, reality can be seen as the product of a superior will and, therefore, as a place where freewill can be exercised.[21] Thus, according to Chesterton, the repetitions in nature on which science is based are not like clockwork but more like a series of theatrical encores:

> All the towering materialism which dominates the modern mind rests ultimately upon one assumption; a false assumption. It is supposed that if a thing goes on repeating itself it is probably dead; a piece of clockwork. People feel that if the universe was personal it would vary; if the sun were alive it would dance. This is a fallacy even in relation to known fact. For the variation in human affairs is generally brought into them, not by life, but by death. . . . A child kicks its legs rhythmically through excess, not absence of life. Because children have abounding vitality, because they are in spirit fierce and free, therefore they want things repeated and unchanged. They always say: "Do it again"; and the grown-up person does it again until he is nearly dead. For grownup people

---

[19] Ibid., 51.
[20] Ibid., 56.
[21] Ibid., 20.

are not strong enough to exult in monotony. But perhaps God is strong enough to exult in monotony. It is possible that God says every morning "Do it again" to the sun; and every evening, "Do it again" to the moon. It may not be automatic necessity that makes all daisies alike; it may be that God makes every daisy separately, but has never got tired of making them.[22]

It is very easy to brush this aside as a flight of fancy, but it does have the great merit of emphasizing first that everything that happens is totally dependent on the will of God, and also that there is normally a great regularity in events, but not by logical necessity. This truth can also be expressed by saying that God gave everything that He created an intrinsic nature, and that normally it behaves exactly in accord with that nature unless, for His own purposes, He decides otherwise. In this way, Chesterton justifies the method of science and also saves free will and hence science itself. It leaves open the possibility of miracles, because God can always decide to do something else; whereas, if events followed each other by strict logical necessity, this would not be possible. God always behaves rationally, and so we can, as a general rule, rely on the regularity of nature; for otherwise all life, including science, would be impossible.

When speaking on the "thrilling romance of Orthodoxy," that is, the vital importance of maintaining the balance of ideas, Chesterton says:

> The Church could not afford to swerve one hair's breadth on some things if she were to continue her great and daring experiment of the irregular equilibrium. Once let one idea become less powerful and some other idea would become too powerful. It was no flock of sheep the Christian shepherd was leading, but a herd of bulls and tigers, of terrible ideals and devouring doctrines, each one strong enough to turn into a false religion and lay waste the world.[23]

One consequence of such a loss of equilibrium is the destruction of science.

---

[22] G. K. Chesterton, *Orthodoxy*, 58.
[23] Ibid., 98–99.

It is important to distinguish between several levels of the scientific understanding of the world. First come the observations of nature, and then the results of measurements and experiments made to probe more deeply than is possible by observation alone. These measurements are the basic facts of science. The next stage is to correlate the facts by mathematical relations, and to try to understand them by making a model of the process or object of study. If the implications of a model agree accurately with a wide range of facts, we begin to have some confidence that it has within it some truth about the world. On these models are erected still higher generalisations; and, at this stage, the process becomes very speculative and subject to revision in the light of further experiments. Indeed, the main purpose of the speculations is to suggest new experiments. Now it very often happens that the speculations are exciting and attract the attention of journalists not familiar with the scientific background. Often the scientists themselves take their speculations more seriously than they deserve, and write popular articles or books about them. These are naturally much influenced by their philosophical or theological beliefs, or lack of beliefs. Hence, the unsuspecting reader is presented with a heady mixture of scientific speculations and personal beliefs that is by no means implied by the basic established scientific facts. This is very typically the case with "scientism," when publicists, often not too well-informed scientifically, present their secularist beliefs in the context of the latest scientific speculations.

Chesterton immediately spotted the fundamental weakness of the advocates of "scientism": they go far beyond the scientific evidence and "simply affirm all the notions that happen to be fashionable in loose intellectual clubs."[24] Scientists like Edison and Sir Arthur Keith, who spoke on spiritual questions in the name of science, were trenchantly exposed. Such men tend to take on the mantle of science: as Chesterton put it, "some men say that Science says this or that; when they mean scientists, and they do not know or care which scientists."[25] Far too many people speak glibly about Einstein's

---

[24] G. K. Chesterton, *The Uses of Adversity* (New York: Dodd, Mead, 1921), 137–38.
[25] G. K. Chesterton, *Come To Think of It* (New York: Dodd, Mead, 1931), 161.

relativity or the new physics and what it means for mankind without having the faintest notion of what it is really about. Far from showing that all is relative, as is frequently maintained, relativity makes even clearer the basic rationality and coherence of the physical world.[26]

Chesterton often referred to the importance for his conversion of the collapse of materialism because of the new physics. With some notable exceptions, scientists now claim much less for science than before, and they no longer maintain that practically the last word has been said about the physical universe. The importance of the new physics is that it undercuts "scientism." Determinism was used to threaten the freedom of the will, and that argument was certainly undercut when scientists started to invoke indeterminism.[27] Chesterton, however, knew that this indeterminism is an insufficient basis for the freedom of the will and he did not fall into that trap. He knew that "the idea of choice is an absolute, and that nobody can get behind it."[28] This is not just academic philosophy: Heitler, for example, ascribed the decline of ethical standards to the influence of determinism and mechanistic concepts.[29]

"Scientism" is the extension of science beyond its proper limits to objects not susceptible to quantitative analysis. If exactitude is set up as the only test of truth, then immediately the whole world of qualities and values is deprived of meaning. Chesterton realised clearly the dangers of this widespread attitude, and put up a spirited defence of the wholeness of man. Jaki has commented that "he was an implacable antagonist of those who, in the name of science—be it anthropology, sociology or psychology—applied their dissecting scalpel to the wholeness of man, and above all to the wholeness of man's mind."[30] The "scientism" of the nineteenth century had evolutionism as a central strand, and Darwinism was invoked to account for the development of man—denying, in the process, his uniqueness. Chesterton

---

26 J. R. Lucas and P. E. Hodgson, *Spacetime and Electromagnetism* (Oxford: Oxford University Press, 1990).
27 S. L. Jaki, *Chesterton, A Seer of Science,* 40.
28 G. K. Chesterton, *All I Survey* (New York: Dodd, Mead, 1933), 102.
29 S. L. Jaki, *Chesterton, A Seer of Science,* 135.
30 Ibid., 53.

diagnosed Darwinism as a union of excellent science and bad philosophy, and exposed its weakness with devastating accuracy. He made it clear that the gradual development from ape to man is perfectly acceptable to the orthodox Christian, as well as being scientifically plausible; but he was also aware that this development is far from being demonstrated. The problems of the origin of life and the origin of consciousness have still not received a scientific answer.

A third unsolved problem is the origin of reason and of evil. No animal except man has made symbols and lived by them, and Chesterton's dictum that "art is the signature of man"[31] remains valid. What was found in the caves of Lascaux and Altimira "were drawings or paintings of animals, and they were drawn or painted not only by a man but by an artist."[32] We know nothing concerning how this change came about, and there is no evidence that it took place slowly. As Chesterton points out, "Monkeys did not begin pictures and men finish them. Pithecanthropus did not draw a reindeer badly and Homo Sapiens draw it well . . . the wild horse was not an Impressionist and the race-horse a Post-Impressionist . . . there is not a shadow of evidence that this thing evolved at all."[33] And in *Come To Think of It*, Chesterton writes, "The tendency of scientists to personify Nature is exemplified by 'natural selection' and the survival of the fittest." The latter term is a mere tautology; and Chesterton continues, "Nature selecting those that vary in the most successful direction means nothing whatever except that the successful succeed."[34] Purposeful action remains incomprehensible within Darwinism, and many prominent biologists now admit the serious difficulties of Darwin's theory.

The real objection to evolutionism, as Chesterton realised, is that it "abolishes forms and all that goes with them, including the deepest kind of ontological form, which is the immortal human soul."[35] Thus, "evolution does not specifically deny the existence of

---

[31] G. K. Chesterton, *The Everlasting Man* (New York: Dodd, Mead, 1925), 16.
[32] Ibid., 10.
[33] Ibid., 17 and 22.
[34] G. K. Chesterton, *Come To Think of It*, 149.
[35] S. L. Jaki, *Chesterton, A Seer of Science*, 76.

God; what it does deny is the existence of man."[36] This is the origin of "the subconscious popular instinct against Darwinism"[37] that arises because "when once one begins to think of man as a shifting and alterable thing, it is always easy for the strong and crafty to twist him into new shapes for all kinds of unnatural purposes."[38] It is just not possible to erect a respectable ethical system on Darwinism; for, as Chesterton writes in *Orthodoxy*:

> [it] can be used to back up two mad moralities, but it cannot be used to back up a single sane one; on the evolutionary basis you may be unhuman, or you may be absurdly humane, but you cannot be human. . . . In neither case does evolution tell you how to treat a tiger reasonably, that is, to admire his stripes while avoiding his claws.[39]

Commenting on the proposal to inject evolutionary thought into every part of the educational programme, Chesterton remarked that "it would not make that education very insistent on the ideas of free will and fighting morality; of dramatic choice and challenge."[40] Again this is no abstract philosophical observation; evolution and the survival of the fittest are among the most potent origins of the first World War and of the racism of today.[41] Empirical science in general, and Darwinism in particular, provide no basis for the equality of man. This equality is safeguarded only by the uniqueness of Christ as man, and by the truth that Christ had an immortal human soul.

It was natural for Chesterton to reflect on the universe as a whole, calling it "a single jewel . . . without peer and without price; for there cannot be another one."[42] He saw that the acceptance of

---

[36] G. K. Chesterton, *Charles Dickens: A Critical Study* (London: Hodder and Stoughton, 1903), 275.

[37] G. K. Chesterton, *What's Wrong With the World* (New York: Cassell and Company Ltd., 1910), 268–69.

[38] Ibid.

[39] G. K. Chesterton, *Orthodoxy*, 110.

[40] G. K. Chesterton, *The Spice of Life and Other Essays* (Beaconsfield:Dufour Editions, 1964), 118.

[41] S. L. Jaki, *Chesterton, A Seer of Science*, 78.

[42] G. K. Chesterton, *Orthodoxy*, 63.

objective reality as prior to mind implies the rejection of debilitating solipsism and the affirmation of the totality of all objects, namely the universe. Positivist thinkers such as Comte, Mill, Pearson, Poincaré, and Duhem had already stripped scientific laws of their bearing on reality, and of these only Duhem insisted on the realism of common sense as the sole means through which scientific laws can be connected with the real world.[43] Thus, Chesterton was alone in moving directly and without hesitation from a strictly positivist preamble not only to a reassertion of reality, but to an assertion that embraced the entire cosmos.[44] The universe is specific and contingent, but it could be otherwise. Chesterton realised "that reality, both in its smallest details and in its vast entirety was most specific,"[45] and he felt in his bones that "this world does not explain itself";[46] that it "must have a meaning, and a meaning must have someone to mean it."[47] This immediately points to its origin in the will of the Creator. While today the specificity of the universe is increasingly recognised, its implications are avoided by talk about nothing turning itself into something. Chesterton clearly saw the absurdity of this idea:

> The world does not explain itself, and cannot do so merely by continuing to expand itself. But anyhow, it is absurd for the Evolutionist to complain that it is unthinkable for an admittedly unthinkable God to create everything out of nothing and then to pretend that it is *more* thinkable that nothing should turn itself into everything.[48]

Chesterton wrote long before the great discoveries that have revealed the universe for the first time as an object of scientific study.[49] The stellar spectra have now shown that all the galaxies are

---

[43] S. L. Jaki , *Chesterton, A Seer of Science,* 95.

[44] Ibid.

[45] Ibid. 120.

[46] G. K. Chesterton, *Orthodoxy,* 63.

[47] Ibid.

[48] G. K. Chesterton, *St. Thomas Aquinas,* 215–16.

[49] S. L. Jaki, *God and the Cosmologists* (Edinburgh: Scottish Academic Press, 1989).

receding from one another; and, projecting back their motions, we find that they were concentrated in a small volume about fifteen thousand million years ago. This, in turn, points to a primeval explosion that marks the beginning of our era. Detailed work in nuclear and elementary particle physics has led to a deep understanding of the processes that took place in the first few minutes of that explosion and of the expansion that followed it. Many quantitative predictions are made by the theory, and they agree with the experimental data, thus supporting the theory. What is remarkable is the extreme specificity of the process.[50] The initial conditions had to be exceedingly finely tuned for the process to develop in the particular way that has led to the evolution of man. It is really exceedingly improbable that we should be here at all. So specific is the development of the universe that it now seems very likely that, from the beginning, it was made as a home for man. This is referred to as the anthropic principle.

"Religion," remarked Chesterton, "means something that commits man to some doctrine about the universe."[51] The fatal mistake of the cosmic philosopher is "to choose as his starting point not the thing but the self or even the phenomena, in so far as they are his mere sensations."[52] Chesterton writes: "A cosmic philosophy is not made to fit man; a cosmic philosophy is constructed to fit a cosmos."[53] As Jaki has remarked, religions fall into two categories:

> in one there is the Judeo-Christian religion with its belief in a linear cosmic story running from "in the beginning" to "a new heaven and earth." In the other are all the pagan religions, primitive and sophisticated, old and modern, which invariably posit the cyclic and eternal recurrence of all, or rather the confining of all into an eternal treadmill, the most effective generator of the feeling of unhappiness and haplessness.[54]

---

[50] P. E. Hodgson, *Theology and Modern Physics* (Aldershot: Ashgate Press) ch. 10.

[51] G. K. Chesterton, *A Miscellany of Men* (London: Dodd, Mead, 1912), 262.

[52] S. L. Jaki, *Chesterton, A Seer of Science,* 114.

[53] G. K. Chesterton, "The Book of Job", *G. K. C. as M. C.* (London: Methuen, 1929), 42.

[54] S. L. Jaki, *Chesterton, A Seer of Science,* 113.

Concerning that treadmill, Chesterton observed: "I am exceedingly proud to observe that it was before the coming of Christianity that it flourished and after the neglect of Christianity that it returned."[55] And elsewhere he writes:

> The final and conclusive argument against the doctrine of eternal recurrence in the unique and unrepeatable Incarnation of Christ. For it is the key to nearly everything in the development of two thousand years; and in nothing is it so much the key to Christendom as in the recurrent reversions to Paganism.[56]

Underlying all Chesterton's writings is a clear and accurate grasp of the central tenets of the Christian creed, that God created the universe out of nothing, that God is completely distinct from the universe, that the universe is continually and utterly dependent on God, and that Christ is God Incarnate. Scientists are intent on discovering the laws of nature, those generalisations that enable us to describe in great detail the workings of the natural world, from the subnuclear particles to the vast galaxies. If God had not created things that behave consistently and, on the whole, rather simply, then science would not have been possible at all. Chesterton reminds us of the contingency of the universe; that it could have been made otherwise and, at any instant, God could decide to change it.

For most people, Chesterton is a jolly journalist, a coiner of startling paradoxes and the writer of ingenious detective stories to be enjoyed on a quiet afternoon. But there is another much less familiar and far more important Chesterton who deserves the most careful study. In the words of Etienne Gilson:

> Chesterton was one of the deepest thinkers who ever existed; he was deep because he was right, and he could not help being right; but he could not either help being modest and charitable, so he left it to others who could understand him to know that he was right, and deep; to others, he apologised for being right, and he

---

55 G. K. Chesterton, *All is Grist* (New York: Dodd, Mead, 1932), 150.
56 G. K. Chesterton, *The Resurrection of Rome* (New York: Dodd, Mead, 1930), 121.

> made up for being deep by being witty. That is all that they can see of him.[57]

Chesterton was right not only on the fundamental tenets of the Christian faith, on God the Creator, on God Incarnate in Christ, who founded a Church to teach in His name through Peter and his successors in Rome; but he was also, as a result, right about the basis of science. That is why there is so much that we can learn from him about the very nature of science and about its place in human culture.

[57] Etienne Gilson, quoted by Stanley L. Jaki in *Chesterton, A Seer of Science,* 127.

CHAPTER 5

Belief in Science and Religion*

BELIEFS IN SCIENCE and religion are quite different from each other. Thus it is sometimes said that scientific research gives us true, exact, reliable, and objective knowledge about the natural world whereas religion is a matter of subjective feeling and personal preference. People accept scientific results without question but consider that it is everyone's right to choose their own religious beliefs. Scientific statements can be proved to be true, but religious beliefs are a matter of personal taste.

To explore this in more detail, we can ask what it means to know. To contrast two examples, Rutherford once asked the professor of geology at Cambridge how old he thought was a sample of the mineral pitchblende he was carrying. He was told about a hundred million years. "I *know* that it is seven hundred million years old," replied Rutherford. That is an example of scientific knowledge. In contrast, one could find undergraduates in the College Chapel singing, "I *know* that my Redeemer liveth." How did they know, and how did Rutherford know?

There is no simple answer to these questions. There are degrees of belief that need to be distinguished. We would readily admit that we believe some things because we have been told by a source we consider reliable, but would not be surprised if further evidence caused us to modify them. Other beliefs we hold so firmly that we cannot imagine any circumstances that would cause us to change

---

* Reprinted with permission from *St. Austin Review* (June 2002): 41.

them; we would even be prepared to die for them. The professor of geology, after listening to Rutherford's explanation, doubtless accepted his conclusion. The undergraduates singing in the chapel might not be so easy to convince that they are wrong.

Many scientific beliefs have eventually turned out to be wrong. The cosmology of Aristotle has been disproved and the theory of phlogiston has gone beyond recall. There are many popular beliefs about the world that have definitely been disproved, or for which there is no good evidence. This is not confined to those who have no scientific training. Thus it is now assumed even by most physicists and repeated in countless textbooks and articles that Einstein has disproved the existence of absolute space and time, that Bohr and Heisenberg have proved that matter is radically indeterministic, and that the Bell inequalities have shown the existence of non-local interactions. Yet all these beliefs are very probably false. Obviously one has to be careful in asserting that a particular scientific statement is true. The need for caution is even clearer in matters of religion. There are numerous different religions with quite different beliefs, and they cannot all be true. More precisely, adherents of each of them hold a complex mixture of beliefs only some of which can possibly be true.

How then can we justify what we call knowledge? If Rutherford had been asked how he knew the age of that sample of pitchblende, he would explain that he had examined a sample of uranium and had found that it decays by emitting alpha-particles and that he had measured the probability of decay per unit time. Alpha particles are the nuclei of helium atoms, and he had also measured the amount of helium in the pitchblende sample, together with the concentration of uranium. Simple arithmetic then gives the age of the sample.

He could well be asked a number of supplementary questions, such as how did he know that some of the helium did not escape from the sample. To this he could reply that he took his sample from the middle of a large piece of pitchblende, or that he had studied the variation of the helium concentration with depth in the sample and had found it to be very small, or that he had repeated the measurement on several samples and had always found essentially the same result. He was thus implicitly relying on a large and established body of knowledge of the behaviour of radioactive minerals.

He could also be asked a much more fundamental question, namely how did he know that there is such a substance as uranium and that all the nuclei in his sample were exactly the same? How did he know that the decay rate of uranium remains constant, which is an assumption implicit in his calculation of the age. If the rate of decay speeds up or slows down during the hundreds of millions of years of the life of the pitchblende, he would obviously get a different result. Might it not depend on the temperature of the ore, which obviously varies greatly through geological time? More fundamentally, might the decay depend on the time elapsed since the universe began? Such questions are more difficult to answer. He could say that in all his experience of radioactive materials, with a wide range of lifetimes, he had never found any evidence that the decay rate changes or depends on the surroundings in any way at all. Furthermore, the decay rate depends on the structure of the nucleus, and how could that change? But our inability to see how it could change does not prove that it does not change. Perhaps the very constants of nature, such as the strength of the nucleon–nucleon interaction, which determine the structure of the nucleus, do change with time. This has indeed been seriously suggested, and studied in great detail and the consequences of such changes have been used to set tight limits on the possible changes.

Finally, how do we know that there is not some other unknown effect that could quite alter our conclusion? This is not an absurd suggestion. Nineteenth-century estimates of the age of the earth, for example, gave results that were far too short to allow enough time for the biological and geological changes required by the theory of evolution. It was the quite unexpected discovery of radioactivity that provided a new source of heat and thus increased the estimates of the age of the earth to an acceptable value.

There is much more that can be said about Rutherford's belief in his estimate of the age of his sample of pitchblende, but in the end all we can really say is that it is the best we can do in the present state of knowledge. It forms a coherent structure that is indeed far stronger than might appear from a description of the parts needed to answer questions such as those posed above. It is checked and rechecked in numerous ways and is very unlikely to be wrong. And yet there is always the possibility of some new knowledge that will cause the answer to be changed. This has happened so often in the history of science that it would be unwise to assume that it can never happen again.

If this can be said for a piece of scientific knowledge that is quite directly linked to actual measurements, the situation for theories is even more tenuous. One of the most impressive scientific achievements of all time, Newton's classical mechanics, supported over the centuries by numerous measurements of the highest precision, has been shown by the development of special relativity to be an approximation to the truth for velocities much less than that of light. This is not to say that it is untrue, but it is no longer believed to be universally valid. There is a strong tendency for each generation of scientist to think that now at last they have gained the final truth about nature, but always in a few decades this is shown to be overoptimistic.

Nevertheless, in spite of all this, science as we have it now is an impressive and largely correct body of knowledge about the natural world. Even though many scientific beliefs are unproved, their credibility is guaranteed by their success. Certainly it is based on many assumptions, but their reliability in practice is convincing evidence of their truth.

So much for belief in science. What can be said about belief in religion? If we asked those undergraduates who were affirming their belief in their Redeemer what was the meaning and the basis of their belief, what would they reply? First, they would explain that by Redeemer they mean the historical personage Jesus Christ, who lived in Palestine about two thousand years ago and was crucified by Pontius Pilate, the Roman Governor of Judea. He died and was buried, so to say that He still lives affirms their belief that He rose from the dead; in other words the statement affirms belief in Resurrection. Taken on its own, this is extremely implausible. If for a moment we accept the truth of the account in the Gospels, He certainly died. Roman soldiers had plenty of experience of death following crucifixion and made no mistake about that. To avoid the possibility that the disciples might steal the body, guards were set over the tomb. The disciples of Jesus were terrified of what might happen to them, and so they kept behind locked doors. And yet soon after they were boldly taking to the streets and preaching that Jesus Christ rose from the dead. Would they be likely to do that unless they were convinced that what they said was true? To this one can say that it is not very sensible to explain the improbable by the impossible. But how do we know that it is impossible? Certainly not on scientific grounds, because science deals only with repeatable events, not with unique events. Furthermore, the same arguments would prove the impossibility of miracles, and yet these certainly occur.

How do we know that the Gospel accounts are correct? Over the centuries they have been exhaustively analysed and found to be coherent and reliable, and the teaching they contain has been found true to life by countless generations of Christians. The structure of belief is retrojustified by experience. The theology forms a coherent whole, in agreement with experience, and taken together the beliefs it enshrines, including the Resurrection, command assent.

At this point we notice that far from being quite different, the grounds for belief in religion and science are remarkably similar. In both, individual beliefs are sustained not by a single chain of reasoning but by their integral connection with a whole complex of tightly interlocking beliefs. The strength of a particular belief depends on the whole. It is always possible to find reasons for rejecting one belief or another, and it is only by understanding the whole, on the basis of knowledge gained by many experiences over a long period of time, that the strength of a particular belief becomes apparent. This explains why a belief is sometimes rejected by persons in good faith, because they have insufficient knowledge of the whole picture.

This is similar to the interpretation of an X-ray picture by a radiologist or a bubble chamber photograph by an elementary particle physicist: their experience enables them to interpret the picture immediately, whereas to anyone else it is quite unintelligible.

In this perspective, the existence of a few counterarguments is seen to be of lesser importance. Many objections can, and are, raised against particular scientific results, but this does not affect the faith of scientists in the validity of the scientific enterprise. They know that in due course these objections will be answered, as has occurred many times in the past. This also applies to arguments against the Christian faith.

So far we have considered belief in science and in religion as quite separate, and have shown their remarkable similarity. If we carry still further our enquiry into the justification of belief in science we find an even greater convergence. Rutherford took for granted that the natural world behaves in a rational and consistent way, that it is at least partly open to the human mind and that whatever he found out about it was not his alone but must be freely shared. These were the beliefs that underlie all science, and they made possible the first viable birth of science in the High Middle Ages. They are very special beliefs; they were not held before then and their absence is why science as we know it never developed in any of the ancient civilisations, despite achievements of the highest order in practically every other sphere of human endeavour. Those beliefs, vital for the development of science, are Judeo-Christian beliefs and it was in the High Middle Ages that they were first held by a whole society. So science is not an activity and a body of knowledge distinct from belief, still less is it contrary to it. Modern science is based on Judeo-Christian beliefs about the natural world, and so is itself a fully Judeo-Christian activity.

CHAPTER 6

Concepts of Belief[*]

A BIOGRAPHY of the distinguished physicist I. I. Rabi contains the following quotations:

> When I discovered physics, I realised that it transcended religion. It was the higher truth. It filled me with awe, put me in touch with a sense of original causes. Physics brought me close to God. That feeling stayed with me throughout my years in science. Whenever one of my students came to me with a scientific project, I asked only one question: "Will it bring you nearer to God?" They always understood what I meant.
>
> Religion tends to erect barriers between people, science tends to tear those barriers down. The practices of religion are defended locally; the practices of science are shared globally. The culture of religion is sectarian; the culture of science, universal. Science is a great intellectual force which liberates the mind from outworn prejudice and provides understanding and illumination.

One's first reaction is that surely he is mistaken; obviously religion is a higher truth than science and brings us closer to God. On second thought, there is something in what he is trying to say, and this deserves more detailed exploration.

First, what is meant by "religion"? I recall a speaker remarking that "Hinduism is not just a religion; it is a way of life." By "religion,"

---

[*] Reprinted with permission from *St. Austin Review* (September 2002): 13.

he presumably meant adherence (whatever that might mean) to a set of beliefs (not precisely formulated) that is only expressed when you fill a box marked "Religion" on some form. Your "religion" in this sense is usually determined by the country in which you happen to live, and it has as much effect on the way you live your life as the colours of your national flag.

"Religion" can also mean a set of beliefs, more or less precisely defined, that do have some influence on our lives. We do not claim any objective validity for them, and we respect the beliefs of others. We can all believe what we like, provided we are sincere.

According to these two views, "religion" is either vacuous or subjective, and in either case it cannot tell us anything about God.

What about science? It has been well-defined as objective knowledge of the natural world, obtained by a systematic process of observation, experiment, and theoretical analysis. A scientific measurement made by a Japanese or a Brazilian, by a Christian or an atheist, provided it is done properly, will give the same result, within the uncertainties of measurement. If there were scientists on other planets, or other galaxies, who studied electromagnetism, they would eventually formulate what we know as Maxwell's equations. The laws of nature describe the behaviour of the natural world made by God; they are God's laws. In this sense science can be said to bring us closer to God: the power, consistency and subtlety of God's laws are faint reflections of His nature.

Now perhaps we can make some sense of the quotations. Underlying them is a wholly inadequate concept of "religion." What then should we mean by "religion"? It can be described as a timeless and objective set of beliefs given to us by God. These beliefs pervade, inspire, and guide our lives. It is a unique set of beliefs; in Newman's words there is only "one, true fold." These beliefs may be expressed in different languages, different ceremonies, but they remain always the same, just as Maxwell's equations would be the same if discovered by Martians, though they would use different mathematical symbolism to write them down.

Though still far from being achieved, scientists aim to provide an integrated and coherent account of the natural world. In talking about their work, scientists often use quasi-religious language. It may be just a convenient shorthand way of referring to the most fundamental aspects of nature, or it may reflect a deeper belief. Many scientists, explicitly or implicitly, regard their work as a religious quest. The mathematician-philosopher Whitehead said that it is the conviction that there is a rational order in nature and that it can be found that provides the scientist with the strength to carry on in spite of difficulties, and this is a religious conviction.

There is an important distinction between the fundamental truths of Christian theology on the one hand and the ways they are expressed in different cultures and the corresponding Church rules on the other. It is the same Mass, whether celebrated in London or Tokyo, or in a Melkite liturgy in the Holy Land. The fundamental truths are unchanging; the rules governing fasting or Mass attendance or even clerical celibacy are adapted to the times. But to ask the Pope to change the moral law is like asking a physicist to change the laws of gravity. If you defy these laws you get hurt.

It is not always recognised that religious beliefs can be objectively true. People say that they will not impose their beliefs on their children; they will let them decide for themselves what to believe when they grow up. They would not say the same for the laws of arithmetic. It is a matter of simple logic: a belief and its opposite cannot both be true, so there can only be one true fold.

It is easy to understand Rabi's words about religion tending to erect barriers between people while science tends to tear them down. If I go to Japan or China to continue my research in nuclear physics with my colleagues there, we are immediately talking about the same problems in the same way. But if I were to start talking about religion it would be very difficult to make any contact at all.

There are deep historical reasons for this. Over the millennia sets of beliefs permeate a culture to such an extent that it becomes difficult to even communicate meaningfully with people brought up in different cultures. Schoolteachers in Africa often find it very difficult to teach physics because the cultures of the children lack the fundamental beliefs about causality and time that are essential to physics and are obvious to European children. Scientists in non-European cultures come to accept beliefs about the nature of the physical world implicitly during their scientific studies, but there is an unrecognised discontinuity between them and the beliefs of their culture. In this way science, by carrying with it the Christian beliefs on which it is based, is preparing the way for Christianity itself, acting as an unseen herald of the Gospel. If we see science in this way, as Christian to its very roots, we can see that it tears down the barriers between people by gradually showing its religious roots and so indeed liberates the mind from outworn prejudice.

True religion provides an integrated account of the whole of reality: our origin and our destiny, our rights and our duties. Our beliefs are real and objective, and we hold them not as abstract propositions but as realities that permeate our lives. Included are the very beliefs that made modern science possible. Nothing is excluded from the influence of these beliefs; they do indeed constitute a way of life.

CHAPTER 7

Is Physics Catholic?*

CAN THERE BE a Catholic physics? Of course not! The idea is absurd. Newton's equations of dynamics, Einstein's relativity, and Maxwell's equations of the electromagnetic field are objective descriptions of the behaviour of the natural world and are just the same for atheists as for Catholics.

Yet there may be more to be said than that. The following remarks are stimulated by Professor Gerald Bradley's article on Catholic Education.[1] He is able to show how holding the Catholic faith affects the teaching of the humanities, but admits that he is unable to do the same for physics, not because it is not possible, but because he is unfamiliar with physics. This is a challenge to Catholic physicists.

One can begin by observing that it is a remarkable historical fact that many of the great civilisations of the past achieved a high level of excellence in the humanities, in philosophy, law, drama, and music, but none of them developed science in the modern sense, that is the detailed knowledge of behaviour of the natural world, expressed by differential equations. Modern science was born in the High Middle Ages, when for the first time in history there was a civilisation permeated by Catholic theology. Included in that theology are beliefs about the natural world—that it is good, rational,

---

* Reprinted with permission from *Fellowship of Catholic Scholars Quarterly* (Fall 2002): 26.

[1] Gerard V. Bradley, "Looking Ahead at Catholic Higher Education" *Fellowship of Catholic Scholars Quarterly* 25(2; Spring 2002): 16.

contingent, and open to the human mind—that form the essential basis of science. These beliefs are lacking in all ancient civilisations.[2] Furthermore, the beginning of physics, and hence of all science, may be identified with the work of the Parisian philosopher John Buridan. He studied the key problem of local motion, and his belief in the creation of the world in time (contrary to the eternal world of Aristotle) led him to formulate the law of inertial motion, later to be expressed quantitatively as Newton's first law. Thus physics, unlike the humanities, is essentially and radically Catholic, as it is based on Catholic beliefs.[3]

The development of science through the following centuries was largely due to the work of Catholics, other Christians, and Jews. The greatest physicist, Newton, was a somewhat heterodox Christian; the second greatest, Einstein, had a strongly Jewish upbringing. Most physicists would choose the gentle Maxwell as the third greatest, another devout Christian. The founder of experimental science, Robert Grosseteste, was one of the first chancellors of the university of Oxford and Bishop of Lincoln.[4] Buridan's pupil Nicholas Oresme, who carried on his work, was a bishop. Copernicus was a canon, Galileo a devout Catholic, and Kepler a Christian. Many Catholics were pioneers of astronomy, among them the Theatine priest Piazzi, the discoverer of Ceres, and the Jesuits' Scheiner, who studied sunspots, and Secchi, a pioneer of meteorology who also made spectral analyses of the sun and of thousands of stars. Another Jesuit, Roger Boscovich, made important contributions to mathematics and astronomy and developed ideas on fields of force holding atoms together that were far in advance of his time. Niels Stensen made important discoveries in medicine, was one of the founders of the sciences of crystallography, geology, and paleontology, and also worked on embroyology and mineralogy. He became a

---

[2] Stanley L. Jaki, *Science and Creation* (Edinburgh: Scottish Academic Press, 1974).

[3] P. E. Hodgson, "The Christian Origin of Science," *Logos* 4(2; Spring 2001): 138, and references therein.

[4] A. C. Crombie, *Robert Grosseteste and the Origins of Experimental Science 1100–1700* (Oxford: Clarendon Press, 1953).

bishop and was canonized. Laplace, one of the greatest developers of Newtonian mechanics and who was often described as an atheist, died a Catholic. Fresnel and Fraunhofer, pioneers of optics were Christians; Galvani, Ampere, and Volta, pioneers of electricity, were all Catholics. Pierre Duhem, the French physicist who founded the discipline of the history of science, was a devout Catholic, as was Alistair Crombie, another historian of science. The Austrian monk Gregor Mendel founded the science of genetics. The theory of the Big Bang was due to the Belgian Abbe Lemaitre. The list is endless.[5]

All this refers to the past. What is the situation today? I can answer only through my own experience. This is not entirely negligible, as I have been engaged on research in nuclear physics, and lecturing and tutoring mathematics and physics, continuously for the past fifty-four years, mainly at Oxford.

Oxford today, despite the presence of Christian symbols, is entirely secular, apart from the theological Colleges. Religion is almost never mentioned in the science laboratories, and I would never raise the subject either to colleagues or students. And yet, looking back, there are several experiences that indicate that this is not the whole story.

Over the years I have become aware that a substantial number of the physics students I tutored at College are Christians; two of them are now Catholic priests and one became a Venerable Archdeacon (it is rather easier for an Anglican than for a Catholic to become Venerable) and is now a bishop. One year when the College had five physics undergraduates in the first year, one of them came to me and said that four of them were active Christians, and they were working on the fifth. I never mentioned Christianity in my lectures on nuclear physics but somehow, as I was told just a few weeks ago, they all knew that I am a Catholic

The graduate students, like the undergraduates, are selected solely on evidence of ability, and over the years I have found that many of them are Christians. One of the very best of my own students applied

---

5 Karl A. Kneller, *Christianity and the Leaders of Modern Science* (Port Huron, MI: Real View Books, 1995).

for entrance to an Anglican theological College, and I was asked to provide a reference. The letter told me that they required candidates to have a second-class degree. I could not resist replying that I regretted that he did not have the required qualification; he had a first-class degree and an excellent D.Phil. Another graduate student in the department obtained a D.Phil in elementary particle physics and is now studying for the priesthood at the Venerable English College in Rome. Another student there, recently ordained, has a Cambridge doctorate in astrophysics.

A very substantial proportion of the science lecturers and professors at Oxford are Christians or Jews, and so are scientists from all over the world with whom I have worked on joint research projects. Those from France, Italy, Spain, Poland, and Slovakia are mostly Catholics, and they include Professor Madurga, the first professor of atomic and nuclear physics at the University of Seville, who was a Jesuit priest. The son of another colleague, Professor van Heerden, sometime professor of nuclear physics at the University of the Western Cape, is the rector of the new seminary in Cape Town, where I had the privilege of giving a few lectures.

One of my colleagues in Oxford once commiserated with me that I was unable, as a physicist, to use my position as a tutor to inculcate students with my religious beliefs. He taught history, and presumably used his tutorials to advance his political opinions. I replied that I simply tried to teach my students how to find the truths of mathematics and physics. He was rather surprised at this, and remarked that physics must be a very constricted subject. I replied that there is an objective truth that can be found by rigorous arguments, and that if I succeeded in training them to seek the truth, whatever the cost, this habit would eventually extend beyond physics, and would lead them to even greater truths.

If it is indeed the case that physics is based on Catholic beliefs about the natural world, then it might well be asked what will happen if these beliefs are removed. Ever since the Middle Ages, science has developed into a self-sustaining enterprise that seems able to exist apart from its origins and to spread over the whole earth. Close examination reveals a somewhat different picture. In Germany, where physics formerly flourished, it was almost completely destroyed by the Nazis. Hitler declared that Germany did not need physics. Many of the best German scientists, particularly the Jews, were expelled from their posts and went overseas, and party hacks put in their places. Only a very few, such as Max Von Laue, firmly opposed the Nazis.[6]

Even more revealing is the situation in Soviet Russia, where it was declared that henceforth science was to be built on the iron rock of dialectical materialism, Engels in his "dialectics of nature" laid down a series of rules, invariably erroneous, that physics is supposed to obey. He castigated a whole galaxy of physicists, even including Newton. For Engels, science is not the source of objective knowledge but the slave of dialectical materialism. The results were not long in appearing. Those who resisted were purged from the Academy. Landau was imprisoned and Einstein's theory of relativity condemned. Genetics was destroyed by the charlatan Lysenko, and Vavilov, the greatest of the Russian geneticists, was exiled to his death in Siberia.[7]

To a lesser extent, we can see the same process insidiously at work in our own society, as it becomes progressively more secularized and divorced from its Catholic roots. The numbers of aspiring physicists in most countries is steadily falling, and with it the number of those who seek only the truth about the natural world, with no thought of their reputation or personal gain.

So modern physics is Catholic through and through. It is rooted in Catholic theology, is sustained by those roots, and if those roots are weakened or destroyed it withers and dies.

---

6 Peter E. Hodgson, "Science in non-Christian Cultures," Lecture 7 of the course "Science and Belief," 1999.

7 Peter E. Hodgson, *The Roots of Science and its Fruits: The Christian Origin of Science and its Impact on Human Society* (London: St. Austin Press, 2002).

PART II
Philosophy
of Science

CHAPTER 8

The Mind of the Universe[*]

DURING THE LAST CENTURY it became possible to study the universe as a whole, spread out in space and time. We now have a firm framework of knowledge and understanding from the primeval explosion about fifteen billion years ago to the present time. Combining our knowledge of nuclear and elementary particle physics it is possible to describe the evolution of the universe from the formation of the nucleons and simple nuclei, the synthesis of heavier nuclei in stars, the development of planetary systems to the emergence of life and its evolution into the myriad of forms that surround us today. Some of this story is known quite well, other parts are still obscure, and obviously we know only a small fraction of what is to be known.

If we stand back and think about it all, several questions arise: did all this stupendous development just happen, or is there a reason behind it all? Is the universe the product of a mind, and is it all done for a purpose? If so, what is that purpose, and does the mind behind the universe care for us in a personal way? These are not scientific questions, but they arise with increasing frequency as the result of scientific advances.

---

[*] A review of *The Mind of the Universe: Understanding Science and Religion* by M. Artigas (Radnor, PA: Templeton Foundation Press, 2000). Reprinted with permission from *Contemporary Physics* 42(2001).

Professor Artigas has chosen the title *The Mind of the Universe* because he believes that "the contemporary scientific world view suggests that the universe is permeated in its innermost being by a rationality whose explanation requires the authorship of a rational mind." His aims are to show "that our present scientific world view provides a most suitable basis for a perspective that includes an end and religious values," but also "to explore the implications of this world view on our ideas about the universe as God's creation, man as God's collaborator and God as the foundation of being, creativity, and values."

He first shows that science itself rests on certain presuppositions and the values implied by the scientific activity itself, namely "the search for truth, rigour, objectivity, intellectual modesty and cooperation with others." The undoubted fact of scientific progress "retro-justifies, enriches and refines" these presuppositions. "The analysis of each of these presuppositions can provide a clue to the philosophical meaning of scientific progress and therefore to its theological relevance."

The detailed exploration of these arguments is divided into four parts, which Artigas describes as follows. "In the first part, I consider which method should be used to study the philosophical and theological implications of science; then I analyse these implications in the following parts, which deal, respectively, with the ontological implications of scientific progress and the corresponding image of divine action, the epistemological implications of scientific progress and the corresponding image of man, and the ethical implications of scientific values. I conclude by examining the results of my study and the plausibility of the naturalistic and theistic positions using criteria similar to those applied to evaluate scientific explanations."

Science and religion can be related in three ways: hostility, indifference, and cooperation, as already analysed by Ian Barbour and John Haught. Since the aims, methods, and results of science differ from those of religion, there is a methodological gap between them. Thus "if there is a personal God, and if the human person possesses spiritual dimensions, these spiritual realities will remain forever outside the possibilities of the methods of experimental science." Many scientists such as Monod, Sagan, Crick, E. O. Wilson, and Weinberg hold materialistic beliefs, but these are in no way supported by their scientific work. Empirical science by itself cannot answer religious questions. Scientism, the belief that science will ultimately solve all problems, is a naïve faith that receives no support from science. Furthermore, it fails to provide any moral guidance, because there is an unbridgeable gap between statements of fact and statements of value.

The development of science can be described as a progressive increase in our knowledge of the order of nature. The ancients considered nature as an organism, and in Renaissance times this was replaced by a mechanistic model that treated the natural world as a purposeless machine. Many hoped that all complex structures would eventually be explained in terms of the interactions of simpler structures, but this reductionism eventually failed even in physics. Studies of the chemistry of self-organising systems and much biological research is providing many examples of emerging order, thus showing how matter can behave in a cooperative way to produce new structural patterns. This self-organisation produces many novelties that cannot be understood as just the sum of the components. This immediately raises the question of teleology, namely whether nature acts for a purpose. Is evolution directed toward a particular end? Dawkins denies this, but his argument is completely deceptive. At a deeper level he argues that there is no need to ask for an explanation of the basic features and even the existence of the physical world since its fundamental units could have come from nothing. Artigas remarks that some physicists may say such things, but they are not supported by any valid physical arguments.

The justification of the methods of scientific investigation has been the subject of many philosophical studies. It is rightly pointed out that we can never be sure that a scientific generalisation or theory is true, because it is inevitably based on limited knowledge. Some writers have used this to argue that science, being fallible, can never contradict religion. Artigas, a physicist himself, firmly rejects this devaluation of science, and sets out to place scientific knowledge on a firm footing. He analyses the views of many philosophers, including Mach, Schlick, Feigl, Popper, Neurath, Kuhn, Lakatos, Feyerabend, Laudan, McMullin, Van Fraassen, Leplin, and Putnam. In each case Artigas first gives their views, then a critical analysis accepting what he considers valid and useful, and finally the reasons why he cannot accept some aspects of their work.

Artigas begins his own account by emphasizing that "creativity and interpretation play a central role in scientific progress." Since it is possible that our observations can be explained by different theories, there is a logical asymmetry between verification and falsification. From this Popper concluded that no theory can ever be verified and so all scientific knowledge is conjectural. Artigas argues that nevertheless "we can be pretty sure about the truth of many scientific statements," and that to "explain how empirical science works we must admit that scientists use subtle kinds of reasoning that go beyond pure formal logic." Thus "the rationality of science does not lie in the application of automatic rules or algorithmic procedures, but includes a sophisticated combination of creativity, argument and interpretation." Even the most elementary concepts, such as mass, time, and temperature, cannot be derived from observation and logic alone. Five criteria may be used to assess scientific theories: explanatory power (e.g., DNA, relativity, and quantum mechanics); predictive power (e.g., Neptune, the deflection of starlight by gravitational forces, the discovery of the omega minus, and the W and Z particles); accuracy of explanation (e.g., Kepler's analysis of the orbit of Mars); the convergence of varied and independent proofs, as the Big Bang theory is supported by the cosmic microwave background and by the abundance of the elements; and finally the mutual support of several theories, as the atomic theory is used in chemistry, biology, and astrophysics. These five criteria enable us to understand how, in spite of logical difficulties, we can reach conclusions that are "good candidates for the status of true knowledge." Thus empirical science enables us to reach true knowledge of the natural world, and "this realism is retrojustified, enlarged and refined by the progress of science."

Science has strongly influenced our image of the human being. Naturalism emphasizes the continuity between human beings and the rest of nature, but "some versions of naturalism carry the methods of empirical science too far and leave no room for the spiritual dimensions of the human being." Like scientism, the claim that all can be explained on the basis of materialism relies on the promise of future achievements. Thus Patricia Churchland holds that if we can determine how the brain works we can maximize rationality in human enquiry. Artigas remarks that this would be fine if it were true, but that he "seriously doubts that a better understanding of how our brain works will enable us to predict which theory of unification we should formulate in microphysics or which new accelerator we should build to test it."

Jaki has emphasized that man is a mysterious union of matter and mind, and that if we ignore his body he becomes a sort of angel and if we ignore his soul he is turned into an ape. The methods of empirical science combine theory and experiment and so require a subject capable of combining them. We are natural beings engaged on empirical studies and in addition we build theories that require us to transcend the natural world. We use scientific arguments to transcend our experiences, thus showing our capacity for objectification and conceptualization. Thus "scientific progress retrojustifies, enriches and refines the epistemological presuppositions of science," and "this is most coherent with the view that man is a co-creator who participates in God's plans." Thus "cultivating science becomes a human task with a divine meaning."

Empirical science is concerned with objective facts and so is often considered to be value-free, thus protecting its autonomy. Pure science is committed to its own goals and its progress is governed by internal criteria, while applied science is governed by extra-scientific values. However the search for truth is itself an ethical value, although not an absolute one, and scientists should be aware of the effects of their actions. As Popper has remarked, science itself cannot produce ethical principles, but this does not imply that there are no such principles; in fact the search for truth presupposes ethics since it requires open-mindedness, detachment, and respect for rational arguments, recognition of our fallibility, and intellectual honesty. Stephen Toulmin and Loren Graham have analyzed the connection between science and values, and this has become increasingly important in psychology, physiology, and sociobiology where science is used to study human beings.

Science is increasingly the cooperative endeavour of many people, and there are now many studies of the sociology of science, pioneered by Robert Merton. He defined four norms that comprise the ethos of science, namely universalism (truth claims are independent of race, nationality, religion, etc.); communism (the findings of science belong to the whole community); disinterestedness (the verification of results by other experts); and organized skepticism (the detailed scrutiny of results). Many authors including André Cournand, Michael Meyer, Jacob Bronowski, H. Richard Nebuhr, and Michael Polanyi have further elaborated the values intrinsic to science. This is not to say, however, that scientists are improved morally by their scientific work, but if they already hold these values they will be better scientists.

Scientists evaluate scientific theories according to certain criteria, and Kuhn lists these as accuracy, consistency, scope, simplicity, and fruitfulness. Ernan McMullin has pointed out that the historical development of science reinforces and clarifies these values, so that we can have some confidence that our theories give a true although incomplete account of nature. This moderate realism is held by most scientists, particularly by those engaged in experimental work.

The relationship between objectivity in morality and objectivity in science has been explored by Alasdair MacIntyre. He distinguishes between internal goods, namely those that show high aesthetic, imaginative intellectual and physical powers, and external goods that are the related rewards, such as money, status, reputation, and power. Since science is committed to the search for objective truth, considered as an internal good, it embodies a moral task. Furthermore, "the historical unity of the scientific enterprise has a moral character, as the continuity of a communal project directed toward the search for truth." Scientific knowledge of the natural world gives us some domination over nature, which can be used for practical ends, such as the improvement of our conditions of life. The applications of science may be good or bad, showing that science must be governed by ethical criteria. Society as a whole is willing to support science as long as it produces useful application, but hostility is easily aroused when it is applied for evil purposes.

The continual progress of science since the seventeenth century has yielded unprecedented knowledge of natural phenomena. Originally this was seen as a road leading from nature to a recognition of its Maker, but from the mid-eighteenth century onward it was seen more as a road toward the independence of the human person from religious constraints. The de-divinization of the world can be understood in two senses: according to the first, "it means that the world is neither a part of God nor can be identified with God." Seeing the world as created by God is a central Christian belief that favoured the birth of modern science. The second sense, held by Schiller and Weber, is that there is no trace of God to be found in the world. Such views interpret "the methodological limitation of empirical science as the denial of anything that cannot be studied using the methods of empirical science." Thus "scientific progress should not be considered a major cause of the de-divinization of the world."

On the philosophical and theological level, Artigas recognizes the methodological gap between them and the sciences, and so proposes an interpretation based on coherence rather than proof. To assess his interpretation he applies the same criteria that scientists use to assess their own theories. His interpretation "in favour of theism and human spirituality possesses a high explanatory power because it accounts for many phenomena that, when seen in the light of agnosticism or atheism, are left completely unexplained." Theists "have no problem in accepting all scientific explanations and, in addition, provide explanations about other problems that would otherwise remain veiled in mystery." This also holds for teleology, as "the present world view provides a great amount of highly sophisticated evidence in favour of the teleological interpretation of the world." His interpretation has predictive power because "it provides a rational basis for responsible and creative human activity." The theistic perspective "respects the real complexity of the world and does not interfere with natural explanations but provides them with their adequate radical foundation," and is "coherent with scientific data stemming from a variety of sources, such as deterministic chaos, evolutionary theory, and natural dynamism."

In a final section, Artigas observes that "the current world view is highly consistent with the emphasis on God's respect toward creation. Divine action should not be conceived as opposed to natural agency; rather, it makes possible the very existence of created causes and fosters their own agency." Thus, "acceptance of Divine purpose makes it possible to understand how necessity, chance and purpose can be combined to bring about our world. Indeed, if naturalistic explanations were to be considered ultimate, we would be forced to attribute to blind natural forces a subtlety and foresight they cannot possess." We can recognize that the detailed and subtle workings of nature revealed by scientific progress shows God's power and wisdom. On a personal level, the extreme sensitivity to initial conditions shown by chaos theory emphasizes the importance of all our actions: everything we do can be transformed into actions directed toward the fulfillment of God's plans.

This brief summary of some of the main themes of Professor Artigas's book may suffice to show its importance and value. He has raised the level of the contemporary debate on the relations between science and religion and provided a sure guide to their complexities. He seems to have read almost every book on the subject, and gives judicious and sympathetic accounts even of views he does not share. As a scientist himself, he does full justice to the value of science and to the subtleties of the scientific method. Whether one agrees with him or not, this is a book that cannot be ignored by anyone interested in these questions.

CHAPTER 9

A Treatise on Truth*

IT IS SURPRISINGLY EASY to overlook the obvious and its obvious implications. Thus, when we send a message, we have to make use of some means to send it. These means themselves carry a message, and sometimes this contradicts the original message. Thus the means used to convey a message are inevitably part of the message. For example, if a philosopher writes a book denying the existence of material objects, he refutes himself because the book itself is a material object. For example "the truth reveals itself in real messages." The message depends on the means used to convey it. Furthermore, "a book is not only an object, it is produced freely and for a purpose" and so implicitly endorses both free will and purposeful human behaviour. It follows from this that philosophers should recognize the reality and use of the means by which they propagate their ideas. Only if this is done can their message be about truth.

In any philosophical discussions, primary consideration should be given to the objects that provide the means for the message. Objects are primary data, so fundamental that they cannot be explained by anything else. This cannot be refuted, because any attempted refutation is itself an act of communication, and this requires objective

---

* Review of *Means to Message. A Treatise on Truth* by Stanley L. Jaki (Grand Rapids, MI: Eerdmans, 1999). Reprinted with permission from *Contemporary Physics* 44(2003): 397.

means. The very act of acknowledging objects is the cornerstone of the philosopher's system of truth.

The first step in any philosophical discourse is of vital importance, and this is provided by the objective recognition of objects. Neglect of this trapped Descartes and Kant in the narrow circle of their own ideas. If one starts with ideas, there is no way back to reality. The recognition of an object is to know the object, and this act of knowledge registering reality is consciousness.

Philosophers seek clarity, especially clear ideas. What could be clearer than immediate reality? Mathematics is taken as the paradigm of exact clarity; yet philosophers have to use words and these are not precisely definable; moreover, words change their meanings with time. There is a sharp distinction between the quantitative and the qualitative, and this means that arguments in philosophy are not the same as those in mathematics. They make sense only if these are about the real world and are addressed to real minds. "Concepts other than quantities have a clarity of their own which cannot be properly rendered in terms of a clarity that quantities alone possess."

The great success of the scientific enterprise from the time of Newton onward led to its being accepted as the paradigm of truth, and philosophers came to think that science is the source and justification of philosophical ideas. This is not so, although it is true that philosophical ideas provide the basis of science. Physicists frequently use models in their attempts to understand phenomena. These may convey partial aspects of the truth but they are corrigible. It is the systems of equations that are permanent. Since the same equations may describe very different phenomena, there is no way to go from the equations to the physical picture. The theory then exists in full independence of all the philosophical and quasi-philosophical factors that helped its erection in the first place.

The differences between the abstract mathematical structure of equations and physical reality do not prevent the equations from being used to manipulate that reality. "The road that connects philosophy and exact science is a one-way road." Science presupposes philosophy; it does not provide it. One can go from philosophy to science, but not from science to philosophy. Philosophy must therefore begin with an unconditional assertion of material reality, embedded in objects.

Physics is the quantitative study of the quantitative aspects of things in motion. It can tell us nothing about how these things came to be; the transition from non-being to being belongs to metaphysics alone.

Science "make sense only if it is done freely and for a purpose." Any protracted activity, such as writing a book or conducting a scientific experiment, is sustained by a purposeful exercise of free will. Nobel Prizes are not given to robots. Any attempts to find out how free will operates serves only to undermine the significance of our immediate understanding that we can act freely, an ontological act. Science tells us nothing about free will since it cannot be observed or measured; it is experienced personally. The Ten Commandments make sense only if we are free to obey them or not. "Free will is a mystery on the natural level in the sense that it cannot be reduced to anything else." The mystery of free will ceases to appear a contradiction in terms only when seen in the context of the infinite power and goodness of God.

Anyone who writes a book does so with a purpose, and in the process makes and uses tools. This activity implies conscious and purposeful action, a characteristic behaviour of mankind. However sophisticated the tools or machines, the man who makes them is immeasurably superior. It is absurd to claim that "an evolutionary process, which is seemingly and allegedly purposeless, could produce a being whose very nature is to act for a purpose." Chance remains a cover-up for ignorance, and necessity is "refuted by the very freedom whereby it is posited." Like reality or free will or causality, the reality of one's acting for a purpose is something irreducible to anything else.

Biologists can only observe and describe the organisms that they study but, if they look at them with the eyes of philosophy, they see everywhere evidence of purpose.

To argue against causality is likewise self-defeating, since the arguments used are intended to cause a change of mind. The founders of quantum mechanics claimed that causality is an illusion, and that all events are basically random. The ontological insensitivity of some physicists is shown by the claim that quantum mechanics enables them to create, at least in principle, entire universes out of nothing. The cosmological steady-state theory similarly postulates the appearance of hydrogen atoms out of nothing, without the action of a creator. The recognition of causality requires no more than the recognition that reality exists independent of ourselves. Scientists must assume that nature is causal, for otherwise there would be no sense in studying it.

While the means is generally a tangible object such as a book, the message is an intangible that needs to be understood by both the sender and the receiver. The act of understanding is so fundamental that it cannot be explained in terms of anything else. These acts are invariably conscious and coalesce into personal identity that persists through space and time. It is an awareness of one's own existence.

Consideration of consciousness raises the question whether there is mind distinct from the body, even though the mind is totally dependent on the body. Thoughts are not material, and mental operations are performed with a sense of freedom and for a purpose. The transference of ideas from one person to another uses causation that is quite different from the contacts of material bodies. Further, non-material activities of the mind are the appreciation of the meaning of "now" and of the concept of nothing. Even more remarkable is man's ability to make symbols of reality, and to develop languages for communication. Our beliefs are not determined by the motions of atoms in our brains, for otherwise we would never know whether they are true. Thus the idea of artificial intelligence is profoundly artificial; computers, however sophisticated, are mere robots. They cannot think and, as Einstein remarked, there is no logical road to discovery, although the process is certainly rational. The history of philosophy shows the importance of avoiding materialism on the one hand and idealism on the other; only by combining matter and mind can a viable science be constructed.

In contemporary society the majority vote determines ethical issues, irrespective of considerations of right and wrong. Thus the means, the numbers, are taken as messages so that actions that not so long ago were considered to be immoral are now generally accepted. This reshaping of morals is engineered by propaganda widely spread by the mass media, and thus absolute values are steadily eroded. This can be prevented only by recognizing irreducible facts concerning messages, namely that they are sent freely and purposefully, and by the realization that we depend on each other. This is the origin of our sense of social justice and hence the recognition of objective moral values.

This is a profoundly original book that richly repays reading and rereading. Starting with the recognition that any message requires a means to transmit it, Jaki shows how this requires the acceptance of objective reality, freedom, purposeful behaviour, and causality, all perennial philosophical subjects that are usually studied in isolation. A particularly valuable feature is that it clarifies the relation between science and philosophy, a relation that is so often misunderstood or inverted.

CHAPTER 10

Science as Salvation*

TRADITIONAL RELIGIONS gave answers to the great questions that we all ask when we think about ourselves: why are we here, what is the purpose of our lives, and is there life after death. If, for one reason or another, we reject our traditional religion, these questions are not stilled, and we try to answer them in other ways. Where can we find salvation? If not in traditional religions, then possibly in the religions of the East, or perhaps in science.

The scientific discoveries of the last three hundred years, and their technological applications, have transformed our culture and made it unlike any other. For the first time all people are unified by easy communications and transport. We know the structure of matter down through the atoms and molecules to the nuclei, nucleons, and quarks, and its evolution through aeons of time from the Big Bang to the present. Modern medicine has banished age-old diseases and extended our life span, and modern agriculture has vastly extended the quality and quantity of our food, thus providing in a rational way what previous generations prayed for in vain.

Scientists have waxed lyrical about the power of science to change our lives. Thus Popper in 1972 claimed that science is "perhaps the

* Review of *Science as Salvation: A Modern Myth and It's Meaning* by Mary Midgley (London: Routledge, 1992), reprinted with permission from *History and Philosophy of the Life Sciences* 18(3; 1996): 397.

most powerful tool for biological adaptation that has emerged in the course of organic evolution." Thirty years earlier Waddington had proclaimed that "science by itself is able to provide mankind with a way of life which is, firstly, fully self-consistent and harmonious and, secondly, free for the exercise of that objective reason on which our material progress depends. So far as I can see, the scientific attitude of mind is the only one which is, at the present day, adapted in both these respects." More recently, Hawking declared that "our goal is nothing less than a complete description of the universe we live in" and that when a satisfactory cosmological theory has emerged "we will be able to take part in the discussion of the question why it is that we and the universe exist. If we find the answer we would know the mind of God."

Whether the average working scientist believes all this is another question. Undoubtedly we are proud of the successes of science, but if pressed to justify it we are liable to take a much more modest view. Influenced by subliminal positivism, we may even deny that science gives us any real knowledge of the world and that all we do is to make some observations and experiments and then seek to falsify some hypothesis concerning their interrelation. This disarms opposition, but at the price of denying the aim of science to provide objective reliable knowledge of the world, to say nothing of the grandiose claims that science provides a new way to salvation.

Most scientists are too busy to think out their positions in detail and in some there is a tendency to oscillate between the two extremes of inflated fantasy and excessive modesty. A critical analysis is badly needed, and this has now been provided by Mary Midgley.

Science first arose in the ages of faith, and the first scientists were very conscious that their work revealed the glories of God's creation. This was indeed the vocation of the scientist, and by following it faithfully he attained salvation. Nowadays God has receded or vanished but "the conceptual maps that he once dominated go on, being used as if they do not need much revision." We all have deep imaginative needs, and if they are not satisfied by religion, other beliefs will take their place.

Aristotelian science attributed purpose to natural phenomena in order to save purpose for mankind. This idea was misplaced, and modern science was made possible by removing purpose and replacing it by accurate description. Science itself, however, remained a most purposeful enterprise. At a higher level, religion provided a purpose for life, and now some scientists see science as taking on this role. In place of God's purpose, evolution is now governed by chance.

Science itself poses a problem: the second law of thermodynamics tells us that the universe is running down to the uniform heat death corresponding to the state of maximum entropy. Long before then the sun will expand and eliminate all life on earth. What then is the purpose of life?

Some scientists have tackled this problem. Already in 1929 the Marxist crystallographer Bernal surmised that man would colonise most of the stars, and organize them for our own purposes. More recently these ideas have been developed by Dyson and by Barrow and Tipler. Paul Davies has speculated that "we might even be able to manipulate the dimensions of space itself, creating bizarre artificial worlds with unique unimaginable properties. Truly, we shall be lords of the universe." To do all this we may have to transfer our consciousness from organic bodies to machines or to computer programs.

Midgley pertinently asks what is the point of it all. Why should salvation be pushed to the indefinite future? The old religions found salvation in the here and now.

Much play is made with the various versions of the anthropic principle. Studies of the evolution of the universe have shown that the emergence of life depends on the fundamental constants of nature having very specific values: if they were ever so slightly different we would not be here at all. It therefore looks as if the universe was made for us, until we reflect that if the constants of matter did not have those values we would not be here to think about it. And why should we suppose that it is all made for us, and not for the ants or the pandas?

Such "desperate tangles" are illustrations of what happens when science is displaced from its proper role as the way we obtain genuine reliable knowledge of the world we live in, a world made by God in which we fulfill our eternal destiny. If this role is denied, and science is inflated to become the ark of salvation, it runs amok and spawns a host of megalomaniacal fantasies.

Working scientists are not so much affected by all this, but it is readily taken up by enthusiastic journalists and influences many who have not the scientific and analytical knowledge to challenge its pretensions. Thus science is given an unreal glorification and prevented from carrying out its essential down-to-earth function.

Scientists frequently pride themselves on their high intellectual standards: They never believe anything until it is supported by overwhelming evidence and until this is forthcoming they suspend judgment. This is of course in sharp contrast to religious believers, who accept a whole range of highly implausible beliefs on little or no evidence. The reality is quite different in several respects. Modern physics is full of the most bizarre and counterintuitive ideas that are accepted by scientists without notable concern. Some, like those associated with special relativity, are clearly proven but others, particularly those associated with quantum mechanics—such as the wave-particle duality, tunneling through potential barriers, and non-local interactions—are not only quite unsupported, but would be derisively rejected in any normal discourse. More fundamentally, science itself rests on a host of prescientific beliefs about the existence and rationality of the world, the laws of logic, the reliability of our senses, the existence of other people, and so on that are hardly ever recognized, let alone analyzed and justified. On the other hand, some religious believers, it is true, are indeed credulous, but if they are to be judged by their more serious thinkers, no one who has ever even glanced at a manual of scholastic philosophy could accuse them of not taking reason seriously. It is also worth noting that some people hold a superstitious attitude toward science, believing uncritically every wild speculation, without knowledge of the extensive research that is necessary before any real conclusion is reached. Rather than considering themselves superior, it behooves scientists to look most carefully at their own beliefs, and acknowledge that radical skepticism is not a viable option. Once this is granted, the way is open to a fruitful discussion of hitherto unexamined presuppositions.

Is it possible for science to stand on its own? Hitherto, the presuppositions supporting this were provided by the belief in God, so what happens when this is removed? We lose the guarantee that nature is ordered and that the order holds throughout the past and the future. When pushed, scientists may retreat into phenomenalism, operationalism, instrumentalism, or idealism, but these cannot be held consistently, and they revert to realism as soon as they re-enter the laboratory. Without beliefs we would not only have no grounds for saying that anything is correct, but also for saying that anything is false.

Science is often presented as objective, and this is indeed true, but not to the extent that it stands entirely on its own. Science is ultimately based on faith, a set of beliefs concerning what is important and what is not. What counts as explanation and provides an integrating scheme that makes sense of our lives? Is this now to be found merely in the gathering of an infinite number of facts, and are we to be satisfied by the vision of mankind existing as computer programs far into the future? We cannot avoid faith in a set of metaphysical beliefs, and it is better to articulate them rationally than to be unaware of their existence.

It is particularly curious that scientists, so meticulous and careful in their professional work, should so readily let their imaginations run wild when they leave the laboratory. Now that they know that Mary Midgley is waiting with her sharp tools to puncture their fantasies this may induce a welcome sense of restraint and caution.

CHAPTER 11

Mystery in Science and Faith[*]

THERE IS A STORY about Lord Kelvin, the great pioneer of electricity, visiting an electrical equipment factory. He was shown round by a young apprentice who did not know the identity of the visitor. Kelvin listened patiently as the young man explained elementary facts about amps and volts, and then asked him: "Please tell me what electricity is." The young man fell silent. "Don't let that worry you," Kelvin remarked, "no one knows what electricity is."

It is just the same with the forces of nature. We do not know what gravitation is, or electrical forces, or nuclear forces. What we can do, and this is of course of the highest importance, is measure their strength and their variation with distance. Thus Newton postulated that the gravitational force between two objects is given by a constant multiplied by the product of their masses and divided by the square of the distance between them. The numerical value of the constant can be found by experiment, and then we have all we need to calculate the motions of the moon and the planets to a very high accuracy. We can do all this, but still we do not know what gravitation is.

Many of Newton's contemporaries refused to admit the validity of what Newton had done, saying that his forces were occult and no part of physics. Newton said that he made no hypotheses about the mechanism of the gravitational force, but the accuracy of his results

---

[*] Reprinted with permission from *Catholic Herald* (9 August 2002): 10.

showed the validity of his theory of gravitation. It is the same for the electrical and nuclear forces.

It is one of the aims of the physicist to explain these forces and to show how they may be connected at a deeper level. More and more experiments are being made, using large high-energy particle accelerators that probe ever finer motions and transformations of the particles. Some progress has been made toward seeing how the forces may be related, but whatever success is achieved the deepest mystery will remain. So we have a magnificent set of theories with a mystery at its heart.

This is quite similar for the beliefs at the heart of our Faith: the Trinity, the creation, the Incarnation. and the Resurrection. These beliefs, together with many others, form a tightly connected, unified whole that illuminates and guides our lives. The more we think about them the more we understand the purpose of our lives, our human rights and duties and our vocations in the life of the Church. As in science, we can go deeper and deeper, but we can never reach the end. There is finally a mystery beyond our comprehension.

Examination of real science, however, shows a strong similarity in its structures of belief to the faith articulated in Christian theology. In each there is detailed knowledge that guides our lives, one in the natural world and the other in the supernatural world, and in each there is a mystery at its heart.

CHAPTER 12

Fraud in Science*

IN RECENT MONTHS there have been two or three well-publicised examples of fraud in science. Such events are rare, but they do happen from time to time, and are of interest from the point of view of morality, scientific method, and the sociology of science. Nowadays the pressure on active research scientists is intense: They must publish or perish. Secure posts in universities and research establishments are relatively few, and there is intense competition for any vacancy. In addition, scientists must compete for funds to support their research.

Suppose that you are about to apply for a vacant post or for more research funding. You have to provide full documentation on your current and proposed research. It is no good saying that you made a spectacular discovery without being able to prove it because you will soon be found out. You have to be more subtle. So what you can do is to "improve" some new measurements that you have made. Suppose that your results seem to indicate something interesting, and you are pretty sure that given more time you could improve the accuracy to the point where the effect is established. It is then tempting to add some fictitious data to genuine data and make it all the more impressive. Such fraud is not easy to detect and may achieve its objective.

Scientists are continually checking each others' results and looking for discrepancies, and fraud is soon found out. This is one of the

* Reprinted with permission from *Catholic Herald* (28 March 2003): 10.

great strengths of science, and ensures that in the long run erroneous results are detected and removed.

In more leisurely times it was much easier. Pasteur urged researchers to spend months and years testing and checking their results, trying to see if there was any possibility that they could be wrong, before publishing their results. In earlier centuries, scientists published results that were not yet securely established in the form of an anagram. If later on they succeeded in establishing the result beyond doubt, they could reveal the key to the anagram and obtain the credit and priority they deserved.

However if the result was not confirmed they could consign it to oblivion without losing their reputation. Galileo did this for his discovery of the phases of the planet Venus, which proved that Venus orbits the sun. It is neither practicable nor fashionable to use anagrams today. Obviously a scientist is wrong and foolish to fake his results, but there are more subtle choices that have to be made in the course of research. If, for example, you are making an accurate measurement of the charge on the electron, there are numerous small corrections that have to be made to take account of disturbing effects. The difficulty is to know when to stop looking for such corrections.

There is a great temptation to stop when your result agrees with the best values obtained by previous workers. It is a matter of delicate judgment, and sometimes courage, to make this decision. Scientific research is not a mechanical process proceeding according to rigid rules; it requires a high degree of judgment and integrity. An instructive example is provided by Millikan's celebrated determination of the charge on the electron. Many other scientists were trying to do this in various places, and they obtained many different results. Millikan claimed that his measurements, each of them made on a single electron, gave closely the same result. Yet when his laboratory notebooks were examined they seemed to tell a different story. Each page contained the results of a series of measurements on a single electron, with the calculations leading to a value for the charge. These were annotated with remarks such as "beautiful—

publish." Some cases however, gave a different result, and these were marked "not an electron—ignore."

Superficially, it looks as if Millikan just selected the cases that gave a good result, and ignored the rest, while claiming that all the electrons he measured gave the same result. This judgment is unjust. He was quite right to reject some of the cases because he recognized that they were due to electrons attached to particles of dust, that would give erratic results. His genius as an experimentalist, and insight into what was going on, enabled him to overcome the difficulties.

The line between unconscious fraud and justified interpretation is thus a fine one, and there are no rigid rules to provide guidance. Ultimately the decision has to be made by the conscience of the scientist.

CHAPTER 13

Beauty in Science*

SCIENCE IS THE SYSTEMATIC STUDY of the natural world, and we see all around us many beautiful things: the colours and symmetries of cacti, snowflakes, and crystals, the graceful movements of the antelope, the flight of birds. To what extent is this beauty found also in science?

"Science is measurement," declared Lord Kelvin, adding that "unless you can measure what you are talking about and express it in numbers, your knowledge is of a meagre and unsatisfactory kind." That is indeed true for those things that can be measured. But beauty cannot be measured. Is there then no beauty in science?

There are two ways to carry out scientific research. Most scientists spend their lives measuring some natural phenomena or devising an experiment to subject matter to extreme conditions and then seeing how it behaves. When they have some results they try to put them into order and to fit them into a theoretical scheme.

There is another way, but it can be followed only by the very greatest scientists. They try to imagine how the world is made at the deepest level. "I want to know how God created the world, I want to think His thoughts," declared Einstein, "the rest are details." He tried to imagine what a light beam would be like if he traveled alongside it and was led to the theory of relativity. The resulting formalism, the Lorentz transformation, is much more beautiful

---

* Reprinted with permission from *The Second Spring*, Vol. 5.52.2004.

mathematically than the transformation until then considered to be obviously true. What do we mean by mathematical beauty? In this case it is the symmetry of the Lorentz transformation, which is just a rotation in spacetime. Relativity predicts results that are contrary to common sense, and yet they are confirmed by experiment. We all thought that velocities add arithmetically, but they do not, and then we realized that we never had good reason to suppose that they do. Some early experimental results with electrons disagreed with relativity, but Einstein was quite unperturbed; a few years later it was found that the experiments were flawed.

It was the same with his theory of gravitation, often called the general theory of relativity. According to Newtonian dynamics, a ray of light should be bent by a gravitational field, and this may be tested by measuring the bending of starlight by the sun. This can be observed only during a total eclipse of the sun, and the critical measurements were made by Arthur Eddington, who led an expedition to the island of Principe off the coast of West Africa in 1918. Einstein's theory predicted twice the deviation of Newton's theory, so the measurements were a critical text of the new ideas. He knew that his theory was correct because it was so beautiful.

Dirac was another great scientist who always looked for beautiful equations. It is not possible to explain in words what we mean by beautiful equation, anymore than it is possible for a musician to explain what constitutes a beautiful symphony or an artist to define what constitutes a beautiful picture. Dirac knew what he meant by a beautiful equation, and even said that he preferred his equations to be beautiful than to agree with experiment, but he knew very well the difficulties of experiments and was confident that any initial disagreements would ultimately be resolved when the experiments had been perfected.

Occasionally in the history of science many beautiful equations are unified in a way that describes a vast range of phenomena. Thus Newton's three laws of motion, together with his theory of gravitation, unify celestial and terrestrial dynamics, including Kepler's three laws of planetary motion. Maxwell's four equations unify all electromagnetic phenomena, and Schrödinger's equation provides a way to study atomic and nuclear phenomena. Einstein's theories of relativity and gravitation similarly describe the behaviour of matter at high velocities. These are supreme examples of beauty and science.

It is interesting to recall that even such great scientists as Einstein and Dirac sometimes lacked full confidence in the congruence between truth and beauty. Thus when Einstein formulated his cosmological theory he found that it predicted the expansion of the universe. Believing this to be incorrect, he inserted an extra term in his equation to prevent the expansion. Soon after, Hubble measured the velocities of the galaxies, and found that the universe is indeed expanding. This has been described as Einstein's greatest blunder.

In a rather similar way, Dirac wrote down a very beautiful equation describing the behaviour of relativistic electrons. He was surprised to find that it predicted not only the familiar negatively charged electrons, but positively charged ones as well. These were unknown, so Dirac assumed that the positively charged particles must be the familiar protons. Soon afterward Anderson discovered positively charged electrons in the cosmic radiation. They were the first anti-particles, and now it is known that every particle has its anti-particle. This is one of the first examples of a fundamental symmetry of nature.

Since that time many more symmetries have been discovered. Sometimes they are broken symmetries that are nearly always, but not quite, obeyed. Further work then shows that full symmetry is restored when two or three broken symmetries are combined. Nature shows a beautiful symmetry at the deepest level.

It has often been remarked that a detailed knowledge of the evolution of the universe shows that it is exceedingly unlikely that we should be here at all. It seems that if the constants of nature had been even very slightly different, it would not have been possible to build even the lightest chemical elements, and so there would have been no life. This led some to say that God must have chosen the constants of nature very carefully so that life is possible. This is called the anthropic principle. Others, not liking this conclusion, suggested that a large number of universes came into existence with all possible values of the fundamental constants, and, of course, we live in the universe where, by some accident, the "right" values occur.

The constants of nature are the velocity of light, the charge on the electron, the strengths of the electric and gravitational fields, and so on. The numbers we use are expressed in units that we choose. It is, however, possible to combine them into groups that are independent of our units, and an example of this is what is called the fine structure constant. The question we can then ask is whether even God can change the fine structure constant. Might it not be like the constant pi, which God cannot change? This is the sort of question that Einstein asked himself; he wanted to know how much freedom God had when He created the universe. We still do not know the answer to that question. For all we know the constants of nature are fixed by mathematical necessity, and if so this would undermine all anthropic arguments.

The knowledge that the natural world is created by God makes a fundamental difference to the way scientific research is carried out. The Belgian Abbe Lemaitre, originator of the Big Bang theory of the evolution of universe, has suggested that "perhaps the believer has the advantage of knowing that the enigma has a solution, that it is in the final analysis the work of an intelligent being; so the problems posed by nature are here to be solved, and the degree of difficulty is without doubt appropriate to the present and future intellectual capacity of humanity. This will perhaps not give him greater resources for his investigations, but it will help to support the feeling of healthy optimism without which a sustained effort cannot be maintained." Commenting on this, Pope John Paul II declared: "I wish all of you this healthy optimism of which Abbe Lemaitre speaks; it is an optimism that takes its mysterious but very real origin in God in whom you have placed your faith."

CHAPTER 14

Chance[*]

WE OFTEN HEAR such phrases as: "I'll chance it," "We met quite by chance," "I think that I have a good chance of winning that race," "Evolution takes place by chance," and so on.

What do these phrases mean? Presumably they imply some beliefs about the natural world, and if so are they justified?

The mathematical theory of probability was developed some years ago, mainly, it seems, to find the best strategies for winning certain card games. A simple example is tossing a coin. We know that the chance of it falling with the head up is just one-half. Similarly with the dice: we know the chance of throwing a six is just one in six, and if we throw two dice the chance of two sixes is just one thirty-sixth. Other games require much more sophisticated analysis but the principle is the same. The same applies to those problems that amused us at school: "If three men and five women enter an eight seat railway carriage and sit down at random, what is the chance that two men will sit opposite each other?" "If there are fifty people in a room, what is the chance that there will be two with the same birthday?" All such problems have a definite answer. Lord Cherwell was once asked whether he intended to take part in a lottery. "Young man," he replied, "I lecture on the theory of probability."

---

[*] Reprinted with permission from *St. Austin Review* (January/February 2004): 30.

It often happens that a word that has a very definite meaning in a particular context is applied to a rather different context where the meaning is not so clear. If we say "we met by chance," we cannot calculate the probability of this happening. Two causal chains, each having a perfectly logical explanation, happen to intersect. Aquinas indeed gives this as an example of chance. In this case there is the complication that two people are involved, each having free will. Would we say that the collision of two particular gas molecules in the air is also a chance event? It rather seems to be stretching the meaning of chance too far.

The French physicist Laplace considered the natural world to be made up of entities that always behaved strictly in accord with inviolable laws. He said that if one knew the positions and velocities of all the particles and the interactions between them, a being of great intelligence could calculate every thing that will happen in the future and also all that has happened in the past. The whole history would be open to his gaze. Of course we cannot do this: we cannot measure the present state exactly, we do not know the interactions, and we cannot do the mathematics. Nevertheless it is a useful way of thinking about one type of theoretical world. It is a world of complete determinism where nothing happens by chance. If we do not like it we have to say why.

First of all, the world is not just a completely determined world. We are in the world, and we have free will. We do not know how, but we can certainly come to a decision and produce a physical effect. If this were not so we would be just robots. The words on this paper would be just the result of interactions between particles. In the words of Whitehead, the world would be just the hurrying of material, endlessly, meaninglessly.

It is not only ourselves, but also God who can act on the world. Everything, ultimately, is caused by God. Aquinas distinguished two types of divine causality, primary and secondary. By primary causality God causes everything, but He also acts by secondary causality when he creates matter and gives it certain definite properties. Thereafter the matter behaves in accord with these properties.

This does not happen by unbreakable necessity, because God has complete power over nature and can suspend or alter the laws of nature. He does this occasionally, as in the case of miracles.

This means that Laplacian determinism is unacceptable. While the natural world usually follows laws, it does not do so by unbreakable necessity: both God and human beings can cause different effects.

In recent years there have been several attempts to find a way for God to act on the world without overriding the laws of nature. These use quantum mechanics, a very successful theory that enables a wide range of atomic and nuclear events to be calculated, but only in terms of probabilities. The world then seems fuzzy and indeterminate. For example, the Heisenberg uncertainty principle tells us that we cannot know both the position and the velocity of a particle like an electron to any desired accuracy. It seems that the more accurately we know the position, the less accurately we know its velocity, and vice versa. It is thus possible that God can act within the limits of uncertainty in such a way that He can bring about the effects he needs without apparently breaking the laws of physics.

This argument is unacceptable for several reasons. Quantum mechanics is an incomplete theory in the sense that it is just one step along the road to understand the natural world. We cannot be sure that it is the final theory. Furthermore, it is essentially a statistical theory and applies to ensembles of similar systems, and so cannot give a complete account of any particular system. There are indeed many phenomena, such as the time of decay of a radioactive nucleus, that cannot be calculated by quantum mechanics. The word fuzzy only applies to a hypothetical world that strictly obeys quantum mechanics, not to the real world. Physics can take no account of Divine intervention or of acts of free will, so in the course of scientific research the world is assumed to be strictly determined.

Since quantum mechanics is a statistical theory, there has been much discussion about whether in the future we can learn more about the deterministic substructure that underlies it. Are there "hidden variables," as they are called, that describe quantum phenomena exactly? There are several possibilities that are being actively studied, but so far no definite conclusion has been reached.

So now we have the natural world that obeys definite laws that scientists seek to know ever more accurately, and yet it remains a world open to the actions of God and to our own free decisions. It is a world of law and order, yet also freedom and responsibility. ⚛

CHAPTER 15

Time*

"PLEASE, WHAT IS TIME?" asked the visitor with an imperfect grasp of English idiom, and was somewhat disconcerted by the reply: "Ah, my friend, that is a very profound philosophical question." He could also have been told that it is a very profound theological and scientific question as well.

What sort of answer would we expect to that question? We cannot expect the clear and definite type of answer we can give to scientific questions such as, "What is the chemical composition of water?" Time is one of those fundamental concepts that can be apprehended but cannot be defined in terms of anything more fundamental because there is nothing that is more fundamental. We can, however, think about it and perhaps gain some insights. As St. Augustine remarked in his Confessions, we all know what time is until someone asks us, and then we fall silent.

Our first experience of time comes through our own bodies. We feel our pulse, we fall asleep and wake again to a new day. We experience just an instant between the past and the future. The past is gone forever and cannot be changed. The future does not yet exist.

We do not know what prehistoric men thought about time, but they knew the progression of the seasons. They banded together and dragged huge monoliths weighing up to fifty tons for miles and miles

---

* Reprinted with permission from *St. Austin Review* (January/February 2005).

to build Stonehenge, carefully aligned so that the sun rises over the heel stone on midsummer day, thus marking the summer solstice. Perhaps such circles were used as primitive calendars, helping farmers to know when to plant their crops. Later, priests were chosen and given the duty to keep track of time. They made increasingly accurate measurements of the movements of sun and stars and prepared calendars to mark the seasons. They found that the year is about 365 and one-quarter days. This was to form the basis of the Julian calendar.

In all ancient civilisations it was believed that after very many years everything will be repeated again, and so on forever. This belief in cyclic time, so strange to us, is very depressing, and is one of the reasons why science never developed in ancient times. Writing on the Doctrine of the Great Year, the belief that history continually repeats itself in a series of unending cycles, Duhem declared: "To the construction of that system all disciples of Hellenistic philosophy—Peripatetics, Stoics, Neo-Platonists—contributed; to that system Abu Masar offered the homage of the Arabs; the most illustrious rabbis, from Philo of Alexandria to Maimonides, have accepted it. To condemn it and to throw it overboard as a monstrous superstition, Christianity had to come." The superstition was indeed broken by the unique incarnation of Christ; henceforth time was not an infinite series of cycles but a linear and purposeful progression from beginning to end.

In Roman times sand and water clocks were adequate to mark the hours of the day, but they were not good enough for the monks who had to regulate their hours of prayer and work. They made mechanical clocks, and the earliest recorded examples are from Dunstable priory in 1283 and Exeter cathedral in 1284. A very sophisticated example dating from 1386, with a double feedback mechanism, is still to be seen in the nave of Salisbury cathedral. Subsequently clocks were placed on towers in the centres of towns and cities to regulate the hours of business. Gradually a sense of time spread through the community.

Curiously enough, this concern with time is characteristic of Western but not of Eastern Christendom. Eastern Orthodox Christians always have had a much more relaxed sense of time. Clocks were only introduced in the monasteries of Mount Athos in the eighteenth century and timekeeping is still casual. "The service will start when it is time," impatient and exasperated visitors are serenely told. This lack of a sense of exact time is probably not unconnected with the failure of science to develop in the East. There is a profound relation between Christianity and time.

The old Julian calendar was based on a year of 365.25 days, whereas the true value is about 365.2564 days. This difference might well be considered small enough, but by the end of the Middle Ages the error added up so that the date was incorrect by about ten days. Pope Gregory XII therefore appointed a commission that included the distinguished Jesuit Papal astronomer Christopher Clavius to advise on how to set things right. The commission recommended that the error accumulated over the centuries should be put right by omitting the days from 4 to 14 October 1582 and that no centenary years should be leap years except when divisible by 400. This calendar is extremely accurate and will not require further correction for thousands of years. Pope Gregory accepted and promulgated the recommendation of the commission. The Gregorian calendar, as it is called, was accepted by Catholic countries, but not by Protestant countries, whose inhabitants were outraged that the Pope was trying to steal ten days of their lives. This difference between Catholic time and Protestant time persisted until 1700 in most countries, except for England and Ireland, where it was violently opposed by the bishops and not accepted for another fifty years. (These different dates have to be remembered by historians who describe events in different countries in that period.) Eventually Gregorian time was generally accepted, although not by the Orthodox Church until 1923. Most of the monasteries on Mount Athos still use the Julian calendar.

Scientists found it necessary to devise more accurate ways of measuring time. Galileo at first used his pulse and then, in his famous experiment on rates of fall, weighed the water that spurted out of a small hole in a jar. A new standard of accuracy was achieved by the pendulum clock. In the times of great voyages of discovery there was a pressing need for an accurate method of determining position at sea. More and more ships were wrecked by running onto rocks at night. It is easy to obtain the latitude by astronomical observations, but determination of the longitude requires an accurate timekeeper, and the pendulum clock is useless onboard due to the motion of the ship. The British Admirality offered a prize to anyone who could make a sufficiently accurate clock for use at sea. The prize was won by John Harrison for his extremely ingenious clock driven by springs. These clocks were very expensive, and were further refined over the years. It was a long time, however, before any but the most wealthy could afford to have a timekeeper for personal use.

Newton, who brought science to maturity, began by defining space and time. "Absolute, true and mathematical time, of itself, and from its own nature, flows equably without relation to anything external," he declared: "All motions may be accelerated and retarded, but the flowing of absolute time is not liable to any change." This definition is of course, circular, and shows the futility of trying to define time. Nevertheless, he formulated his three laws of motion and principle of gravitation and thus founded dynamics. Henceforth it was clear that we live in four-dimensional spacetime: every event has its position marked by three spatial and one temporal number. It is situated at a definite point on a four-dimensional grid that extends to infinity in all directions.

These equations of Newton imply a serious problem. They contain only second derivatives of time, and so are unchanged if we reverse the direction of time. Every phenomenon should therefore be reversible. However, if we see a film of a glass shattering, we know very well the direction of time. If the film is run backward we know it is wrong. Yet everything is governed by Newton's equations. So where does this directionality of time come from? This was a subject of great discussion in the nineteenth century, especially by Maxwell and Boltzmann. The answer is contained in the new statistical mechanics, which shows that what we consider as time-reversed events are not impossible, but only extremely improbable. The question of time-reversal invariance is a live contemporary problem in elementary particle physics.

In the early years of the twentieth century, Einstein thought about the way used to transform the spacetime coordinates of an event in one coordinate system to those in another moving with uniform velocity relative to the first. He realized that the Galilean transformation that everyone used, and considered obviously true, was unsatisfactory when applied to lightwaves. Applying fundamental symmetry considerations, and assuming the constancy of velocity of light in all coordinate systems, he obtained what was already known as the Lorentz transformation. This is more elegant than the Galilean transformation, as it is just a rotation in spacetime. Moreover it agrees with experiments of ever-increasing precision. Some of its predictions appear contrary to common sense: velocities do not add arithmetically, and moving clocks appear to run slow, but this simply shows how unreliable is common sense. This is hardly surprising, as these effects show only for velocities approaching that of light, and we have no direct experience of such behaviour. The theory of relativity tells us something more about time. In the following years clocks of ever-increasing accuracy were made, particularly by using oscillating quartz crystals and atomic vibrations. Scientific measurements are made in milliseconds, nanoseconds, picoseconds. Some of the nuclear reactions I study take about 10^{-22} seconds (this means one divided by ten thousand million million million).

All this keeps physicists amused, but gives us no help toward understanding the fundamental problem of God and time. God is timeless and unchangeable. " I hear no more the busy beat of time," declared Gerontius as he sped toward his maker. God did not decide, one fine day, to create the universe: He created time, space, and matter together. There is no time before the creation. For God, all is an ever-present now: past, present, and future are spread out before Him. So then He must know everything that I will do in the future; in particular He knows what decisions I will make. Are we then not just robots following a plan that God has known from all eternity?

What then becomes of my free will, of my responsibility to choose right rather than wrong? We can say that God knows how I will freely choose, but how can I choose freely if he already knows what I will chose? I don't know the answer to these questions, and I doubt if anyone does. We must await the answer at the end of time. ✲

PART III
Modern Physics

CHAPTER 16

Relativity and Religion:
The Abuse of Einstein's Theory[*]

IT IS FREQUENTLY maintained that the theory of relativity, along with quantum mechanics, demolished the
nineteenth-century picture of the universe and created a
new world picture that differs radically from that of
Isaac Newton.

After Einstein's theory was published in 1905, it took physicists
some time to absorb its implications, but by 1912 the conservative
Max Planck could say, "This new way of thinking . . . well surpasses
in daring everything that has been achieved in speculative scientific
research, even in the theory of knowledge. . . . This revolution in
the physical *Weltanschauung*, brought about by the relativity principle, is to be compared in scope and depth only with that caused by
the introduction of the Copernican system of the world" (quoted in
Holton 1982, xii). The reception of the general theory of relativity
was even more dramatic, and the scene was described by Alfred
North Whitehead:

> It was my good fortune to be present at the meeting of the Royal
> Society in London when the Astronomer Royal for England

[*] I am very grateful to Sarah Nelson and John Lucas for illuminating comments
and suggestions, and I acknowledge with particular gratitude the book edited by
Gerald Holton and Yehuda Elkana, *Albert Einstein: Historical and Cultural Perspectives* (1982), which has provided much valuable information. Reprinted with
permission from *Zygon* 38 (2; 2003): 393. Some of the material in this article is
used in *Theology and Modern Physics* (Aldershot: Ashgate Press, 2005).

announced that the photographic plates of the famous eclipse, as measured by his colleagues in Greenwich Observatory, had verified the prediction of Einstein that rays of light are bent as they pass in the neighbourhood of the sun. The whole atmosphere of tense interest was exactly that of a Greek drama: we were the chorus commenting on the decree of destiny as disclosed in the development of a supreme incident. There was dramatic quality in the very staging: the traditional ceremonial, and in the background the picture of Newton to remind us that the greatest of scientific generalisations was now, after more than two centuries, to receive its first modification. Nor was the personal interest wanting: a great adventure in thought had at length come safe to shore. (1925, 15)

The event was widely publicized, and thereafter Einstein became a public figure, the very personification of scientific genius. Einstein's theory, according to a perceptive writer,

. . . overturned the concepts of absolute space and time which formed the framework within which the laws governing the behaviour of matter were described in Newtonian physics. By disproving the existence of temporal simultaneity, demonstrating the variability of the lengths and masses of bodies moving at high velocity, establishing the equivalence of mass and energy, and tying together space and time in a four-dimensional manifold of varying curvature, Einstein created a world picture that differed radically from that of Newton in its theoretical principles. (Graham 1981, 35)

To this list may be added time dilation, namely that moving clocks appear to run slow. Many of these implications of the theory, well-confirmed by experiment, seemed contrary to common sense and engendered the feeling that familiar and traditional landmarks had melted away.

The word *relativity* was taken by many to mean the denial of any absolutes, and the equivalence of mass and energy seemed to mark the end of nineteenth-century materialism. Many physicists, such as Sir Arthur S. Eddington and Vladimir A. Fock, used its ideas to support their religious or political beliefs (Graham 1982, 107). Relativity has also been enthusiastically welcomed by artists and novelists, but in ways that deserve Wolfgang Pauli's devastating remark on a scientific paper: "It is not even wrong" (Cropper 2001, 257).

The purpose of this article is to examine these questions and to see the real connection between relativity and religion. It will be shown that Einstein's theory is principally concerned with establishing the objective and invariant features of the world, that its apparently paradoxical aspects are readily understandable, and that absolute space and time remain at the basis of physics. To do this, we first recall Newton's concept of absolute space and time and then the approach of Einstein, which led him to realize the general applicability of the Lorentz transformation, which gives the relation between the coordinates of two systems moving relative to each other with a constant relativistic velocity. (This was described by Hendrik Antoon Lorentz and named after him.) The consequences of this transformation are then explored, and relativity is found to be a natural extension of classical physics. The interpretation of relativity due to Lorentz based on absolute space and time is shown to be consistent with the formalism of relativity and also to provide the basis of physics. The interpretations of relativity are then compared with those of quantum mechanics, and their similarities and differences discussed. The final section is devoted to the connection between relativity and religion.

Although this article is concerned only with the special theory of relativity, J. L. Synge (1964) has rewritten Einstein's theory of gravitation (often referred to as the general theory of relativity) in a form based on absolute space and time.

As in the case of quantum mechanics, it is important in such discussions to distinguish between the formal mathematical structure of a scientific theory and the various interpretations that have grown up around it. The former constitutes the physics, and its success in no way endorses the validity of the interpretations.

Newtonian Space and Time

The concepts of absolute space and absolute time, independent of the existence of any physical objects, are basic to Newtonian physics.

In formulating his concepts of space and time, Newton was strongly influenced and guided by his theological beliefs and saw them as the sensorium of God:

> Does it not appear from phenomena that there is a Being incorporeal, living, intelligent, omnipresent, who in infinite space, as it were His sensory, *sees* the things themselves intimately, and thoroughly perceives them, and comprehends them wholly by their immediate presence to Himself: of which things the images only carried through the organs of our sense into our little sensoriums, are there seen and beheld by that which in us perceives and thinks. (Barbour 1989, 628)

God is omnipresent and eternal, and so all space and time is equally present to him:

> He is eternal and infinite . . . ; that is, his duration reaches from eternity to eternity; his presence from infinity to infinity. . . . He is not eternity and infinity, but eternal and infinite; he is not duration or space, but he endures and is present. He endures forever, and is everywhere present; and, by existing always and everywhere, he constitutes duration and space. Since every particle of space is *always*, and every indivisible moment of duration is *everywhere*, certainly the Maker and Lord of all things cannot be *never* and *nowhere*. (Newton, *Principia* 941)

Newton concluded that motion "must be referred to some motionless thing such as extension alone or space" (Barbour 1989, 617). Extension has "its own manner of existence which fits neither substance nor accident" (p. 618). In *De Gravitatione*, Newton describes the properties of space in more detail:

> . . . space extends infinitely in all directions. For we cannot imagine any limit anywhere without at the same time imagining that there is space beyond it. . . . The parts of space are motionless. . . . The parts of duration and space are only understood to be the same as they really are because of their mutual order and position; nor do they have any hint of individuality apart from that order and precision, which consequently cannot be altered. . . . Space is

the disposition of being qua being. No being exists or can exist which is not related to space in some way. God is everywhere, created minds are somewhere, and body is in the space that it occupies; and whatever is neither everywhere nor anywhere does not exist. . . . The positions, distance and local motions of bodies are to be referred to the parts of space. . . . Lastly, space is eternal in duration and immutable in nature, and this is because it is the emanent effect of an eternal and immutable being. (Barbour 1989, 619)

Within this rationalist perspective, Newton formulated in his *Principia* the following definitions of space and time:

Absolute space in its own nature, without relation to anything external, remains always similar and immovable. Relative space is some moveable dimension or measure of the absolute space; which our senses determine by its position to bodies; and which is commonly taken for immoveable space; such is the dimension of a subterraneous, and aerial or celestial space, determined by its position in respect of the earth. Absolute and relative space are the same in figure and magnitude; but they do not remain always numerically the same. For if the earth, for instance, moves, a space of our air, which relatively and in respect of the earth remains always the same, will at one time become part of the absolute space into which the air passes; at another time it will be another part of the same, and so, absolutely understood, it will be continually changed.

Absolute, true and mathematical time, of itself, and from its own nature, flows equably without relation to anything external, and by another name is called duration; relative, apparent, and common time, is some sensible and external (whether accurate or unequable) measure of duration by the means of motion, which is commonly used instead of true time; such as an hour, a day, a month, a year. (Newton, *Principia,* 408–9; Barbour 1989, 623–24)

Thus,

. . . the flowing of time is not liable to any change. . . . As the order of the parts of time is immutable, so also is the order of the parts of space. . . . All things are placed in time as to order of succession;

and in space as to order of situation. It is from their essence or nature that they are places. . . . These are therefore that absolute places; and translations out of these places are the only absolute motions. (Barbour 1989, 624–25)

These definitions are metaphysical, so that it makes sense to speak of doubling the speed of clocks or enlarging space. Without the concept of metaphysical time as an ultimate reference this would have no meaning, and similarly for space. Such definitions need to be supplemented by more physical definitions if they are to be of practical use. Absolute space can be defined physically as the unique reference frame that, if it exists, can be recognized as such by all observers irrespective of their velocities with respect to that frame. Absolute time can be defined in a similar way.

We can think of absolute space as constituting a three-dimensional coordinate right-angled grid extending uniformly in all directions to infinity. Each event is situated within that frame, and its position is specified by the values of the three coordinates. Space and time exist independently of any material objects. In *De Gravitatione*, Newton considers the nature of space and by implication time: "It is not substance; on the one hand, because it is not absolute in itself, but is as it were an emanent effect of God, or a disposition of all being; on the other hand, because it is not among the proper dispositions that denote substance, namely actions, such as thoughts in the mind or notions in the body" (Hall and Hall 1978, 132). In this passage Newton makes it clear that space is not absolute in itself but only as an emanative effect of God. Space and time are in no way part of God, but God being implies infinite space and time. They "are uncreated and co-existent with God and yet ontologically dependent on him for their being" (Craig 2000).

However, for practical purposes,

. . . because the parts of space cannot be seen, or distinguished from one another by our senses, therefore in their stead we use sensible measures of them. For from the positions and distances of things from any body considered as immoveable we define all places, and then with respect to such places we define all

motions, considering bodies as transferred from some of these
places into others. And so, instead of absolute places and motions
we use relative ones; and that without any inconvenience in common affairs; but in philosophical disquisitions, we ought to
abstract from our senses and consider things themselves, distinct
from what are the only sensible measures of them. For it may be
that there is no body really at rest, to which these places and
motions may be referred. (Barbour 1989, 625)

Newton also remarked that "it is necessary that the definition of
place and hence of local motion, be referred to some motionless
thing such as extension alone or space so far as it is seen to be truly
distinct from bodies" (Barbour 1989, 617).

Newton thus clearly distinguished these absolute notions of
space and time from the results of our attempts to measure space
and time, which he called relative. When we make our measurements we do not know whether we are moving relative to absolute
space and also whether this has any effect on the results of our
measurements. As we improve the accuracy of our measuring apparatus, we may hope to obtain results that approach the values corresponding to absolute space and time, but we cannot be certain of
this. Newton's attempt to measure absolute space by using the
curvature of the fluid surface in a rotating bucket is able to determine absolute rotation but not absolute motion. This absolute rotation is relative to the whole universe. This may be identified as the
ultimate reference frame as there is no sense in saying that the whole
universe is rotating, since there is no external reference point. His
first Law of Motion does however require absolute space for it to be
meaningful (Jammer 1954, 99–103).

It may be remarked, in parenthesis, that even Newton, who so
clearly recognized the impossibility of determining absolute position, nevertheless found it very difficult to absorb all of its implications, for in his treatment of the solar system he makes the
hypothesis that "the centre of the system of the world is at rest"
(Newton, *Principia,* 231). Furthermore, due to the invariance of
Newtonian mechanics under the Galilean transformation (the laws

of motion are the same in all systems moving relative to each other with constant velocities), it is not possible to give an invariant meaning to the statement that two events occurring at different times took place in the same positions in space.

In establishing his concepts of space and time, Newton took a God's-eye view of the world. He considered space to be God's sensorium, and since God is omnipresent this establishes absolute simultaneity. Even on the physical level, there is nothing contradictory in conceiving signals being propagated with an arbitrarily large velocity.

Newton's theology thus had a fundamental role in establishing his concepts of space and time. God is explicitly mentioned in the first edition of the *Principia*, and on 10 December 1692 Newton wrote to Richard Bentley, "When I wrote my Treatise about our System, I had an Eye upon such principles as might work with considering Men, for the Belief of a Deity, and nothing can rejoice me more than to find it useful for that purpose" (Cohen 1978, 280).

In the subsequent years there were many discussions of space and time. The nineteenth-century French physicist Henri Poincaré was undecided between relativism and absolutism (Holton 1973, 188). He considered defining time with reference to the sensorium of Newton's *"intelligence infinie"; "une sort de grand conscience qui verrait tout, et qui classerait tout dans son temps"* ["a supermind that sees everything, and orders everything in his own time-frame"], but could not accept this because the infinite intelligence, *"si meme elle existerait, serait impénétrable pour nous"* ["even if it exists, will be impenetrable to us"]. Poincaré was a physicist who used his great abilities to develop and improve existing theories but failed to make the creative leap that enabled the whole problem to be seen in a new light. That was finally achieved by Einstein (Stachel 1990).

Einstein's Concept of Space and Time

In contrast to Newton, Einstein developed his concepts of space and time from the point of view of a human observer, considering how space and time are actually measured, and postulating the constancy of the velocity of light in all inertial systems. This implies the Lorentz transformation, which in turn shows that relative motion affects the measured time, so that moving clocks appear to run slow. This constitutes the essential difference between Einstein and Newton. Einstein's approach is more attuned to the necessity of defining concepts in such a way that they can be measured, but this does not affect the validity of Newton's absolute space and time.

Einstein always looked for the most general principle underlying phenomena. In his early years he was strongly influenced by the philosopher Ernst Mach, and so he developed his concept of space and time from the point of view of an observer, considering how space and time are actually measured. At that time, he was a pure empiricist (Reiser 1930, 51–52) and identified reality with what is given by sensations. He learned about the current theories of electromagnetic phenomena by studying the works of Hermann Helmholtz, James Clerk Maxwell, Gustav Kirchoff, Heinrich Hertz, and Ludwig Boltzmann, and especially the textbook of August Foppl. It is notable that the latter work retains the ether and absolute motion and draws attention to precisely the same problem, namely, that of the relative motion of a magnet and an electrical circuit, that Einstein considers at the beginning of his pioneering paper of 1905. In his major work *The Science of Mechanics*, Mach criticized "the conceptual monstrosity of absolute space" because it is "purely a thought-thing which cannot be pointed to in experience" (Holton 1973, 221). It is thus notable that this paper of Einstein's contained two very general hypotheses that are certainly not empirical, namely, the constancy of the velocity of light and the extension of the principle of relativity to all branches of physics (Holton 1973, 232). This principle maintains that the behavior of phenomena and the laws governing them are independent of the reference frame used to describe them. Contrary to the usual accounts of the genesis of the special theory of relativity, Einstein was not greatly influenced by the result of the Michelson-Morley experiment, showing that it is not possible to detect the motion of the earth through a postulated aether (Holton 1973, 261–352). The essential difference between him and Newton is that Einstein's approach is more attuned to the necessity of defining concepts in such a way that they can be measured, and contained features of rationalism and extreme empiricism that were both essential to Einstein's achievement (Einstein 1949, 679; Holton 1973, 246, 259). This does not affect the validity of Newton's absolute space and time.

The reactions to Einstein's paper ranged from the enthusiastic welcome of the positivists to the guarded skepticism of Max Planck. Thus, the positivist Josef Petzoldt hailed the theory as "the victory over the metaphysics of absolutes in the conception of space and time" (Holton 1973, 275). Although Planck (1960) defended Einstein's work, he opposed Mach's view that "nothing is real except the perceptions" and maintained that "the basic aim of science" is "the finding of a *fixed* world picture independent of the variation of time and people" (Holton 1973, 227). In the years following 1905, more physicists came to accept relativity, partly because it explained the result of the Michelson-Morley experiment in a convincing way (unlike the ad hoc Fitzgerald contraction—the apparent contraction of a moving body in its direction of motion) and partly because of its inner consistency (Wien 1909, 32).

The theory of relativity is essentially concerned with the mathematical transformation of quantities measured in one reference frame to those measured in another frame moving with a constant linear velocity relative to the first. Until Einstein, this transformation was believed to be the Galilean transformation. It is a basic requirement of physics that the behavior of phenomena, and hence the laws governing them, is the same whatever frame is used to describe them. Einstein noticed that Maxwell's equations, which describe all electromagnetic phenomena, are not invariant under the Galilean transformation. They are, however, invariant under a transformation already described by Lorentz. The Lorentz transformation becomes the same as the Galilean transformation for velocities small compared with the velocity of light, and so the difference is normally imperceptible. Einstein explored the consequences of assuming that the Lorentz transformation is applicable generally and not just to electromagnetic phenomena, and he deduced many surprising consequences that were abundantly confirmed by experiment.

Since the Lorentz transformation is equivalent to a rotation in spacetime, the length of the vector representing the spacetime interval between any two events is invariant. Thus, relativity theory reveals the quantities that remain invariant during the transformation from one reference frame to another.

It is possible to derive the Lorentz transformation in many different ways (Lucas and Hodgson 1990, 152), showing that it is fundamental in the sense that to deny it entails the denial of many well-accepted beliefs. One of the simplest, though not the most elegant, ways to obtain it uses the constancy of the velocity of light in all reference frames, together with some necessary symmetry principles. In many respects the Lorentz transformation is simpler and more elegant than the Galilean transformation, as it can be expressed as a rotation in spacetime. As Frederick Lindemann has remarked, "if only scientists had had their wits about them, they ought to have been able to reach the Relativity Theory by pure logic soon after Isaac Newton, and not to have to wait for the stimulus given to them by certain empirical observations that were inconsistent with the classical theory" (Harrod 1959, 57). It is therefore more properly seen as an extension of classical physics rather than a component of the new physics. Einstein himself made a similar remark, stressing the continuity of physics: "With respect to the theory of relativity it is not at all a question of a revolutionary act, but of a natural development of a line which can be pursued through centuries" (Seelig 1956, quoted by Holton 1973, 176). Writing to Conrad Habicht in 1905, Einstein described his forthcoming paper as making use of a "*modification* of the theory of space and time" (Holton 1974, 362).

In the years following the publication of the theory, Einstein's empiricism waned, and he increasingly came to believe in the capacity of reason to grasp reality and in the importance of wide-ranging theories. No longer are facts alone the final court of appeal. Thus he was unmoved when the results of the experiments of Walter Kaufmann (1906) disagreed with the prediction of his theory. He was confident that the experiment was faulty, as indeed proved to be the case. It was the same for his theory of gravitation. In a letter to Mach (25 June 1913) he remarks that the next solar eclipse will show whether it is correct or not (Holton 1973, 228). However, as recorded by Ilse Rosenthal-Schneider (1980), when he received a telegram giving the results of Eddington's 1919 expedition and she congratulated him warmly, he was quite unmoved and simply said, "I knew that the theory is correct." When she asked him what he would have done if the result had been otherwise, he replied, "Then I should have been sorry for the dear Lord—the theory is correct" (Holton 1973, 287). This story is somewhat puzzling because Einstein knew very well that theories that do not agree with experiments just have to be abandoned, yet it serves to emphasize his strong belief in the order of nature and its openness to the human mind. Max Jammer has suggested a possible explanation of Einstein's remark. Since he knew that the theory was correct, "the only way in which the expedition could have noticed a different result was if nature had arranged circumstances in a very unusual and painful way for this particular experimental test not to work. Sooner or later it would have worked out, and Einstein would have been sorry for the dear Lord to have gone to so much trouble in order to produce a different result in this case" (Elkana 1974, 389).

Relativity has several apparently paradoxical features, but their subsequent experimental verification provides retrospective confirmation of their correctness. An example of this is provided by the non-additivity of velocities. It seems perfectly obvious that velocities add, as indeed they do in Newtonian dynamics. Newton himself says so explicitly in Scholium IV of the *Principia* (Barbour 1989, 624). Thus, if I throw a ball from a moving train in the direction of motion of the train, the velocity of the ball as viewed by a stationary observer is simply the sum of the velocity of the train and that of the ball relative to the train. This expectation is, however, based on the simple fallacy that if a number can be attached to a physical entity, then if there are two such entities the number corresponding to both of them together is the sum of those entities individually. This is true for apples: a bag with two apples together with a bag with three apples gives a total of five apples. However, this is not generally true. It is false for gradients, for example, because tangents are not additive. It is also false for velocities, as can be shown from the experimental fact that the maximum velocity is that of light (Whittaker 1948, 50). Instead of simple additivity, the formula for the addition of two velocities contains an extra term that ensures that whatever velocity is added to that of light, the sum remains that of light.[1] Of course the difference from simple additivity is vanishing small for velocities that are small compared with that of light.

It also seems strange that bodies in motion should contract and that they should live longer.[2] These effects also follow from the Lorentz transformation, but it should be noted that these statements apply to what is measured by a stationary observer and not to anything experienced by the body itself. Such effects are not small for velocities near to that of light. Thus, when relativistic neutral pions decay into two photons, these photons would have nearly twice the velocity of light if velocities were additive, whereas their measured velocity is just that of light. Muons, with a half-life of about two microseconds, are produced by the decay of pions high in the earth's atmosphere and penetrate far below ground. In the absence of time dilation, they would be expected to have a range of only about $(3 \times 10^{10}) \times (2 \times 10^{-6})$ cm, or 600 meters. This provides striking evidence for the theory of relativity.

Similarly, the variability of mass with velocity seems very strange. The word *mass* indicates the amount of stuff, so how can this change?

---

[1] The formula for the addition of velocities is $V = (v_1 + v_2)/(1 + v_1v_2/c^2)$. It may be derived from the Lorentz transformation (Lucas and Hodgson 1990, 57). A simple and direct derivation attributable to Whittaker is given on p. 8.

[2] The Lorentz transformation can be derived in several ways (Lucas and Hodgson 1990, 57, 189). A simple form is

$$\begin{pmatrix} \gamma & i\beta\gamma \\ -i\beta\gamma & \gamma \end{pmatrix} \begin{pmatrix} x \\ ict \end{pmatrix} = \begin{pmatrix} x' \\ ict' \end{pmatrix}$$

Since $\gamma = (1 - v^2/c^2)^{-1/2}$ is always greater than one, this immediately implies that bodies in motion appear to contract and to live longer. The apparent lifetime is $\tau = \gamma t$, which is called the proper time.

This raises the question of the relativistic definitions of velocity and momentum, energy and force. It is possible to define them in several ways, subject always to the condition that they reduce to the non-relativistic forms in the limit of velocities small compared with that of light. It is also desirable that the definitions lead to transformation equations that are as simple as possible. If the Newtonian definition of velocity as the derivative of the position with respect to Newtonian time is retained, it is not covariant under the Lorentz transformation. However, this condition is satisfied if we define velocity as the derivative of the position with respect to the proper time.[3]

If we define acceleration as the second derivative of the position with respect to Newtonian time we obtain rather complicated transformations (Leighton 1959, 35) and also introduce the additional concepts of longitudinal and transverse mass, which have no practical use (Born 1962, 276). Once again, double differentiation with respect to the proper time gives accelerations that transform by the Lorentz transformation. Multiplying the Lorentz transformation for velocity by the rest mass m_0 gives the transformations for momentum and energy. We find that the relativistic momentum is given by the product of the mass and the velocity as in Newtonian physics. If we keep the Newtonian definition of velocity, indeed we find that the mass varies with velocity. But if we use the relativistic definition of velocity, we retain an invariant mass.[4] It is only when we insist on retaining Newtonian definitions that we obtain a variable mass; if we accept the relativistic definitions, which is obviously more sensible, we have an invariant mass. Thus, it is not an experimental fact

---

[3] To obtain the transformation for velocities, the Lorentz transformation is differentiated with respect to the proper time, giving

$$\begin{pmatrix} \gamma_v & i\beta\gamma_v \\ -i\beta\gamma_v & \gamma_v \end{pmatrix} \begin{pmatrix} \gamma\beta_x \\ i\gamma \end{pmatrix} = \begin{pmatrix} \gamma'\beta'_x \\ i\gamma' \end{pmatrix}$$

[4] Now multiply by the invariant rest mass m, giving

$$\begin{pmatrix} \gamma_v & i\beta\gamma_v \\ -i\beta\gamma_v & \gamma_v \end{pmatrix} \begin{pmatrix} m\gamma\beta_x \\ im\gamma \end{pmatrix} = \begin{pmatrix} m\gamma'\beta'_x \\ im\gamma' \end{pmatrix}$$

As $v \to 0$, $\gamma\beta \to v/c$, so $m\gamma\beta$ may be identified as the relativistic momentum.

that the mass depends on the velocity, despite many published statements to the contrary.

The momentum-energy transformation also implies that the total energy of a particle is the sum of its kinetic energy and its rest mass, implying that mass is a form of energy.[5] This implication of relativity has been abundantly verified, particularly by several well-known nuclear reactions.

The replacement of the Galilean transformation by the Lorentz transformation can be described as "tying together" space and time, because time now depends on the spatial coordinates and on the relative velocity of the two coordinate frames. This was lyrically described by Hermann Minkowski when he declared, "henceforth space by itself, and time by itself, are doomed to fade away into mere shadows, and only a kind of union of the two will preserve an independent reality" ([1923] 1952, 75). Contrary to this rhetoric, however, it remains true that space and time are different, if only because it is possible to move at will in all directions in space but only and inexorably forward in time. Causality is now limited to the light cone, so that an event can only be influenced by events in its past light cone and can only influence events in its forward light cone.

The dependence of time on the spatial coordinates and on the relative velocity of the two frames implies that the absolute simultaneity of events cannot be established. This does not imply, however, that temporal simultaneity has been disproved, since it does not exclude the possibility that absolute space and time can be established in some other way, as may be possible in the context of the Big Bang theory.

Thus, because a theory does not presuppose the existence of absolute space and time, it does not follow that these concepts are meaningless or that they have been disproved.

Lorentz's Concept of Space and Time

Following Newton, Lorentz retained the concepts of absolute space and time, while admitting that there seems to be no way that they can

---

[5] The second component $m\gamma \approx m + (1/2)\ m\beta^2$, or $mc^2\gamma = mc^2 + (1/2)\ mv^2$, and this is the sum of the rest energy $E = mc^2$ and the kinetic energy $(1/2)\ mv^2$.

be established or detected. This does not, however, imply there are no practical differences between his interpretation of the relativistic formalism and that of Einstein. Newton and Lorentz both accepted the possibility of instantaneous action at a distance, without having any physical explanation of how this can occur. It is, however, incompatible with Einstein's interpretation because it implies the affirmation of the absolute simultaneity of two distant events (Popper 1956, 20). Thus, experiments like that of Alain Aspect (Aspect, Dalibard, and Roger 1983) designed to test the Bell inequalities could provide a proof of the correctness of the Lorentz interpretation.

The acceptance of absolute space means a return to the concept of the aether, and indeed this has already been reappearing in elementary particle theory, where what is called the vacuum is teeming with virtual particles. Lorentz's interpretation also allows time dilation to be derived in a physical way by considering a light clock (Craig 2000).

Once we accept absolute space, absolute time is implied by the success of our continuing efforts to construct more and more accurate clocks. These ever-closer approximations give the time in our reference frame, and this can be related to the absolute time in the absolute spatial system.

Thus, there is nothing in the formalism of special relativity to exclude the concepts of absolute space and time (Earman 1970). Although it was not possible to measure or detect them in Newton's or Einstein's days, this can now be done in principle by reference to the unique singularity of the Big Bang. Absolute time can be measured from that event, and an absolute spatial system is provided by the cosmic microwave background radiation. The expanding universe provides an inertial system, and anisotropy measurements can detect motion with respect to that frame (Rosen 1968). The times taken for the return of two light rays traveling equal distances parallel and perpendicular to earth's motion will differ by a very small amount that depends on the rate of expansion of the universe. This is far below the level of detectability in a Michelson-Morley experiment but would be easily measured if the experiment could be done over cosmic distances. For a distance like that to "the nearest quasar (about three billion parsecs) it amounts to some two hours" (Ne'eman 1974, 6). Such an experiment is impracticable, but E. K. Conklin (1972) has determined the absolute velocity of the earth by measuring the anisotropy of the cosmic microwave background and finds it to be 140 kilometers per second in a known specified direction. Such measurements can be made by any observer, and so this satisfies the conditions for absolute space. Such a preferred reference frame is required by realist interpretations of quantum mechanics (Hardy 1992). If the universe is finite, its center of gravity also provides an absolute point in space, but this cannot be determined. Of course, such considerations do not provide measures of space and time with anything like the accuracy required for practical purposes, but this does not affect their value in defining absolute space and time.

Interpretations of Relativity and Quantum Mechanics

It is notable that there is a remarkable similarity between the interpretations of relativity and of quantum mechanics. In both cases there is a formal mathematical structure that has proved able to give extremely accurate accounts of experimental data, together with widely different interpretations of the formalism. There is more debate about the interpretations in the case of quantum mechanics than there is for relativity, but in both of them two principal interpretations can be identified. Relativity can be interpreted by the positivism of Einstein or by the realism of Lorentz, while quantum mechanics can be interpreted by the positivism of Bohr or by the realism of Einstein. In both cases the positivistic theory is generally preferred by the majority of physicists. This may be due partly to the physicist's dislike of being drawn into metaphysical discussions and partly to the prestige of Einstein, as the sole originator of theory in the case of relativity, and the prestige of Bohr, in his position as the leader of the main school of theoretical physics at the time in the case of quantum mechanics.

It is also remarkable that in both cases one of the interpretations was due to Einstein, but in the case of relativity as a positivist and in the case of quantum mechanics as a realist. This is a reflection of the maturing of his philosophical beliefs as a result of his scientific creativity (Holton 1973, 197–217; Jaki 1978, 183–93). In his early years, when he formulated his theory of relativity, Einstein was profoundly influenced by the sensationalism of Ernst Mach, but subsequently, driven by his scientific creativity, he repudiated this view. He knew from his own experience that it is not possible to construct science just by the ordering of sensations. In his autobiographical notes, Einstein remarked that "in my younger years, Mach's epistemological position influenced me very greatly, a position which today appears to me essentially untenable" (Schilpp 1949, 21). He realized that it is not possible to construct science by ordering sensations: "The mind can proceed so far upon what it knows and can prove. There comes a point where the mind takes a higher plane of knowledge, but it can never prove how it got there. All great discoveries have involved such a leap" (Clark 1973, 552). Einstein found it more fruitful to take a God's-eye view of the world: "I want to know how God created the world. I am not interested in this or that phenomenon, in the spectrum of this or that element. I want to know His thoughts; the rest are details" (Jammer 2000, 124, 234). According to Max Born, Einstein "believed in the power of reason to guess the laws according to which God has built the world" (Born 1956, 205). In his later years, especially during his arguments with Bohr on the interpretation of quantum mechanics, Einstein adopted a realist stance and did not hesitate to speak of unobservables. When he was challenged about this by Philip Frank, he replied, "A good joke should not be repeated too often," and to a similar question by Leopold Infeld, he remarked, "Yes, I may have started it, but I regarded these ideas as temporary. I never thought that others would take them so much more seriously than I did" (Clark 1973, 327).

Relativity and Religion

Modern science is rooted in Christian beliefs about the rationality and contingency of the natural world (Jaki 1978), and our concepts of space and time derive from the theological beliefs of Newton and Einstein (Jammer 2000). However, as Einstein remarked, "an important non-reciprocal relationship holds between religion and science: science is greatly dependent upon religion, but not vice-versa" (Ferré 1980, quoted by Jammer 2000, 133).

Many people thought that the advent of the theory of relativity heralded the end of absolute values. The then Archbishop of Canterbury, Randall Davidson, was told by Lord Haldane that "relativity was going to have a great effect on theology, and that it was his duty as head of the English Church to make himself acquainted with it." The archbishop took this advice seriously, obtained several books on the subject, and tried to read them. He did not have much success in his attempts to understand relativity and indeed was driven to a state of intellectual desperation. He therefore asked Einstein what effect relativity would have on religion and was told, "Do not believe a word of it. It makes no difference. It is purely abstract science" (Bell 1935, 1052; Jammer 2000, 125, 155). According to another version of the story, Einstein replied, "None. Relativity is a purely scientific matter and has nothing to do with religion" (Thomson 1936, 431). So that was that.

The archbishop comes out of this story rather well. In the first place, he actually listened to what he was told and went to the trouble of getting some books on relativity and trying to understand what it was all about. He made the usual assumption that any highly educated arts man can in a few hours master any scientific subject but soon realized his mistake. Then, instead of forgetting about the whole matter, he asked a scientist for his advice and chose a scientist who really knew about the subject. If only his example were followed today, we would be spared the acutely embarrassing spectacle of churchmen and churchwomen moralizing on scientific and technical matters without having understood the first thing about them.

"Einstein repeatedly emphasized his belief that physics did not directly relate to his social views, but this reassurance only increased the bewilderment of lay people." He was strongly opposed to any attempts to use physics to support religious, social, or political beliefs and dismissed the mass enthusiasm for relativity as "mostly psychopathological" (Graham 1982, 119). In spite of Einstein's disclaimer, relativity has had a great effect on moral and sociological affairs, but this is due to misunderstandings of the theory and not to the theory itself. It also can happen that ideas developed within science can stimulate or suggest developments in other fields without there being any logical connection, and examples of this can be found in the philosophical works of Percy Bridgman and Karl Popper (Holton 1982, xiii). Wider applications of relativity, such as those to artistic interpretation, sometimes betray a basic misunderstanding of the theory. It is thought that relativity means that objects can be viewed in many different ways and that their sum gives the total view. On the contrary, relativity tells us that our descriptions are independent of the coordinate system in which they are expressed and that each one of them gives a complete description (Holton 1982, xiv).

The theory of relativity is concerned with the quantities that remain invariant during transformations between reference frames. Einstein "did not use the expression 'theory of relativity' in his original paper and for two years afterward he called it *'invarienten theorie'* [theory of invariants]" (Holton 1973, 382). The mathematician Felix Klein and the physicist Arnold Sommerfeld also thought "that the name 'theory of relativity' should be replaced by 'theory of invariants' because the theory is merely a theory of the invariants of the Lorentz transformation or, in the case of general relativity, of a more general transformation." "The term 'theory of relativity' is an unfortunate choice," wrote Sommerfeld, "its essence is not the relativity of space and time but rather the independence of the laws of nature from the viewpoint of the observer. The bad name has misled the public to believe that the theory involves a relativity of ethical conceptions, somehow like Nietzsche's *Beyond Good and Evil*" (Jammer 2000, 33–34). If the theory had been called the theory of invariance, we would have been spared all this trouble.

It does make sense to talk of absolute time, and it may be possible to identify an absolute frame of reference. There is a real difference between past and future, so relativity does not prevent us from trying to influence future.

If relativity sometimes appears strange and unfamiliar, the fault lies in our own inadequate conception of nature. God's world is more subtle than we thought. In Einstein's own words, *"Raffiniert ist Herrgott, aber boschaft er ist nicht"* ["God is subtle, but not malicious"](Pais 1982, vi).   ✺

References

Aspect, A., J. Dalibard, and G. Roger. 1983. *Physical Review Letters* 47: 1804.

Barbour, J. B. 1989. *Absolute or Relative Motion?* I. The Discovery of Dynamics. Cambridge: Cambridge University Press.

Bell, G. K. A. 1935. *Randall Davidson.* Oxford: Oxford University Press.

Born, M. 1956. *Physics and Relativity.* London: Pergamon.

———. 1962. *Einstein's Theory of Relativity.* New York: Dover.

Clark, R. W. 1973. *Einstein: The Life and Times.* London: Hodder and Stoughton.

Cohen, I. B., ed. 1978. *Isaac Newton's Papers and Letters on Natural Philosophy.* Cambridge, MA and London, England: Harvard University Press.

Conklin, E. K. 1972. "Velocity of the Earth with Respect to the Cosmic Background Radiation." *Nature* 222: 971.

Craig, W. L. 2000. Private communication.

Cropper, W. H. 2001. *Great Physicists.* Oxford: Oxford University Press.

Earman, J. 1970. "Who's Afraid of Absolute Space?" *Australasian Journal of Philosophy* 48: 288, 317.

Einstein, A. 1905. "Zur Electrodynamik bewegter Korper." *Annalen der Physik* 17.891.

———. 1949. "Autobiographical Notes. " In *Albert Einstein: Philosopher-Scientist.* Ed. Paul Arthur Schilpp, 1–95. Evanston, IL: Library of Living Philosophers.

Elkana, Y., ed. 1974. *The Interaction between Science and Philosophy.* Atlantic Highlands, NJ: Humanities Press.

Ferré, E. 1980. "Einstein on Religion and Science." *American Journal of Theology and Philosophy* 1: 20.

Graham, L. R. 1981. *Between Science and Values.* New York: Columbia University Press.

———. 1982. *Science and Philosophy in the Soviet Union.* New York: Columbia University Press.

Hall, A. R., and M. B. Hall, eds. 1978. *Unpublished Scientific Papers of Isaac Newton.* Cambridge: Cambridge University Press.

Hardy, L. 1992. "Quantum Mechanics, Local Realistic Theories and Lorentz-Invariant Theories." *Physical Review Letters* 68: 2981.

Harrod, R. F. 1959. *The Prof: A Personal Memoir of Lord Cherwell.* London: Macmillan.

Heisenberg, W. 1971. *Physics and Beyond: Encounters and Conversations.* London: George Allen and Unwin; New York: Harper and Row.

Hodgson, P. E. 2000. "God's Action in the World: The Relevance of Quantum Mechanics." Zygon: *Journal of Religion and Science* 35 (September): 505–16.

Holton, G. 1973. *Thematic Origins of Scientific Thought: Kepler to Einstein.* Cambridge: Harvard University Press.

———. 1974. "Finding Favour with the Angel of the Lord." In *The Interaction between Science and Philosophy.* Ed. Yehuda Elkana, 349–87. Atlantic Highlands, NJ: Humanities Press.

———. 1982. "Introduction." *Albert Einstein: Historical and Cultural Perspectives.* Eds. Gerald Holton and Yehuda Elkana, vii–xxxii. Princeton, NJ: Princeton University Press.

——— and Yehuda Elkana, eds. 1982. *Albert Einstein: Historical and Cultural Perspectives.* Princeton, NJ: Princeton University Press.

Jaki, S. L. 1978. *The Road of Science and the Ways to God.* Chicago: University of Chicago Press.

———. 1988. *The Absolute beneath the Relative.* Lanham and London: University Press of America.

Jammer, M. 1954. *Concepts of Space.* Cambridge: Harvard University Press.

———. 2000. *Einstein and Religion.* Princeton, NJ: Princeton University Press.

Kaufmann, W. 1906. "Uber die Konstitution des Electrons." *Annalen der Physik* 19: 487.

Leighton, R. B. 1959. *Principles of Modern Physics.* New York: McGraw-Hill.

Lucas, J. R., and P. E. Hodgson. 1990. *Spacetime and Electromagnetism.* Oxford: Clarendon Press.

Minkowski, H. [1923] 1952. "Space and Time." In *The Principles of Relativity* by A. Einstein et al. Notes by A. Sommerfeld. Trans. W. Perrett and G. B. Jeffery. New York: Dover.

Ne'eman, Y. 1974. "Concrete versus Abstract Theoretical Models." In *The Interaction between Science and Philosophy.* Ed. Yehuda Elkana, 1–25. Atlantic Highlands, NJ: Humanities Press.

Newton, I. [1686] 1999. *Principia.* Trans. I. Bernard Cohen and Anne Whitman. Berkeley: University of California Press.

Padgett, A. G. 1993. "Eternity and the Special Theory of Relativity." *International Philosophical Quarterly* 33: 219.

Pais, A. 1982. *Subtle is the Lord . . .* Oxford: Clarendon Press.

Planck, M. 1960. *A Survey of Physical Theory.* New York: Dover.

Popper, K. 1956. *Quantum Theory and the Schism in Physics.* Ed. W. W. Barclay III. London: Hutchinson.

Reiser, A. 1930. *Albert Einstein.* New York: A. and C. Boni.

Rosen, N. 1968. *Inertial Systems in an Expanding Universe.* Proceedings of the Israel Academy of Sciences and Humanities (Section of Science), 12.

Rosenthal-Schneider, I. 1980. *Reality and Scientific Truth: Discussions with Einstein, Von Laue and Planck.* Detroit, MI: Wayne State University Press.

Schilpp, P. A., ed. 1949. *Albert Einstein: Philosopher-Scientist.* Evanston, IL: Library of Living Philosophers.

Seelig, C. 1956. *Albert Einstein: A Documentary Biography.* London: Staples.

Stachel, J. 1990. "The Theory of Relativity." In *The Companion to the History of Modern Science.* Eds. R. C. Olby, J. R. R. Christie, and M. J. S. Hodge, 442. London and New York: Routledge.

Synge, J. L. 1964. *Relativity: The General Theory.* Amsterdam: North-Holland.

Thomson, J. J. 1936. *Reflections and Recollections.* London: G. Bell and Sons.

Whitehead, A. N. 1925. *Science and the Modern World.* Cambridge: Cambridge University Press.

Whittaker, E. T. 1948. *From Euclid to Eddington.* Cambridge: Cambridge University Press.

Wien, W. 1909. *Uber Electronen.* 2d ed. Leipzig: B. G. Teubner.

CHAPTER 17

Interpretations of
Quantum Mechanics*

Introduction

THE DEVELOPMENT of quantum mechanics has stimulated intense discussion about the nature of the microworld, and it is now widely believed that it is radically
indeterminate and statistical, and its reality has been doubted. Since the
affirmation of the reality of the world, its intelligibility, and its openness
to the human mind are central to the philosophy of St. Thomas, it is
appropriate to discuss this question at a Thomistic Institute.

The Realism of the Scientist

Experimental scientists, who struggle daily in the laboratory to
understand the physical and biological world, are instinctively convinced that they are gradually, in spite of many difficulties, obtaining valid and enduring knowledge about a real, objective word. It is
a familiar experience to be confronted by an apparently unintelligible phenomenon, to have an idea about what is going on, to base a
theory on that idea, and then to show that using it they can explain
quantitatively what is already known and also to make predictions
about new phenomena that are subsequently verified. This is intelligible if we are gradually finding out about the world but not if we
are simply projecting our ideas on the world. Often scientists have
struggled for a long time to interpret the world according to their

---

* Lecture to the Thomistic Institute, University of Notre Dame, Indiana, 1997.

own ideas, only to be forced by the evidence to adopt a different view. Planck's discovery of the quantum is an example of this.

The basic conviction underlying all scientific research is that its purpose is to learn about the structure and interactions of an objectively existing world. This world exists independently of us, it was here before we were born and will be here after we are gone. For scientific research to be possible, the world must be rational and consistent, and at least partly open to the human mind. These realistic beliefs are seldom explicitly formulated, but are implicitly held by all working scientists, especially those engaged in experimental research. They were expressed by Einstein when he wrote: "The belief in an external world independent of the perceiving subject is the basis of all natural science." (Einstein 1941). This is underlined by the writings of many scientists. Thus John Houghton has recently said:

> An important element in the attitude of scientists is the idea of transcendence, the idea that in science we are dealing with something objective and "given." It is basic to scientific enquiry that there is objective reality to be discovered and described—there is something to be found "out there." The facts and descriptions resulting from scientific enquiries are not invented by scientists as they pursue their work; rather, they are there to be discovered. (Houghton 1995)

In his Tarner lectures Michael Redhead (1995)noted that:

> Physicists in their unreflective and intuitive attitude to their work, the way they talk and think among themselves, tend to be realists about the entities they deal with, and while being tentative as to what they say about these entities and their exact properties and interrelations, they generally feel that what they are trying to do, and to some degree successfully, is to get a "handle on reality."

Richard Feynman expressed himself with his usual inimitable directness when asked about the counterintuitive nature of the rules of quantum electrodynamics:

. . . you'll have to accept it. Because it's the way nature works. We looked at it, carefully. Looking at it, that's the way it looks. You don't like it? Go somewhere else. To another universe, where the rules are simpler, philosophically more pleasing, more psychologically easy. I can't help it, okay? If I'm going to tell you honestly what the world looks like to the human beings who have to struggle as hard as they can to understand it, I can only tell you what it looks like. (Dudley and Kwan 1996)

The instinctive belief among working scientists that we are trying to find out about a real external world comes through very clearly in a series of interviews conducted by Lewis Wolpert and broadcast by the BBC. These were subsequently published under the title *A Passion for Science*, by Lewis Wolpert and Alison Richards (1988). Thus the physicist Michael Berry says:

Physics describes the real world. It isn't a sort of low level mathematics, which it would become if one lost contact. It's very important always to realize that there are phenomena, that there is a world outside our heads that we're trying to explain. Otherwise it's a curious game, a form of self indulgence which I think is intellectually not very worthwhile. (Wolpert and Richards 1988, 47)

The biologist Stephen Jay Gould spoke in a similar way, but also showing that he was aware of the subjective elements in scientific research:

Radicals in the history of science will actually claim something close to relativism. They may not deny that there's an empirical truth out there somewhere, but it's in a fog, so distantly behind cultural presuppositions that you can never find it, so you might as well not talk about it. Therefore, for them, the history of the field really is the history of changing social context and psychological predisposition. I don't take that position at all. I can't—an empirical scientist cannot. If I didn't believe that in working with these snails I was really finding out something about nature, I couldn't keep going. I'd like to be honest enough to admit that everything I'm doing is filtered through my psychological presuppositions, my cultural vices, and I think that honesty is very important because you have to subject yourself to continuous scrutiny. If you really believe that you're just seeing the facts of nature in the raw you'll never be aware of the biasing factors in your own psyche and in your prevailing culture. But that's quite a separate issue from whether something is true or not. The truth value of a statement has to do with the nature of the world, and there I do take the notion that you can test and you can refute, and so I have fairly conventional views about that. (Wolpert and Richards 1988, 146)

This realism derives from the belief that the universe was created by God and endowed with definite and determinate properties that ensure that nature behaves consistently the way it does, and not in any other way (Jaki 1974; Hodgson 1995). This guarantees that it has an intrinsic rationality and stability, and makes it possible for us to learn about it. Scientists aim to discover the properties given to matter by God, and the natural laws that describe its behaviour. They do this by observation and experiment, and then try to integrate that knowledge into a coherent whole by models and theories. Scientific theories are attempts to understand the world, and as they become more sophisticated and in closer accord with a wide range of experimental data they approach asymptotically to the true description of reality given by the natural laws. They are thus only partly true, and are subject to revision and development, but nevertheless contain definite truth about the world. This is the philosophy of moderate or methodological realism (Gilson 1955, 1990; Tanzella-Nitti 1992).

By contrast, many philosophers this century held a very different view, namely that the scientist is simply correlating sense impressions into the most convenient and economical pattern, and that it is meaningless to ask what is really there. How can we know except through our sense impressions, and why should there be anything beyond them? This, however, fails to explain why scientists are always making experiments of greater and greater precision, thus obtaining data that is more difficult to fit into a pattern. This would be unintelligible if all we wanted to do was to correlate our sense impressions but is a fully justified and indeed necessary procedure if what we want to do is to understand the world more deeply. More recently, however, positivism has been increasingly discredited, and has indeed been described as "nearly all false" by one of its leading exponents (Ayer 1978).

The Quantum World

The discoveries of the present century in atomic, nuclear, and elementary particle physics have, however, revealed strange phenomena that apparently make it hard to be a realist (Lucas 1995). Electrons, we are told, can be both waves and particles, and perhaps both at once, and the more accurately we know their positions the less we know about their momenta. Quantum systems exist in a superposition of states represented by a wave function, and this collapses to a definite state only through the intervention of an observer. Non-local interactions can take place between two particles without any detectable signal passing from one to the other, a "spooky action at a distance." Even the laws of logic seem to be confounded. How can all this be reconciled with realism? To answer this question we follow Einstein's advice and pay more attention to the deeds of the scientists than to their words.

Quantum mechanics was formulated to solve the severe difficulties encountered by attempts to understand atomic structure. In 1912 Bohr proposed a model of the atom known as the old quantum theory. He suggested that the electrons revolve about the nucleus in circular orbits and applying the quantum condition he was able to derive the spectrum of the hydrogen atom. Classically, however, such electrons would rapidly spiral into the nucleus, and so Bohr had to forbid this. The result was a theory that was in excellent agreement with experiment but was contrary to the laws of electromagnetism.

This was the situation around 1920. Physicists were reduced to a state of despair. The only theory that even began to make sense of atomic structure was totally unacceptable classically. The distress was poignantly expressed by H. A. Lorentz, one of the greatest of the classical physicists, who wrote in 1924: "I lost the certitude that my scientific work was bringing me close to objective truth and I no longer know why I continue to live. I am only sorry not to have died five years ago when everything appeared clear." Pauli, one of the most brilliant of the younger physicists, was so upset that he said he wished he had become a movie comedian instead of a physicist.

Soon after, Heisenberg proposed the matrix form of quantum mechanics and Schrödinger developed his wave mechanics, and these were shown by Pauli, Schrödinger, and Eckhart to be mathematically equivalent. They provided a way to calculate the observable quantities of atomic systems, and so at last it was possible to go forward again. Wave mechanics is much easier to handle mathematically, and is much more appealing physically, so this is the formalism most generally used.

Quantum mechanics was formulated in the 1920s when positivism was very influential among European philosophers, and several of the leaders had links with the Vienna Circle. It is thus not surprising that many of the pioneers of quantum mechanics thought along positivist lines, so that many of the paradoxes that are encountered in the quantum mechanical analysis of the material world were described in positivist terms. Thus if there is a question that cannot be answered experimentally it is considered to be meaningless. This is the Copenhagen interpretation associated with the writings of Bohr and many of his colleagues.

They believed that in quantum mechanics physics has reached the end of the road, so that no further progress is possible (Popper 1956). This belief was strengthened by von Neumann's proof of the impossibility of hidden variables. They also believed that the wave function of a system contains all that can be known about a system. Given these beliefs the quantum paradoxes are inevitable.

Einstein, however, believed that since quantum mechanics does not provide, even in principle, the answers to many physically reasonable questions, it must be incomplete, and showed this in a paper with Podolsky and Rosen. He maintained that quantum mechanics is an essentially statistical theory that gives the average behaviour of a large number or ensemble of similar systems, but an incomplete account of the behaviour of each individual system. Quantum mechanics is a very successful theory, but it is just one step along the road toward the understanding of the world. Feynman has indeed pointed out that the possibility that quantum mechanics fails at large distances is consistent with our present knowledge.

If we examine the way quantum mechanical calculations are compared with experiment, we find that they are always compared with quantities such as a decay half-life or a differential cross-section that are obtained as the result of measurements on a large number of systems, and are thus statistical quantities. Furthermore, quantum mechanical calculations ignore the effects of the surrounding materials, and treat the system as if it were poised in empty space. All measurements, however, are made on systems interacting with their surroundings.

The so-called quantum paradoxes only arise when we take statistical statements about the average behaviour of a large number of systems to describe completely each individual system. When this is corrected, the quantum paradoxes are resolved, and a fully realistic account of the world is restored. This will be illustrated by considering several experiments.

Real and Imaginary Experiments

Experiment is the essential basis of science. Without careful and systematic experiments we would still be at the level of speculation attained by the ancient Greeks. The vital role of experiments in science is often underemphasized or even practically ignored in books on the philosophy of quantum mechanics, possibly because they are usually written either by theoretical physicists who are more at home in the abstract world of symbolism than in messy laboratories, or by philosophers who have never in their whole lives been anywhere near a laboratory.

The lack of understanding of how experiments are actually done, and all the laborious cross-checking that is carried out, accounts for the bloodless (and often incorrect) descriptions of experiments often found in books on the philosophy of science. One philosopher of science, who was previously an experimental elementary particle physicist, was so incensed by this that he wrote a book called *The Neglect of Experiment* (Franklin, 1987).

Books on the philosophy of science frequently contain descriptions of experiments, complete with drawings of the apparatus and accounts of the results, that omit to inform the reader that the experiment has never actually been done. It is what is called an imaginary (or thought or *gedanken*) experiment. Such experiments have an important and valued role in the development of science. They serve to clarify our concepts and may suggest actual experiments. Nevertheless, it cannot be too strongly emphasized that, to use the title of a paper by another exasperated physicist, "Unperformed Experiments Have No Results" (Peres 1978).

The danger of confusing real and imaginary experiments is obvious; if the experiment is actually done it may give a result that confounds our expectations. That is indeed one of the reasons why we do experiments. An example of this occurred in the early years of the wave theory of light. Fresnel applied the wave theory to explain diffraction and interference, and his paper was submitted to a jury for a prize. One of the jury, Poisson, made some calculations himself, and found that the wave theory predicted that a white spot should appear at the centre of the shadow cast by a small spherical obstacle. Since this was obviously absurd, he concluded that the wave theory should be rejected. Thus far it was an imaginary experiment. However Arago actually did the experiment, and found the white spot just as predicted.

If experiments are neglected, all that remains are the writings of the founders of quantum mechanics and of later commentators. These are frequently studied by philosophers with great erudition as if they were sacred texts. Since the founders were physicists, they were unfamiliar with philosophical terms and often write in a confusing way. It is then all too easy to read into their writings ideas and beliefs that they did not hold. This perhaps accounts for the wide variety of books on the philosophy of Niels Bohr. Whatever one may think of Bohr's ideas, he was grappling with real problems of physics, and unless one understands physics one has no hope of understanding what he is trying to say.

Another failure of many of these philosophical writings is lack of understanding of the mathematical basis of quantum mechanics. All physics, and especially quantum physics, is written in the language of mathematics. Quantum mechanics is a formal mathematical theory of great power and beauty, and a knowledge of the mathematical structure is essential for an understanding of the theory. Of course, it can be described in words, and this is done in many popular books, some by the founders themselves. But at most these books can only give some imperfect glimpses of quantum mechanics, like a written description of a great symphony or the translation of a poem into a foreign tongue.

In a valid physical argument it is highly desirable that the physical understanding and the mathematical formalism are held together in a perceived unity. Before beginning a formal calculation one should have some qualitative idea of how the phenomenon under study is likely to behave.

Ideally the calculation confirms quantitatively this physical intuition. Occasionally our physical intuition fails us, and such cases require special care. Not only should the physical intuition be controlled by mathematical argument, but also our mathematics should be controlled by our intuition. If it is not, it is fatally easy to make an invalid inference, an unjustified approximation, or simply an error, without realizing it. This union of physical insight and mathematical formalism is not always easy in classical physics; it is much more difficult in quantum mechanics. An example that will be discussed later is von Neumann's argument for the impossibility of hidden variables. This was generally accepted for twenty years until Bohm constructed a counterexample and then, and only then, Bell found a restrictive flaw in the argument. Niels Bohr "never trusted a purely formal argument or mathematical argument: 'No, no' he would say, 'You are not thinking; you are just being logical.'" (A Centenary Volume, 136, 1985)

Physicists understand this very well, but are less sensitive to another danger. It is equally hazardous for them to try to talk about the meaning of quantum mechanics without some grasp of philosophical ideas and their history. Many philosophical positions have been analyzed in detail, and may be expressed precisely by a recognized vocabulary. It is quite essential to realize that there is not a one-to-one correspondence between ideas and words. Our everyday words such as "real," "object," and "substance" have specialised meanings in the contexts of particular philosophies. Physicists frequently use analogies and models, and in their hands, as for the philosophers, words like "space," "time," and "energy" take on a new and more precise meaning. But although they do this, physicists seldom analyze with precision just what they are doing, and their knowledge is like knowledge of dynamics of a cyclist, or that of hydrodynamics of a dolphin.

Thus, in response to the toast *Science* by the president of the Royal Academy of Arts on 30 April 1932, Rutherford said:

> Quite recently there has been much interest taken by the cultivated public in the metaphysical aspects of science, especially those of theoretical physics. Some of our publicists have boldly claimed that the old ideas which served science so well in the past must be abandoned for an ideal world where the law of causality fails, and the principle of uncertainty, so valuable in the proper domain of atomic physics, is pushed to extremes. The great army in its march into the unknown discusses with interest, and sometimes amusement, these fine spun disputations of what is reality and what is truth. But it still goes marching on, calling out to the metaphysicians "there are more things in heaven and earth than are dreamt of in your philosophy." (Oliphant 1972)

Rutherford's attitude to philosophy is not uncommon among physicists, but it is dangerous even to the progress of physics itself. Rutherford himself was seriously misled on one occasion by false philosophical arguments that he was unable to counter; this story will be told later on.

Thus a discussion of the philosophy of quantum mechanics rests on three pillars—the experimental, the mathematical, and the philosophical—and without any one of these, inevitably ends in disaster.

It is, of course, part of our task to relate these together, and this immediately raises the traditional problems of the philosophy of science. This includes the relation of theory to experiment and of theory to explanation.

One problem in particular is of such importance that it should at least be mentioned now. It has roots far in the past, when there was much discussion about whether the purpose of a physical theory is just to "save the phenomena" or to give a real explanation. If the former, then the theory is simply a formal mathematical structure that enables one to calculate the results of all experiments. What more can one want? A physicist wants a great deal more. He is convinced that he is finding out about a real world, objectively existing apart from himself, and he wants to understand its inner workings. A calculational recipe, however successful, leaves him unsatisfied.

But suppose, as is arguably the case for quantum mechanics, one has a theory that is extremely successful as a calculational scheme, but seems not to make sense. He can either put up with it, and say that there is nothing more to be done, resigning himself to the resulting paradoxes. Or he can try to probe deeper, but he then finds that he can achieve conceptual clarity at the cost of much greater formal complexity. As a practical physicist, interested in calculating the results of experiments, he may feel that there is more loss than gain. But he may remain unsatisfied, for often a deeper physical understanding is essential for successful calculation. He will therefore feel that although at present the lack of understanding can be endured by practical people, in the end it is dangerous to shut the door to future advances. It is useful to remember that:

> since all possible experiments have not yet been done, the choice is going to be based on one's guess of the outcome of these experiments when they are performed in the future and on our philosophical inclination. There is no reason why everyone should agree about what that best choice (of future experiments) is. Divergences of opinion must be expected that cannot be reconciled by logical argument. Tolerance is in order! (Schommers 1989, 86)

The Quantum Paradoxes

There are several experiments that illustrate the strange behaviour of the quantum world, bringing into sharp relief the problems of its nature. These experiments will now be described.

Diffraction by a Single Slit

The diffraction of light by a single slit is familiar from optics. The form of the diffraction pattern may be calculated from Huygens's wave theory and is in excellent agreement with the observations. The measurement of the diffraction of an electron beam by a slit is very difficult and it was first made by Jonsson in 1961. The results are identical, and it is very natural to say that therefore electrons are waves. Certainly we can say that the observations are well accounted for by a wave theory, but this does not mean that the electrons are waves.

Whittaker has remarked that the vibrations of an elliptic membrane and the gyrations of a variety artiste are both governed by Mathieu's equation, but that this does not imply that the phenomena are the same.

An important feature of diffraction by a single slit is the reciprocal relation between the width of the slit and the width of the diffraction pattern: if one is increased, the other is reduced and vice versa. More exactly, the product of the two widths is always greater than Planck's constant h divided by 4π. This is the Heisenberg uncertainty principle, usually interpreted as meaning that the more accurately we determine the position of an electron, the less we know about its momentum and vice versa. This has led to the belief that matter is inherently fuzzy, or even that the electron does not have a definite position and momentum.

Diffraction by a single slit has been analyzed quantum mechanically by Beck and Nussenzweig (1958).

Diffraction by a Double Slit

The diffraction of light by two parallel slits is also familiar from optics, and the result is an interference pattern. In the outer regions the diffraction is similar to that from a single slit, but in the central region there is an interference between the waves passing through one slit with those passing through the other slit. The corresponding experiment for electrons featured as an imaginary experiment for many years, until it was finally done by Jonsson in 1961. In this experiment the slit width was 0.5 micron, and they were spaced 2 microns (2×10^{-4} cm) apart. This may be compared with the wavelength of the 50 KeV electrons that were used, which is 0.05 Angstroms, or 5×10^{-8} cm.

Experiments on electron scattering show that they behave as point particles down to distances of the order of 10^{-15} cm. (Jackson 1975, 791). It is thus very natural to suppose that an electron goes through one slit or the other, so if the particle theory is correct we would expect to see just the superposition of two single slit diffraction patterns, and not the interference pattern that is observed. There is no possibility that electrons going through one slit interfere with electrons going through the other slit, because the electron intensity can be adjusted so that only one electron goes through the apparatus at a time. The interference pattern thus builds up gradually, electron by electron.

It might be thought that we could determine which slit a particular electron traversed, but this would destroy the interference pattern. To observe the interference pattern the separation of the slits has to be comparable with the wavelength of the electrons, and this is so small that it is not possible to insert a detector.

Radioactivity

Many nuclei are radioactive; they emit alpha-particles or electrons (beta decay). If we take a sample of a radioactive material, containing a very large number of atoms, we find that the probability that a particular nucleus decays is a constant, independent of time. As a consequence, the radioactivity of the sample decays exponentially with time. The rate of decay is characterised by the half-life, defined as the time it takes for the radioactivity of a sample to decay to half its initial value.

We can measure the time that a particular nucleus decays, but we cannot predict it or influence it in any way. It appears to be a totally random quantity. It is only the half-life that can be measured, using a sample containing a large number of nuclei. Like any statistical quantity, the measurements of the number of nuclei decaying in successive time intervals fluctuates around the value corresponding to the exponential decay curve, so the greater the number of nuclei in the sample, the more accurate is the value found for the half-life.

In the early days of nuclear physics, the half-lives of many radioactive decays were measured, together with the corresponding energies of the emitted particles. It was found by Geiger and Nuttall that for each series of alpha-particle decays the logarithm of the half-life is linearly related to the logarithm of the energy. Beta decay is more complicated because a neutrino is also emitted, and so it will not be further discussed.

The first great success of quantum mechanics was Gamow's explanation of alpha-particle decay. He was able to derive the Geiger-Nuttall law, showing how the half-life depends on the energy, using the concept of tunnelling. The mathematics is so simple that we may fail to notice the conceptual difficulties. We do not of course believe that the tunnels are real; we calculate the attenuation of the wave as it passes through the potential barrier. As soon as it emerges, it is a particle with a definite trajectory that we can see in a cloud chamber or detect with a counter. Yet how can the alpha-particle be first a wave and then a particle?

Radioactive decay also raises problems about causality. If all nuclei of the same type are identical, then why do they decay at different times? If they are not identical, then how do they differ? If one believes that quantum mechanics provides a complete description of reality, then no reason can be given why a particular nucleus decays at one time rather than another. All we can measure is the time variation of the decays in a sample; this is a statistical quantity which tells us little about each individual event.

The Quantum Mechanical Formalism

The problems that caused physicists so much anguish in the 1920s were resolved by the development of quantum mechanics. It is not possible to derive the formalism of quantum mechanics from anything else, though it can be made to appear plausible. It is perhaps better to regard it as a series of postulates that enable observable quantities to be calculated. The essential postulate is that to every observable—that is, something that can be measured—there corresponds a mathematical operator. The state of a physical system is represented by a wave function ψ that is an eigenfunction of the operator, and the possible values of the physical quantity are the eigenvalues of the operator. Thus the operator acts on the wave function and the result is the wave function again, but now multiplied by a number that is one of the possible values of the physical variable corresponding to the operator.

The first application of quantum mechanics to the nucleus was made by Gamow. He wanted to understand alpha decay, in particular the enormous range of half-lives. He assumed that the alpha-particle can exist inside the nucleus and calculated its wave function. This is the problem of a particle in a potential and the solutions are waves. The alpha-particle is kept inside the nucleus by the attractive nuclear forces that are represented by a potential barrier. This region is classically forbidden, so that the solution of the wave equation is a rapidly falling exponential. Outside the nucleus the solution is a wave once again. The wave function must be continuous over the whole region and when this condition is applied it is found that the amplitude of the wave outside the nucleus is very small, and that the lower the energy of the alpha-particle the smaller the amplitude. This immediately explains the enormous range of half-lives and the Geiger-Nuttall law.

This example shows how quantum mechanics may be used to solve problems in atomic and nuclear physics. It has now been used for about seventy years with outstanding success. There is no other serious way of tackling problems. In most cases the difficulties are the choice of interaction potential and the solution of the Schrödinger equation.

Interpretations of Quantum Mechanics

Quantum mechanics is an outstandingly successful theory, but what does it mean? What is this wave function? Is the electron a wave or a particle? What really happens when an alpha-particle "tunnels" through a potential barrier? Most physicists just can't be bothered with what they regard as sterile philosophical questions. They are far too busy solving real problems to waste their time on fruitless discussions of this type. Quantum mechanics gives good results, so what more can you want? If pressed, they become embarrassed and shifty and produce what they remember of Bohr's ideas, before hastily changing the subject and retreating into their laboratories. Other physicists, perhaps more philosophically inclined but certainly in a minority, may produce fairly well-articulated views. They cannot stand what Popper has called the great quantum muddle, and have definite views on how it might be resolved.

It must be emphasized that quantum mechanics and the problems of its interpretation are quite distinct from each other. This is evident in books on quantum mechanics. The writers usually feel that they must say something about the problems of interpretation, and so devote a few pages to remarks about the Heisenberg uncertainty principle and the double slit experiment. What they say is usually neither very precise nor consistent with what other writers say. Then, with a sigh of relief, they get down to the more congenial task of describing how to use quantum mechanics to solve practical problems.

Although these problems are distinct, they are nevertheless related. It is not satisfactory to accept confusing concepts, even though it is possible to ignore them in practice. Conceptual clarity is important in physics. Furthermore, if one adopts the wrong interpretation it can have a very deleterious effect on one's physics. Some examples of this will be given later on. So I believe that it is important, especially for physicists, to think hard about the interpretation of quantum mechanics.

There are many interpretations of quantum mechanics, but the most fundamental difference is that between the interpretations of

Bohr and Einstein. Their ideas developed over the years, and it is not always easy to be clear about what they said, but the fundamental difference is in the completeness of the theory. Bohr believed that the wave function contains all that can be known about a physical system. Consequently, it is meaningless to ask any questions about entities that cannot be calculated by the quantum mechanical formalism.

Thus it is meaningless to ask which slit the electron went through in the double slit experiment, or what the alpha-particle is doing when it goes through the potential barrier. This view of Bohr is generally known as the Copenhagen interpretation.

The other view, due to Einstein, is that the wave function describes the average properties of a large number (or ensemble) of similar systems. This leaves open the possibility that in the future there will be a more detailed theory that will enable the quantum paradoxes to be resolved. On this view, quantum mechanics is rather like thermodynamics, which describes the properties of a gas in terms of macroscopic quantities like pressure and temperature. We know, however, that these may be expressed as averages over the motions of a large number of molecules.

The debate between the supporters of these two views, and many other views, is still very much alive. Bell (1966) has remarked that "I hesitate to think that it (quantum theory) might be wrong, but I know that it is rotten."

These two interpretations will now be described.

The Copenhagen Interpretation

The question of the interpretation of quantum mechanics is a philosophical one, and thus depends on the philosophical views, explicit or implicit, of the physicists who first thought about it. During the early decades of the twentieth century, when quantum mechanics was developed, the philosophy of science was much influenced by the ideas of Ernst Mach, a nineteenth-century physicist who wrote on the foundations of mechanics. Reacting against the excessive mechanism of the Victorian physicists, he believed that the aim of physics is to achieve the most economical description of our observations and measurements, and that any discussion of what is really there is quite superfluous. This line of thought developed into the positivism of the Vienna Circle. Bohr himself was also strongly influenced by the philosopher Hoffding, a friend of his father who often came to his home when he was a boy. Subsequently, he attended Hoffding's lectures at the University of Copenhagen, and in later years frequently discussed with him the problems of the interpretation of quantum mechanics (Faye 1991).

Following the thought of Mach and Hoffding, Bohr and Heisenberg emphasized that what is important in physics is to have a way of calculating the results of experiments; all else is superfluous. According to Bohr (1935), "physics is not about the world, it is about the way we think about the world." This was echoed by Heisenberg (1938): "[T]he laws of nature which we formulate mathematically in quantum theory no longer deal with the particles themselves but with our knowledge of the elementary particles," and by Born (1949): "Quantum mechanics does not describe an objective state in an independent external world, but the aspect of this world gained by considering it from a certain subjective standpoint." Heisenberg (1938) also said that: "The conception of objective reality . . . has thus evaporated . . . into the transparent clarity of a mathematics that represents no longer the behaviour of particles, but rather our knowledge of this behaviour." They further maintained that "quantum mechanics was the last, the final, the never-to-be-surpassed revolution in physics." Thus "physics has reached the end of the road; that a further breakthrough is no longer possible, although, of course, much is still to be done by way of elaboration and application of the new quantum mechanics."

This view was developed into what is now known as the Copenhagen interpretation of quantum mechanics, which is to be found in practically every textbook, and in the popular literature— and as a result it has been uncritically accepted by most physicists.

The act of measurement and its connection with the reality of the world according to the Copenhagen interpretation has been described by Schommers (1989, v):

Within the standard Copenhagen interpretation the world (or any system) consists of *options* which are equally *unreal*. By the *act of observation* a system is forced to select one of its options and this becomes real, i.e., within the Copenhagen interpretation of quantum theory, reality is produced by the act of observation, so that any real system (for example, an electron) cannot be thought of as having an independent existence; we know nothing about what it is doing when we are not looking at it. Within the Copenhagen interpretation, nothing is real unless we look at it. As soon as we stop looking at it, it ceases to be real.

This idea of the system deciding was earlier discussed by Jordan (1934):

[When its position is being measured] the electron has to make a decision. We force it to take up a well-defined position: before that it was not in general here or there; it has not yet decided on its position. It is we who produce the facts we observe.

This seems equivalent to attributing free will to electrons, and indeed to everything else.

Although quantum mechanics provides rules for calculating observables such as the frequencies of spectral lines, it gives little or no physical picture of what is actually happening. The atom can no longer be described in terms of particles moving along orbits. It is then necessary to find a way to link the concepts used to describe the atomic world with the actual observations made in the laboratory. It thus became of prime importance to consider the nature of physical measurements. Concepts such as position and momentum are meaningful only in the context of actual experimental operations.

The Gamma Ray Microscope

As an example, Heisenberg considered the measurement of the position of an electron. To do this, one could use a gamma ray microscope of high resolving power, and this requires the use of light of short wavelength and therefore high energy.

However the shorter the wavelength the greater the recoil velocity of the electron and hence the greater the uncertainty in its position. There is a reciprocal relation between the precision of the measurements of position and velocity of an electron. It should be noted, however, that there is an inconsistency in the argument because the light is assumed to be first a wave and then a particle. Bohr also pointed out that the finite aperture of the microscope is vital to the argument, and also that the analysis requires a wave interpretation of the scattered light quanta. Indeed, the very formulae for the energy and momentum of the light quantum embody the wave-particle duality. To combine these two views, Bohr developed his idea of complementarity—wave and particle are not antithetical; "they are complementary—mutually exclusive and yet jointly essential" (Cassidy 1992, 243).

Margenau and Cohen (1967) have listed four difficulties in drawing conclusions about Heisenberg's uncertainty principle from the gamma ray microscope. Firstly, Δx refers to the position before the measurement, whereas Δp refers to the period after the measurement. To avoid this difficulty one would have to maintain that measurements do not determine what is, but what will be, or both. Secondly, the argument depends on classical electrodynamics, so the results should be both controllable and predictable. If the interactions are considered mysterious, the argument begs the question. Thirdly, if quantum mechanics is a deeper theory than classical mechanics, so that it reduces to classical mechanics as a limiting case, it is not possible to use classical reasoning to derive a quantum mechanical result. Finally, the symbol Δ must refer to a large number of interactions, and then some of the disturbances are large but others are small, and it is not clear how this can be so. They conclude that there is no way of removing these four difficulties.

Causality and Determinism

The limit to the precision of measurement has important philosophical implications according to Heisenberg. The strict formulation of determinism—that if we know the present we can calculate the future—is inadequate because now we cannot know the present accurately. This led Heisenberg to declare that "in a certain sense the law of causality becomes invalid" (Cassidy 1992, 228). The implication is that the laws of quantum mechanics are generally statistical. Born (1953) has also remarked: "It seems to me important to emphasize that the new quantum mechanics gives up determinism, which has dominated natural research until now" (256).

The Meaning of the Wave Function

There was also intense discussion about the meaning of the wave function. Schrödinger interpreted it as a matter wave, giving the matter density over all space, while Born considered it as a probability wave, so that the wave function gives the probability of finding a particle at the point r. The former allows a continuum interpretation, while the latter allows discrete quantum jumps.

Since we can only calculate probabilities, it is "fruitless and senseless" to seek further information about the motion of the electron. Bohr explained "that we can never know nature as it really is, but only as it appears to be as we become part of the experiment itself. Furthermore, since quantum mechanics is complete, there is no hope of ever improving on this." Another consequence is that "all past and all future experimental research is and will be subsumed under quantum mechanics. Future research would never alter the fundamental validity of quantum mechanics, nor would it offer any hope of surmounting the laws imposed by the uncertainty relations" (Cassidy 1992, 234).

An even more radical view seemed to follow from Dirac's formulation of the relation between matrix and wave mechanics. According to this, the world is essentially discontinuous, rendering the notion of velocity strictly meaningless. Heisenberg concluded "that the path only comes into existence through this: that we observe it" (Cassidy 1992, 236).

Another characteristic of the Copenhagen interpretation is brought out by Bohr in his reply to the Einstein-Podolsky-Rosen (EPR) argument, considered later. To respond to Einstein he argued that no two objects that have once interacted can, at a later time, be observed separately. With the great rapidity of interaction, and the time that has elapsed since the Big Bang, it would therefore seem that everything interacts with everything, and so no system can be isolated. If these interactions are appreciable, as Bohr requires, this makes science impossible.

The Copenhagen interpretation blurred the distinction between observer and observed, object and subject, physics and nature. Every observation destroys the independence of the observed phenomenon, forces a descriptive scheme on the experiment and introduces uncertainties in measurement through the uncertainty relations (Cassidy 1992, 253).

Over the years the thought of Bohr and Heisenberg was developed in a series of lectures and books. Bohr has been variously described as a positivist, a realist, an idealist, a pragmatist, and an operationalist. It is clear that he does not fit easily into any of the philosophical categories and, like that of most physicists, his thought is not expressed with philosophical precision. He had many supporters among the founders of quantum mechanics, including Pauli, Born, and Rosenfeld, and naturally they did not always express their ideas in the same way. The spread of the Copenhagen interpretation was rapid, partly because of the missionary fervour of its proponents, most of whom worked with Bohr at some time, and then returned to their home countries to occupy prestigious chairs.

It is not easy to find in their writings a definitive expression of the Copenhagen interpretation, but a list of its main features has been compiled by Stuart (1991):

1. The completeness postulate that the wave function completely specifies what can be known about a particular quantum state;

2. The superposition principle that a quantum state represented by a linear superposition of allowable quantum states is itself an allowable quantum state;

3. The Heisenberg uncertainty principle;

4. The probability interpretation of the wave function;

5. The principle of inseparability that the object under investigation is inseparable from the experimental apparatus used to observe it;

6. The principle of complementarity; and

7. The correspondence principle.

He went on to show that there are many inconsistencies between these features.

The Copenhagen Interpretation
of the Quantum Paradoxes

Further insight into the Copenhagen interpretation is provided by the way it deals with the quantum paradoxes. The single slit diffraction pattern shows that the more accurately we try to measure the position of an electron, the less accurately we know its momentum and vice versa. These are known as conjugate variables. Energy and time are another pair of these variables. According to the Copenhagen interpretation this constitutes a fundamental limitation to our knowledge, so that it is meaningless to speak of the exact position or momentum of an electron.

The problem of the double slit is that neither the wave nor the particle picture seems to be satisfactory: if the electrons are waves, then why are they detected like particles, each at a particular point on the screen, whereas if they are particles, then they must go through one slit or the other, and then how does the interference pattern arise? This dilemma may be avoided by concentrating on what is actually observed. Since the Copenhagen interpretation admits only observable quantities, the question about which slit the electron traverses is dismissed as meaningless. We cannot observe which slit it goes through, so that is a non-question.

Bohr developed his idea of complementarity to deal with this situation. We can arrange the experiment in one way or another, and if we ask a particle-like question, then we get a particle-like answer, and similarly for waves. The objects we study are thus sometimes waves, sometimes particles (Bohr 1935). We can have either one description or the other, but not both together, and each tells us part of what is happening. This also applies to conjugate variables. Thus we measure position with a fixed ruler, but if we want to measure momentum we use a moveable detector that recoils. Our measuring instrument must be either fixed or moveable, so we cannot measure both position and momentum together (Hughes 1989, 229).

Since the wave function refers to only one system, the uncertainties Δx and Δp must be interpreted as intrinsic limits to the precision of measurement. This in turn implies that quantum mechanics is the ultimate theory that is the limit of physical research.

There are several other answers to the wave-particle dilemma. Thus Mott (1964) says that only particles have real existence; waves being the collective behaviour of many particles. De Broglie (1954) thought of the particle as being carried along by the wave, while Bunge (1967) used the concept of "quantons," which are neither waves nor particles, but combine aspects of both.

In a similar way it is maintained that it is meaningless to ask why a particular nucleus decayed at a particular time. Since the wave function completely specifies the nucleus, the decay has no cause. This led Heisenberg (1938) to declare that "the validity of the principle of causality has been definitely disproved."

In all these examples the system is initially described by a wave function that is a superposition of all possible eigenstates, and it is the act of measurement that projects this on to a single state. This is called the collapse of the wave function. This is a most curious phenomenon. The word itself is misleading; in ordinary speech, collapse implies motion through space from one configuration to another. But no one really supposes that the wave function collapses in this literal way; certainly no one has specified the equations of motion followed by the collapsing wave function. Nevertheless there has been considerable debate about what is meant by the collapse of the wave function. This has been dramatised by the stories of Schrödinger's cat and of Wigner's friend; taken together they show that the Copenhagen interpretation ends in solipsism.

The formalism of quantum mechanics enables us to calculate the probability that a system will collapse into a particular eigenstate. This probability refers to a single system, and so must refer to our knowledge of the system, not to the system itself. This in turn implies that physics is not concerned with the world but with our knowledge of the world.

Hidden Variables

The situation is reminiscent of the relation between the macroscopic and microscopic theories of gases. The thermodynamic variables such as pressure and temperature enable the bulk behaviour of a gas to be described and calculated. A more detailed account is given by the kinetic theory of gases, which considers a gas to be composed of a large number of molecules in rapid motion. Averaging over their motions gives us the thermodynamic variables. Thus, in "a complete physical description, the statistical quantum theory would take an approximately analogous position to the statistical mechanics within the framework of classical mechanics" (Einstein, quoted in Schilpp 1949).

In the case of atoms and nuclei, however, we have only the macroscopic theory, quantum mechanics. Is there a corresponding microscopic theory, describing the detailed behaviour of the electrons and other particles in terms of microscopic or hidden variables?

The Copenhagen interpretation avoids the quantum paradoxes by concentrating on the observables and dismissing any questions about the underlying reality as meaningless. Thus according to Heisenberg, "objective reality has evaporated." Normally, however, a physicist faced with a phenomenon he does not understand will try to postulate some hidden mechanism to render it intelligible. The Copenhagen interpretation explicitly rejects any such "hidden variables." The impossibility of hidden variables was proved mathematically by von Neumann in 1932, and this greatly strengthened the Copenhagen interpretation. What he actually proved was that, on the basis of some general assumptions, dispersionless ensembles cannot be incorporated into the formal structure of quantum mechanics. This leaves open the question whether these assumptions are unduly restrictive and also the more fundamental question whether quantum mechanics is a complete account of reality.

Nevertheless, von Neumann's proof was believed for many decades to exclude the possibility of hidden variables. The situation changed when Bohm in 1952 succeeded in constructing a hidden variable theory, and although this was in some respects unappealing and fruitless, it nevertheless showed that there is something wrong with von Neumann's proof. Subsequently, in 1966 Bell identified the key assumption in von Neumann's proof, namely that "any real linear combination of any two Hermitian operators represents an observable and the same linear combination of expectation values is the expectation value of the combination." This is true for quantum mechanical states, and von Neumann very reasonably assumed that it is true of the hypothetical dispersion-free states. However Bell showed, by a single counterexample—namely the measurement of the two spin orientations σ_x and σ_y that this assumption is false. Jauch and Pirion (1963) proposed a new version of von Neumann's argument, but Bell showed that it is subject to the same objection.

The next development was A. M. Gleason's work (1957) on the axiomatic basis of quantum mechanics, which apparently yielded von Neumann's result, without any assumptions about non-commuting operators. However, Bell showed that Gleason assumed that "the measurement of an observable must yield the same value independently of what measurements may be made simultaneously." Thus the whole experimental arrangement must be considered. The implication of this is that "the implicit assumption of the impossibility proof was essential to its conclusion" (Bell 1966, 451). There is thus no reason to believe that hidden variables are excluded and with them a fully determined theory of quantum mechanics.

Einstein's Interpretation of Quantum Mechanics

Einstein always refused to accept the Copenhagen interpretation, maintaining that "the belief in an external world independent of the perceiving subject is the basis of all natural science." In a letter to Schlick, he wrote:

> In general your presentation fails to correspond to my conceptual style in so far as I find your whole orientation so to speak too positivistic. . . . I tell you straight out: Physics is the attempt at the conceptual construction of a model of *the real world* and of its lawful structure. (Broda, 1983)

In a letter to Schrödinger on the 22 December 1950 he remarked:

> You are the only contemporary physicist, besides Laue, who really sees that one cannot get around the assumption of reality—if only one is honest. Most of them simply do not see what a risky game they are playing with reality—reality which is something independent of what is experimentally established. (Przibram 1967, 39).

Einstein believed that quantum mechanics, successful though it undoubtedly is, constitutes just one step on the long road of our efforts to understand the world. The wave function tells us the average behaviour of an ensemble of systems, not all that we can know about a single system. Quantum mechanics is a logically complete theory of statistical events, but not of each particular event. Nature is much richer than we know and there is a microstructure still undiscovered whose average behaviour is what we measure and calculate by quantum mechanics. Working physicists have always used concepts that are not directly linked to measurements. This has been defended by J. J. Thomson:

> I hold that if the introduction of a quantity promotes clearness of thought, then even if at the moment we have no means of determining it with precision, its introduction is not only legitimate but desirable. The immeasurable of today may be the measurable of tomorrow. It is dangerous to base philosophy on the assumption that what I know not can never be knowledge. One day we may find ways of measuring these "hidden variables." (Rayleigh 1942)

In a letter to Schrödinger on the 9 August 1939, Einstein wrote: "I am as convinced as ever that the wave representation of matter is an incomplete representation of the state of affairs, no matter how practically useful it has proved itself to be." After discussing Schrödinger's cat, he goes on:

> If one attempts to interpret the psi-function as a complete description of a state, independent of whether or not it is observed, then this means that at the time in question the cat is neither alive nor pulverised. But one or the other situation would be realized by making an observation. If one rejects this interpretation then one must assume that the psi-function does not express the real situation but rather that it expresses the contents of our knowledge of the situation. This is Bohr's interpretation, which most theorists today probably share. But then the laws of nature that one can formulate do not apply to the change with time of something that exists, but rather to the time variation of the content of our legitimate expectations. . . . I am as convinced as ever that this most remarkable situation has come about because we have not yet achieved a complete description of the actual state of affairs. (Przibram 1967, 35)

As Popper (1956) has emphasized, quantum mechanics is always used to tackle statistical problems. The results of quantum mechanical calculations, such as the half-lives of radioactive decay or scattering cross-sections, are statistical quantities that can only be found by measuring a large number of similarly prepared systems. The spread of the measured values is a consequence of their statistical nature; it is only if we make the mistake of attaching the properties of an ensemble of similarly prepared systems to a single system that we generate unnecessary paradoxes.

According to Einstein, the Copenhagen interpretation avoids problems rather than solving them. As he wrote to Schrödinger on 31 May 1928: "The Heisenberg-Bohr tranquillising philosophy— or religion—is so delicately contrived that, for the time being, it provides a gentle pillow for the true believer from which he cannot very easily be aroused. So let him lie there (Przibram 1967, 31).

It is sometimes said that only Einstein in his old age supported the idea of a deterministic substratum to quantum mechanics, so it should be mentioned that he was not the only physicist to oppose the Copenhagen interpretation. In different ways Planck, Schrödinger, Landé, Fermi, and Dirac all spoke against it. Planck repeatedly called for a revival of determinism and objectivity in atomic physics. Fermi early on expressed doubts about the validity of the Copenhagen interpretation, criticizing its tendency "to refrain from understanding things" (Tarozzi and van de Merwe 1988). This was echoed by Santos when he remarked that the Copenhagen interpretation hides rather than solves problems. In his Nobel Prize lecture in 1976, Murray Gell-Mann, referring to the search for an adequate philosophical presentation of quantum mechanics, remarked: "Niels Bohr has brainwashed a whole generation of theorists into thinking that the job was done fifty years ago."

Not long before he died Dirac (1979) said in a lecture that:

> [I]t seems clear that the present quantum mechanics is not in its final form. Some further changes will be needed, just about as drastic as the changes which are made in passing from Bohr's orbits to quantum mechanics. . . . It might be that the new quantum mechanics will have determinism in the way that Einstein wanted. I think it is very likely, or at any rate quite possible, that in the long run Einstein will turn out to be correct, even though for the time being physicists will have to accept the Bohr probability interpretation—especially if they have examinations in front of them.

More recently, 't Hooft (1997) has written: "The history books say that Bohr has proved Einstein wrong. But others, including myself, suspect that, in the long run, the Einsteinian view might return."

Even Bohr and Heisenberg occasionally spoke in a way that recognized the limitations of quantum mechanics. In a letter to Dirac on 29 August 1930 Bohr speculated about the possibility of a minimum fundamental length about the size of an electron or proton, below which quantum mechanics is no longer applicable: "I believe firmly that the solution of the present troubles will not be reached without a revision of our general physical ideas still deeper than that contemplated in the present quantum mechanics" (Cassidy 1992, 289). Heisenberg endorsed the same idea in an article in

1938 when he said that the fundamental length, now identified as the critical length of meson theory, marks the lower boundary, the "limits of applicability of the present quantum theory" (Cassidy 1992, 407). In a subsequent article on cosmic ray showers, he speculated that the non-linear field interactions due to strong coupling at distances less than the critical length provided "access to the region in which the present quantum mechanics fails" (Cassidy 1992, 411). Throughout his writings, like other physicists, Heisenberg repeatedly referred to science as "the quest for reality" (Cassidy, 148).

There is a very considerable body of research in the foundations of quantum theory that regards the Copenhagen interpretation with considerable reservation. For example, in the epilogue to a conference on "Open Questions on Quantum Physics" we read, "such an acknowledgement of unsolved conceptual problems in the foundations of microphysics is by contrast inadmissible within the purview of the stagnant philosophy of the Copenhagen interpretation, which culminated in the absurd myth of the completeness of the quantum formalism." Thus "it therefore appears evident that a radical emancipation from the negative philosophy of the Copenhagen school is a necessary precondition if one is to look for a real solution of the main quantum paradoxes" (Tarozzi and Van der Merwe, 1985).

Indeed, as Popper has pointed out, emancipation from the Copenhagen interpretation already took place long ago since "most physicists who quite honestly believe in it do not pay any attention to it in actual practice" (Bunge, 1967). They think about it only when they are asked about the foundations of quantum mechanics; in their everyday work they ignore it completely.

Following its demise as a component of serious physics, the Copenhagen interpretation has acquired a new life following Bohr's enthusiastic extension of the notion of complementarity to the life sciences, the mind-body problem, and parapsychology. It has become invaluable to all who want to pose as gurus of the new mysticism, to promote subjectivism, and to reconcile irreconcilables at the expense of facing reality.

It is now necessary to see how the quantum paradoxes are viewed by Einstein.

Einstein's Solution of the Quantum Paradoxes

According to Einstein, quantum mechanics gives only the result of measurements on an ensemble of similarly prepared systems. Indeed all atomic and nuclear measurements whose results can be calculated by quantum mechanics fall into this category. It is thus possible that the result of each measurement is precisely determined by events that are at present undetectable.

Thus in the case of the single slit, the trajectories of the individual electrons differ slightly, and they impinge on different parts of the region in the slit, so it is not surprising that they reach different parts of the screen. It is not true that measurements of the position and momentum of an electron cannot be made with greater precision than that specified by the Heisenberg uncertainty principle. The width of the slit specifies the uncertainty in position, and the spread of the diffraction pattern gives the uncertainty in the transverse momentum. But if we place a particle detector at the screen, we can determine the point of arrival of each electron, and hence we can measure its transverse momentum with an accuracy much greater than that corresponding to the distribution as a whole. Thus while it remains true that we cannot predict the transverse momentum of the electron after it has passed through the slit, nevertheless a subsequent measurement enables it to be determined to an accuracy much greater than specified by the uncertainty principle. Thus physics gives us no ground for saying that the position and momentum of an electron are unknowable within the limits of the uncertainty principle, and still less that it does not have position and momentum (Ballentine 1970).

The wave-particle duality is thus simply a category confusion. On the one hand we have particles moving along definite trajectories with definite momenta, and on the other we recognize that due to their interactions with the slits and with other matter and radiation these trajectories have a certain probability distribution calculable from Schrödinger's equation. The so-called wave nature of these particles is no more an intrinsic property than, for example, actuarial statements are intrinsic properties of a particular individual.

In the case of radioactive decay, each decay process is determined by the motions of the nucleons in the nucleus before the decay, or perhaps by some external influence. Thus the nuclei before decay all differ in their internal dynamical structure. We do not yet know how this structure could determine the instant of decay, and still less how we could ever find out enough to calculate this, but these are problems for the future.

In all these experiments the quantum mechanical calculations are compared with the results of a large number or ensemble of measurements. The half-life of a radioactive decay can only be determined by measuring very many decay events, and the same applies to the interference pattern in the double slit experiment and the angular distribution in a scattering problem. The time of decay of a particular nucleus, or the point on the screen where one electron arrives, or the direction in which one particle is scattered, is of no scientific interest on its own, at least in the context of the present development of scientific theories. It is thus very natural to say with Einstein that quantum mechanics describes the behaviour of ensembles of similarly prepared systems, and gives only a partial account of the behaviour of each individual system. The very fact that quantum mechanics cannot tell us about the details of each individual system is a strong argument for supposing that it is an incomplete theory. Since the wave function simply gives the probability of a system to be in a certain state, the difficulties associated with the collapse of the wave function disappear. Probabilities are not material entities and so the very notion of collapsing is inapplicable.

It will be noticed that all these interpretations of the quantum paradoxes postulate some hidden process that determine the observed outcome, but say little or nothing about the process itself. That is a notable characteristic of the Einstein's interpretation: while the Copenhagen interpretation shuts the door to further advances in understanding, Einstein leaves it open, and thus provides the stimulus to further thought and experimentation.

There have been many attempts to probe deeper into the quantum world, and to try to give a more detailed account of what we observe; some of these will be described later.

Einstein and others who thought like him also devised a whole series of thought experiments designed to show the inadequacy of the Copenhagen interpretation. Some of these were attempts to show internal inconsistencies in quantum mechanics, and are described in the remainder of this chapter. Others, such as the Einstein-Podolsky-Rosen thought experiment, attempt to show its incompleteness and are considered later.

Schrödinger's Cat

This is an experiment that could easily be done, but one may hope that this is considered unnecessary. It is indeed one of the most famous of the thought experiments. Schrödinger imagined a cat that is incarcerated in a sealed opaque box that contains a phial of poison that may be broken by a hammer triggered by the decay of a radioactive nucleus. Since the time of the decay is unknown we do not know at any particular instant whether the cat is alive or dead. Before we open the box, the cat is in a quantum mechanical superposition of states, one corresponding to it being alive and the other to its being dead. When I open the box, according to the Copenhagen interpretation, I collapse the wave function, and at that time the cat becomes definitely either alive or dead.

According to the Einstein interpretation, the cat dies at a certain time whether we know about it or not, and when we open the box we find out what had already occurred. There is another consequence of the Copenhagen interpretation that is less well-known. Suppose there is an observer, known as Wigner's friend, outside the room that contains the box with the cat inside. If he cannot see into the room he does not know whether I have found the cat to be alive or dead, and so for him the wave function of the interior of the room contains both possibilities. It is only when he opens the door and looks into the box that his wave function collapses. Thus his wave function must be different from mine. I am the only person who can collapse my wave functions, and thus my wave function, and hence my science, is unique to me. This solipsistic conclusion is radically opposed to the universal belief that scientists are all engaged in a common search to understand the same objective reality.

Feynman has remarked:

> [D]oes this then mean that my observations become real only when I observe an observer observing something as it happens? This is a horrible viewpoint. Do you seriously entertain the thought that without the observer there is no reality? Which observer? Any observer? Is a fly an observer? Is a star an observer? Was there no reality in the universe before 10^9 B.C. when life began? Or are you the observer? Then there is no reality in the world after you are dead? I know a number of otherwise respectable physicists who have bought life insurance. By what philosophy will the universe without man be understood? (Gribbin and Gribbin 1998)

Michael Redhead (1995)has asked:

> [W]hether it has to be human consciousness, or whether a humble mouse idly looking at the unfortunate cat can resolve it into life and death; or what about the cat's own self-consciousness, could this result in the cat's own demise. I think it would only be reasonable to take such a solution of the measurement problem seriously if there were absolutely no other viable way of proceeding. . . . Quantum mechanics may be queer, but it is certainly not clear that it is that queer.

Einstein's Box

At the Como Conference in 1932, Einstein proposed a thought experiment designed to circumvent the energy-time uncertainty relation. He imagined an opaque box from which a photon is allowed to escape by a shutter controlled by a clock. The box can be weighed before and after the photon emission, giving the energy of the photon. Since both the time and the energy can thus be measured to arbitrary accuracy, the uncertainty relation is violated.

Bohr was initially very upset by this argument, and retired to discuss it with his friends. By the next morning he emerged with the solution to the problem, which ironically used Einstein's own general relativity theory.

Einstein's Particle

Unlike the two previous examples this one is little-known, mainly because it was written in German and published in an article in a book of papers presented to Max Born. Einstein considered a particle that bounces back and forth in one dimension between perfectly reflecting walls. The solution of the Schrödinger equation for a particle in a box is a sine wave with frequency and phase adjusted to ensure that it goes to zero at the walls. If we calculate the expectation value of the momentum of the particle we find that it is zero, which is indeed correct for a large number of particles hitting the walls at random times. But for just one particle, the momentum is zero only instantaneously when it is being reflected, and the rest of the time it has a definite positive or negative value. There could hardly be a clearer demonstration that quantum mechanics applies to ensembles of systems, and fails to describe the motions of individual systems.

The essays were intended to honour Born, and we can only hope that he appreciated the irony of being presented with such a cogent argument against his own position.

The Einstein-Podolsky-Rosen (EPR) Thought Experiment

The thought experiment of Einstein, Podolsky, and Rosen (1935) is often referred to as a paradox, but it is more correctly described as an argument for the incompleteness of quantum mechanics. It is sometimes considered to be a definitive statement of Einstein's mature views, but it is now known that he neither wrote the paper nor much liked the argument it contained, and that he preferred a rather different argument for incompleteness (Howard 1990).

The argument is set within the context of definite beliefs about the nature of science and of reality. First of all they specify a completeness condition that must be satisfied by any acceptable scientific theory: "Every element of the physical reality must have a counterpart in the physical theory." This is followed by a sufficient condition for the existence of elements of physical reality: "If, without in any way disturbing the system, we can predict with certainty the value of a physical quantity, then there exists an element of physical reality corresponding to that physical quantity."

They then describe a thought experiment that shows how both the position and the momentum of a particle can be determined exactly. To do this, they imagine a particle that breaks up into two identical particles that recoil with equal velocities in opposite directions. A measurement of position is made on one of them at a particular time, and a measurement of momentum on the other at the same time. Since the particles have equal velocities in opposite directions, the measurement of the position of one particle immediately gives the position of the other particle, and similarly for the momentum measurement. Thus both the position and the momentum of each particle may be determined with unlimited accuracy, contrary to the uncertainty principle implied by quantum mechanics. Thus quantum mechanics is incomplete.

In his reply, Bohr (1935) maintained that if two particles have interacted they remain thereafter a single system, so that a measurement on one automatically and instantaneously affects the other. Thus if we measure the position of one particle accurately, the momentum of the other is automatically rendered indeterminate, however far away it may be. This immediately implies a holistic universe in which it is impossible to isolate any system. But if everything is liable immediately to influence everything else, it is difficult to see how any consistent account of the universe is attainable. Such influences, of course, exist in classical mechanics, through the gravitational and electromagnetic fields for instance, but such influences are either negligible or cancel out or can be allowed for. Thus measurements on what to all intents and purposes is an isolated system can indeed be made. What Bohr is saying is quite different, namely that the influence of one system on the other is large, immediate and (apparently) is not in any sense transmitted through the intervening space. This is what is called a non-local interaction. If one holds with Bohr that quantum mechanics is complete, then non-locality follows. The positions of Einstein and Bohr are thus each logically coherent, but imply very different views of science and indeed of the physical world.

At this point it must be admitted that the above account is an attempt to present the arguments as clearly and simply as possible. Whether they indeed reflect accurately the views of Einstein and Bohr is another and rather different question. Partly this is a matter of history, which is not our primary concern, and partly it is a matter of finding out what Einstein and Bohr really thought. The difficulty concerning Einstein and EPR has already been mentioned; that concerning Bohr is due to the notorious obscurity of his writings. Although there have been numerous accounts of his thought, it remains likely, in the words of Bell, that no one really understands him. Our concern is thus with the arguments themselves, not with whether or not they were really held by Einstein or Bohr or indeed anyone else.

To take up again the story of the EPR argument, when it was first published, and for many years afterward, it remained a thought experiment. However in 1964 Bell reformulated the experiment in a way that was experimentally practicable, at least in principle. He considered two identical particles A and B each of spin one-half coupled together in a singlet state with total spin zero. Now suppose that they separate and as before fly apart in opposite directions. It is then possible to make spin measurements on each of them along two different directions. We now measure the joint probability Pab of finding particle A with spin component along the direction a and particle B with spin component along the direction b.

These measurements are repeated for other directions a' and b' and Bell (1964) was able to show that these quantities satisfy the inequality

$$|Pab - Pa'b| + |Pab' + Pa'b'| \leq 2$$

It is, however, easy to choose the directions a, a', b, and b' so that this inequality is violated. It is concluded that at least one of the assumptions made in the derivation of the Bell's inequality is false. These assumptions have been listed by D'Espagnat (1979) as realism, induction, and locality, and preferring to retain realism and induction, he concluded that locality must be violated. If this is so, it is a refutation of what is known as local realism, the belief that it is possible to separate two systems so that they can no longer interact with each other. This is equivalent to saying that no influence can propagate faster than the speed of light.

There are, however, several other derivations of the Bell inequality that do not mention non-locality, so it is difficult to maintain that this is critical to the argument. However all derivations assume the existence of joint probability distribution for the measurement of the two spin directions on the same particle (Brody and de la Pena 1979). Since this is known to be forbidden by quantum mechanics, it is to be expected that the Bell inequality differs from the quantum mechanical prediction.

The non-existence of the joint probability distribution can be easily shown. A particular measurement with definite settings of the two detectors can give say P_{ab}, but then it is not possible to measure any other correlation coefficient because the wave function of the system has been disturbed by the first measurement.

The consequences of the violation of the Bell inequality may also be shown by the following argument. The derivation of the inequality makes two assumptions:

1. It is possible to go beyond quantum mechanics by a hidden variable theory.

2. Two systems that have once been in contact can move so far apart that all interactions between them become negligible. This is the locality assumption.

Since the inequality is violated, one or other of these assumptions must be false. If it is the first assumption, then there is no hope of improving on quantum mechanics. If, however, the second is false, then science itself becomes impossible, for everything influences everything else, as there is no possibility of isolating a single system for study.

It is, however, desirable before choosing between these alternatives to see if there are other possibilities. It will be seen that the above argument requires two other assumptions:

3. No other assumption is required to prove the inequality.

4. There is no other way of proving the inequality.

These two assumptions are both false. Examination of several alternative proofs shows that many of them do not mention locality, which is therefore irrelevant. All of them, however, require the joint measurability assumption; this is the assumption that if two successive spin measurements are made on the same particle, the result of the first measurement does not influence the result of the second.

Thus what we can conclude from the violation of the Bell inequality is that joint measurability is false. This is, however, just what is required by quantum mechanics, so the violation of the inequalities is to be expected, and implies nothing new about locality or the possibility of hidden variables.

The Denial of Reality

Many physicists are inclined to dismiss all discussion of the interpretations of quantum mechanics as so much inconclusive philosophical waffle that may amuse people with a taste for such things but which is totally irrelevant to the serious day-to-day work of the practical scientist. This is not so. The first is the need for conceptual clarity. Many students of quantum mechanics are repelled by the quantum paradoxes. They cannot imagine an entity that is both a wave and a particle, they cannot understand the tunnels in alpha decay, and they are baffled when they are told that it is meaningless to ask which slit the electron went through in the double slit experiment. It is not unknown for students to be put off physics entirely by such talk.

Our philosophical beliefs, whether they are implicit or explicit, are vitally important and whether we recognize them or not they inevitably affect our actions. This is particularly so in quantum mechanics. Does it imply a denial of reality, is it to be identified with reality, or does it tell us something about reality, in a limited and probabilistic way? The remorseless inner logic of the consequences of our philosophical presuppositions may be illustrated by many examples from the history of atomic and nuclear physics.

According to the Copenhagen interpretation, only statistical statements are permitted, and all reference to an underlying reality are excluded. With this perspective, it was quite natural that Bohr, Kramers, and Slater (1924) were willing to envisage that atomic processes are essentially statistical, so that the principles of the conservation of energy and momentum are not valid for each individual event. This radical proposal was soon found to be incompatible with the measurements of Bothe and Geiger (1924), which showed that the conservation laws do indeed hold for each individual event.

Another example is provided by the widespread scepticism in the early years of the present century concerning the reality of atoms, expressed, for example, by Mach and Ostwald. As Einstein remarked, "the antipathy of these scholars toward atomic theory can indubitably be traced back to their philosophical attitudes. This is an interesting example of the fact that even scholars of audacious spirit and fine instinct can be obstructed in the interpretation of facts by philosophical prejudices" (Schilpp 1949). It is not surprising that Mach ended his life as a Buddhist (Blackmore 1972).

Saying that no further advance is possible and that certain questions must not be asked prevents all further progress. A particularly striking example of this is provided by the fate of Rutherford's early speculations on the shell structure of nuclei (Wilson 1984). Years before, he had shown that atoms have a structure and it was recognized that the electrons in the atom are arranged in a series of shells. Naturally he thought about the structure of nuclei and devised experiments to investigate it. Bohr, however, thought of the interior of the nucleus as an undifferentiated soup that occasionally presents a particle to the outside world.

From such events, he maintained, it is not possible to deduce anything about the pre-existence of the particle in the nucleus. Rutherford and Bohr frequently discussed this problem, and ultimately Rutherford was convinced that Bohr was correct and abandoned his attempts. Ten years after Rutherford's death, experimental evidence for the shell structure of nuclei began to accumulate and now it is accepted as a basic and essential feature of nuclei and the foundation of nuclear spectroscopy.

While it is true that the apparatus available to Rutherford was probably not sufficiently sensitive to detect the shell structure, Bohr's views certainly hindered the development of nuclear structure physics. If Rutherford had recognized the importance of philosophical presuppositions he would have been better equipped to resist Bohr's arguments.[1]

Another example of the debilitating effect of philosophical beliefs is provided by Heisenberg's refusal, in his capacity as a senior scientific advisor, to allocate funds for the construction of a new accelerator to look for quarks on the grounds that this was the wrong approach. On being questioned about this decision, he replied that the world is made up of mathematical resonances (Ferré 1980). This story lends additional weight to a comment of Popper:

> The metaphysical belief in causality seems more fertile in its various manifestations than any indeterminist metaphysics of the kind advocated by Heisenberg. Indeed we can see that Heisenberg's comments have had a crippling effect on research. Connections which are not far to seek may easily be overlooked if it is continually repeated that the search for any such connections is "meaningless." (Popper 1972, 248)

The effects of this discouragement are still strong today.

---

[1] Rutherford's hearty contempt for philosophy is shown by his remark to the celebrated philosopher Samuel Alexander: "When you come to think of it, Alexander, all you have said and all you have written during the last 30 years— what does it amount to? Hot air! Hot air!" (Eve 1939).

The overwhelming majority of physicists, particularly those who struggle daily in the laboratory, instinctively reject these debilitating beliefs and continue to believe, in the words of Einstein, that "something deeply hidden had to be behind things." To pursue scientific research within the framework of the opposing belief that all we are doing is trying to correlate our sense-impressions is to cut oneself off from the source of scientific creativity.

Realist Theories of Quantum Mechanics

Once it is admitted, following Einstein, that the quantum mechanical wave function represents the behaviour of an ensemble of similar systems, the way is open to investigate the detailed structure of the underlying determinist reality. Can this be described in terms of hidden variables, in much the same way that the velocities of the molecules provide the deterministic substructure to thermodynamics, and to the apparently erratic fluctuations of the Brownian motion? Some of the answers to this question have been sketched in the section on hidden variables, and in this section two of these theories are described in more detail.

One can hold the ensemble theory and use it to resolve at a certain level the quantum paradoxes created by the Copenhagen interpretation without having any specific idea about the nature of the hidden variables. One can indeed hold the ensemble interpretation without having any such ideas, and this leaves the way open to further advances. It is then important to try to develop such theories, because this will not only give much greater insight into quantum mechanics, but could also lead to predictions at variance with quantum mechanical calculations. If such predictions were confirmed by experiment, this would open up a whole new realm of physics.

The Pilot Wave Theory

It has already been remarked in the section on hidden variables that von Neumann's proof of the impossibility of hidden variables received a severe setback when Bohm succeeded in developing such a theory, known as the pilot wave theory. An early form of this theory was indeed proposed as long ago as 1927 by de Broglie, but it was immediately criticized by Pauli and so was not further developed. Many years later, Bohm showed how Pauli's criticism could be answered. If that had been realized in 1927, de Broglie's ideas might have been adopted as the interpretation of quantum mechanics and, since this is deterministic, all the confusion about the indeterminacy of the quantum world would have been avoided (Bohm and Hiley 1993; Cushing 1994; Holland 1995).

According to Bohm, every particle is accompanied by a wave that acts on the particle through the quantum potential. It is as if the particles are surfing the waves. If we specify the initial position of the particle and the form of the wave function, the numerical solution of Bohm's equations then gives the motion of the particle for all subsequent positions and times. Many calculations using this formalism have been made, including the case of a Gaussian wave packet incident on a square potential barrier, alpha decay, and also two Gaussian wave packets on each side of a square potential barrier, which correspond to the situation in a neutron interferometer (Bohm and Hiley 1993).

This formalism may be extended to include particles with spin, and can then account for all the fundamental features of non-relativistic quantum mechanics, including the correlations between separated particles in the Einstein-Podolsky-Rosen experiment.

The pilot wave theory shows how it is possible to construct a fully deterministic theory that gives some insight into the processes that are treated by quantum mechanical calculations. It is, however, a purely formal theory that fails to give any physical insight into why the particles behave as they do, and the origin of the quantum potential and how it acts on the particle. For this we must look to physical theories, and one of these, stochastic electrodynamics, is the subject of the next section.

Stochastic Electrodynamics

Every physical system is subject to the influence of its surroundings through the medium of gravitational and electromagnetic forces, and bombardment by photons, electrons, and neutrinos, to mention just a few. In classical physics we argue that most of these influences are irrelevant to the variables of interest, or average out, or can be allowed for, and this allows us to consider a system in isolation and to set up its equations of motion. Another possibility is to include some of the outside influences explicitly and to average over them subsequently; this is what we do in statistical physics. If neither of these methods were practicable, science would be impossible.

Quantum mechanics is an attempt to formulate the physics of a closed system (that is, to assume that all external influences are negligible) in a situation where the external influences are, in fact, not negligible. This is the root of the difficulties with quantum mechanics, and to solve the difficulties it is necessary to identify these external influences and to take them into account.

There have been many attempts to do this, both formally and by physical models. The formal stochastic theories are conceptually clear and mathematically simple, and have many useful applications. However they provide only mathematical models without any reference to the underlying physical processes. They thus provide a mathematical illustration of the ensemble interpretation, but no deeper physical understanding. The physical models are thus more satisfactory, and we concentrate our attention on one of them, stochastic electrodynamics.

This theory identifies the external influence on quantum systems as the fluctuating background electromagnetic field. Any charged particle experiences this field due to the motions of all other accelerated charged particles. This field must account for the stability of atomic structures, since they would rapidly collapse if electrons are classical particles moving in the absence of any external background.

If we consider the motion of an electron, taking into account the possibilities of emission and absorption, its equation of motion is the Newtonian one with the addition of emission and absorption terms; this is the Braffort-Marshall equation. This form of the equation requires several approximations before a solution is practicable, and even then it is difficult. The important question is, of course, to see if it can give the same eigenvalues and eigenfunctions as the Schrödinger equation. The calculations that have been made so far are unsuccessful.

This question can be partially answered by studying the corresponding harmonic oscillator problem. In this case the equilibrium distribution has the same form as the Wigner distribution and from it all the quantum results are obtained, including the energies of the allowed states. However these are not equilibrium states but average values of the instantaneous energy. This energy fluctuates around the mean values and the fluctuations are highly correlated so that the widths of the absorption and emission lines have the quantum mechanical values. Agreement with the quantum mechanical results is also found when a magnetic field is applied to the harmonic oscillator. It is also possible to incorporate spin.

In cases where a Markov approximation to the stochastic electrodynamical process can be made, the Schrödinger equation can be derived and hence all the quantum mechanical results follow. In other cases, where non-Markovian aspects are important, there are extra terms in the Schrödinger equation; these could lead to differences from the quantum mechanical result that could be experimentally tested.

The character of the background field depends on the surrounding medium. In the case of the double slit problem, the configuration of the background field is influenced by which of the slits is open. If the particle goes through one slit, it is the field that "knows" whether the other slit is open, and thus determines the motion of the particle.

The stochastic theory thus provides a conceptually simple way of tackling problems that, like quantum mechanics, have only one undetermined constant, that of Planck. It is unfortunately, and perhaps not surprisingly, complicated, so that only a few simple cases can be worked out. In this respect it is opposite to quantum mechanics, which is conceptually difficult but computationally elegant, allowing a large range of problems to be solved. Furthermore, stochastic electrodynamics is an open theory, in that further developments are very likely that will allow it to be extended to solve a range of problems (De la Pena and Cetto 1996).

Stochastic electrodynamics also provides a very natural explanation of radioactive decay. The coupling to the background radiation causes the height of the potential barrier to fluctuate, so that there is a finite probability for the particle to escape. As found experimentally, the larger the fluctuation required to allow escape, the longer the half-life.

The pilot wave theory and stochastic electrodynamics provide just two of many possible realist theories of quantum mechanics. There are several others, including decoherent histories and spontaneous localisation. Thus the Bohr-Einstein debate has already been resolved, and in favour of Einstein: what Einstein desired and Bohr deemed impossible—an observer-free formulation of quantum mechanics, in which the process of measurement can be analyzed in terms of more fundamental concepts—does, in fact, exist (Goldstein 1998).

Philosophical Implications

The philosophical implications of quantum mechanics, and their theological consequences, thus come not from the results of physical experiments, but from the philosophical premises inherent in the various formulations. The Copenhagen interpretation is based on positivism, so it not surprising that causality is denied and physics is reduced to the correlation of sense impressions. If, on the other hand, one adopts a realist position, one is thus free to believe that physical reality is a strictly determined system that we only partly understand. The root error in so many contemporary discussions is to suppose that, because it is so outstandingly successful, quantum mechanics gives a complete account of the physical world. We know, however, that there are many physically reasonable questions that cannot be answered, even in principle, by the formalism of quantum mechanics.

If we accept that quantum mechanics is an incomplete theory, then we can ask what future advances are conceivable. It is possible that new phenomena will be found that are not in accord with quantum mechanical calculations (Lokajicek 1997), and this will necessitate a reformulation of the theory, either a small extension or a radical revision. We will then have a theory that agrees with quantum mechanics for some phenomena, but not for others, and where it differs from quantum mechanics it is confirmed by experiment. Such a situation is similar to that between Newtonian dynamics and relativistic dynamics.

Another possibility is that a new theory, possibly along the lines of the realist theories mentioned above, provides a way to calculate the results of observations that cannot be obtained from quantum mechanics, such as the time of decay of a radioactive nucleus or the direction in which a particle is scattered. Such a theory will give the same results as quantum mechanics when averaged over a large number of systems, but will also give a more detailed account of the behaviour of each individual system. This situation would be similar to the relation between thermodynamics and the kinetic theory of gases: one theory describes measurable quantities in terms of macroscopic quantities such as temperature and pressure, and the other in terms of the motions of the individual particles. The kinetic theory is a microscopic theory that gives greater insight into physical reality, but the trajectories of individual particles are never calculated or compared with the results of measurements.

In this case, quantum mechanics remains a complete and correct theory at a certain level, in the sense that it is logically complete and accounts perfectly for a certain range of phenomena, namely the statistical averages of measurements on ensembles of similar systems. It does not, however, account for the behaviour of each individual system, and this is done by the new microscopic theory.

This account of quantum mechanics shows that it gives no support to the various philosophical propositions that have been associated with it nor, a fortiori, to any additional theological speculations.

Realism in Physics

In its most general sense, realism is the belief in an objective external world existing independently of the observer. As science develops we learn more about the objects that constitute the world. A century ago the world was viewed as a mechanism following Newton's laws, and efforts were made to build mechanical models of electromagnetic phenomena. These failed, and now electromagnetic fields are themselves accepted as real objects. It may be that quantum phenomena will ultimately force a further reappraisal of what we should call real, but it remains unacceptable to attribute contradictory properties or intrinsic indeterminism to them. Although reality cannot be assigned to wavefunctions, it is conceivable that non-local interactions may be demonstrated, but physicists have already shown that this can be accepted without abandoning realism.

These discussions of realism in quantum mechanics are of vital importance for the conduct of physics.

Another example of the debilitating effect of positivism is provided by Bridgman, who earned the Nobel Prize for his work on the properties of material under very high pressures. He is also notable for his works on operationalism, a variant of positivism that maintains that the meaning of physical quantities is to be found in the operations used to measure them. Once again, this is a denial of the underlying reality, so it was not surprising that Bridgman made no attempt, as a physicist, to relate his newly found data on the properties of matter to their underlying atomic structure, a line of research that has since been followed energetically by physicists not inhibited by their philosophical beliefs. Neither did Bridgman link his data with theories of stellar evolution, a subject closely connected with the physics of high pressures. Indeed, he poured scorn on modern cosmology as a branch of metaphysics, and urged upon physicists the essential difference between laboratory physics and cosmology, which he equated to the difference between science and non-science (Jaki 1978).

References

Ayer, A. J. 1978. "Logical Positivism and Its Legacy." In *Men of Ideas,* eds. B. McGee. London: BBC Publications, 131.

Ballentine, L. E. 1970. "The Statistical Interpretation of Quantum Mechanics." *Reviews of Modern Physics* 42: 358.

Beck, G., and M. Nussenzweig. 1958. *Nuovo Cimento* 9. 1068.

Bell, J. S. 1966. "On the Problem of Hidden Variables in Quantum Mechanics." *Reviews of Modern Physics* 38: 447.

———. 1964. "On the Einstein-Podolsky-Rosen Paradox." *Physics* 1.195.

Blackmore, J. T. 1972. *Ernst Mach: His Work, Life and Influence.* Berkeley: University of California Press.

Bohm, D. 1952. "A Suggested Interpretation of the Quantum Theory in Terms of 'Hidden' Variables. I and II. *Physical Review* 85: 166, 186.

——— and B. J. Hiley. 1993. *The Undivided Universe: An Ontological Interpretation of Quantum Theory.* London: Routledge.

Bohr, N. 1935. "Can Quantum Mechanical Description of Reality be Considered Complete?" *Physical Review* 48: 696.

———, H. A. Kramers, and J. C. Slater. 1924. "The Quantum Theory of Radiation." *Philosophical Magazine* 47: 785.

———. 1985. *A Centenary Volume.* eds. A. P. French and P. J. Kennedy. Cambridge, MA: Harvard University Press, 136.

Born, M. 1949. *Natural Philosophy of Cause and Chance.* Oxford: Clarendon Press.

———. 1953. *Scientific Papers Presented to Max Born.* London: Oliver and Boyd.

Bothe, W., and H. Geiger. 1924. "Ein Weg zur Experimentellen Nachprufung der Theorie von Bohr, Kramers and Slater." *Zeitschrift für Physik* 26: 44.

Bransden, B. H., and C. J. Joachain. 1989. *Introduction to Quantum Mechanics.* London: Longmans, 53.

Broda, E. 1983. *Ludwig Boltzmann.* Woodbridge, CT: Ox Bow Press.

Brody, T. A. 1993. *The Philosophy Behind Physics.* Eds. L. de la Pena and P. E. Hodgson. New York: Springer.

———, and L. de la Pena, 1979. "Real and Imagined Non-localities in Quantum Mechanics." *Nuovo Cimento* 54B: 455.

Bunge, M. 1967. *Quantum Theory and Reality.* New York: Springer.

Cassidy, D. C. 1992. *Uncertainty: The Life and Science of Werner Heisenberg.* New York: W. H. Freeman.

Cushing, J. T. 1994. *Quantum Mechanics: Historical Contingency and the Copenhagen Hegemony.* Chicago: University of Chicago Press.

de Broglie, L. 1954. *The Revolution in Physics.* London: Routledge and Kegan Paul

de la Pena, L., and A. M. Cetto. 1996. *The Quantum Dice. An Introduction to Stochastic Electrodynamics.* Dordrecht: Kluwer.

D'Espagnat, B. 1979. "The Quantum Theory and Reality." *Scientific American,* November 1979: 128.

Dirac, P. A. M. 1979. "Early Years of Relativity." In *Albert Einstein: Historical and Cultural Perspectives.* The Centennial Symposium in Jerusalem. Eds. Gerald Holton and Yehuda Elkana. Princeton, NJ: Princeton University Press, 84.

Dudley, J. M., and A. M. Kwan. 1996. "Richard Feynman's Popular Lectures on Quantum Electrodynamics." The 1979 Robb Lectures at Auckland University. *American Journal of Physics* 64: 694.

Einstein, A. 1953. "Elementare uberlegungen zur Interpretation der Grundlagen der Quantum-Mechanik." In *Scientific Papers Presented to Max Born.* London: Oliver and Boyd, 33.

————.1934, 1941. *The World As I See It.* London: Bodley Head.

————, B. Podolsky, and N. Rosen. 1935. "Can Quantum Mechanical Description of Reality be Considered Complete?" *Physical Review* 47: 777.

Eve, A. S. 1939. *Rutherford.* Cambridge: Cambridge University Press, 240.

Faye, J. 1991. *Niels Bohr: His Heritage and Legacy.* Dordrecht: Kluwer.

Ferré, F. 1980. Private communication. See also W. Heisenberg, in *The Nature of Scientific Discovery.* Ed. O. Gingerich 1975. Washington: Smithsonian Institution Press, 565.

Fine, A. 1972. "Some Conceptual Problems of Quantum Theory." In ed. R. G. Colodny. *Paradigms and Paradoxes.* Pittsburgh: Pittsburgh University Press, 3.

Franklin, A. 1987. *The Neglect of Experiment.* Cambridge: Cambridge University Press.

Gell-Mann, M. 1976. Nobel Prize Lecture.

Gilson, E. 1990. *Methodical Realism.* Front Royal, VA: Christendom Press.

————. 1955. *History of Christian Philosophy in the Middle Ages.* London: Sheed and Ward.

Gleason, A. M. 1957. "Measures on the Cloised Subspaces of a Hilbert Space." *Journal of Mathematics and Mechanics* (6): 885.

Goldstein, S. 1998. "Quantum Theory without Observers." Parts One and Two. *Physics Today* 51(3); 51 (4).

Gribbin, J. and Gribbin, M. 1998. *Richard Feynman—A Life in Science.* London: Penguin Books, 264.

Heisenberg, W. 1938. "Die Grenzen der Anwendbarkeit der Bisherigen Quantentheorie." *Zeitschrift für Physik.* 110: 251.

Hodgson, P. E. 1995. "The Christian Origin of Science." Coyne Lecture, Cracow.

Holland, P R. 1995. *The Quantum Theory of Motion: An Account of the de Broglie-Bohm Causal Interpretation of Quantum Mechanics.* Cambridge: Cambridge University Press.

Houghton, J. 1995. *The Search for God.* London: Lion Press, 203.

Howard, D. 1990. "Nicht sein. Mame was nicht sein derf," or the "Prehistory of EPR, 1909–1935; Einstein's Early Worries about the Quantum Mechanics of Corporate Systems." In *Sixty-Two Years of Uncertainty: Historical, Philosophical and Physical Enquities into the Foundations of Quantum Mechanics.* Ed. Arthur I. Miller, NATO ASI Series. Erice 1989. New York: Plenum Press.

Hughes, R. I. G. 1989. *The Structure and Interpretation of Quantum Mechanics.* Cambridge, MA: Harvard University Press.

Jackson, J. D. 1975. *Classical Electrodynamics.* New York: Wiley, 791.

Jaki, S. L. 1974. *The Road of Science and the Ways to God.* Chicago: Chicago University Press, 228.

————.1978. *Science and Creation.* Edinburgh: Scottish Academic Press.

Jauch, J. M., and C. Pirion. 1963. *Helvetica Physica Acta* 26: 827.

Jonsson, C. 1961; 1974. *Zeitschrift für Physik* 161:454; *American Journal of Physics* 42: 4.

Jordon, Pascual. 1934. "Quantenphysicalische Bermerkungen zur Biologie and Psychologie." *Erkenntnis.*4.215.

Lokajicek, M. 1997. Lecture to the Thomistic Institute. University of Notre Dame, Indiana.

Lucas, J. R. 1995. "Prospects for Realism in Quantum Mechanics." *International Studies in the Philosophy of Science* 9: 225.

Merzbacher, E. 1961. *Quantum Mechanics.* Hoboken, NJ: Wiley, 22.

Mott, N. F. 1964. "On Teaching Quantum Phenomena." *Contemporary Physics* 5: 401.

Oliphant, M. 1972. *Rutherford: Recollections of Cambridge Days.* Amsterdam: Elsevier, 60.

Peres, A. 1978. "Unperformed Experiments Have No Results." *American Journal of Physics* 46: 745.

Popper, K. R. 1982. *Quantum Theory and the Schism in Physics.* Ed. W. W. Barclay. London: Hutchinson.

Przibram, K., ed. 1967. *Albert Einstein, Max Planck, and H. A. Lorentz. Letters on Wave Mechanics.* Translated and Interpreted by Martin J. Klein. London: Vision Press.

Putnam, H. 1965. In *Beyond the Edge of Certainty.* Ed. R. G. Colodny. Upper Saddle River, NJ: Prentice-Hall.

Rayleigh, Lord. 1942. *The Life of Sir J. J. Thomson.* Cambridge: Cambridge University Press.

Redhead, M. 1995. *From Physics to Metaphysics.* Cambridge: Cambridge University Press, 9.

Schilpp, P., ed. 1949. *Albert Einstein: Philosopher-Scientist.* Cambridge: Cambridge University Press, 49, 672.

Schommers, W., ed. 1989. *Quantum Theory and Pictures of Reality.* New York: Springer.

Schrödinger, E. 1926. "Quantisierung als Eigenwert Problem." *Annalen der Physik.* 79: 734.

Stuart, C. I. J. M. 1991. "Inconsistency of the Copenhagen Interpretation." *Foundations of Physics* 21: 591.

Tanzella-Nitti, G. 1992. *Questions on Science and Religious Belief.* Tucson: Pachart Publishing House.

Tarozzi, G., and A. van der Merwe. 1985. *Open Questions in Quantum Physics.* Bari Workshop 1983. Dordrecht: Kluwer.

_____. 1988. *The Nature of Quantum Paradoxes.* Dordrecht: Kluwer.

't Hooft, G. 1997. *In Search of the Ultimate Building Blocks.* Cambridge: Cambridge University Press.

Tonamura, A., J. Endo, Y. Matsuda, T. Kawasaki, and H. Ezawa. 1989. "Demonstration of Single-Electron Buildup of an Interference Pattern." *American Journal of Physics* 57: 117.

von Neumann, J. 1955. *Mathematical Foundations of Quantum Mechanics.* Princeton, NJ: Princeton University Press.

Wilson, D. 1984. *Rutherford: Simple Genius.* London: Hodder and Stoughton.

Wolpert, L., and A. Richards. 1988. *A Passion for Science.* Oxford: Oxford University Press.

Zeilinger, A. 1986. "Testing Quantum Superposition with Cold Neutrons." In *Quantum Concepts in Space and Time,* eds. R. Penrose and C. J. Isham. Oxford: Oxford University Press.

CHAPTER 18

God's Action in the World: The Relevance of Quantum Mechanics*

IT IS A BASIC CHRISTIAN BELIEF that we are all totally dependent on God, that God cares for us and guides our lives. And yet, according to the scientific account, the world is like a vast machine behaving in a deterministic manner following mathematical equations. If we maintain that God gave matter its properties and started its motions on the day of creation, this implies that it continues to act strictly in accord with these laws. How then can we also believe that God acts upon the world?

It has been suggested that this question can be answered by considering the properties of the quantum world (Pollard 1958, 139; Polkinghorne 1988, 333; Russell 1988, 343; Tracy 1995, 289; Murphy 1995, 325; Ellis 1995, 359; Clayton 1997, 194).[1] Quantum mechanics, it is argued, has shown that the microworld is essentially indeterministic and so this provides the means whereby God, by acting within the limits of quantum uncertainty, can affect the world without violating the laws of physics. In this way we can maintain the rule of scientific law and also allow God to act freely.

---

* Reprinted with permission from *Zygon* 35 (2000): 505 Some of the material in this article is used in *Theology and Modern Physics* (Aldershot: Ashgate Press 2005).

[1] "The clear and determinate character of physical processes, as Sir Isaac understood it, has dissolved at its constituent roots into the cloudy and fitful quantum world" (Polkinghorne 1988, 333). "The overwhelming impression one gets from quantum physics is of the irreducibly statistical character of experience" (Russell 1988, 343).

This proposal raises a number of questions that deserve critical attention. To determine whether they are sufficient to achieve their object, we must first ask if the minute interventions constrained within the limits of the uncertainty principle are able to produce macroscopic effects. We need also to confirm that material reality is indeed an indeterministic system, and this raises the question of the relation between quantum mechanics and reality. In particular, does quantum mechanics give a complete or an incomplete account of the quantum world? We can also ask if this conception of God's action is consistent with our existing knowledge of divine intervention. Are there instances where other laws of nature are violated?

It is useful to recall that the history of interpretations of quantum mechanics could well have been very different. Soon after the formulation of quantum mechanics, de Broglie proposed the deterministic pilot wave theory, but soon abandoned it following criticisms by Pauli, which were long afterward shown by Bohm to be unfounded (Cushing 1994, Ch. 9). The difficulties of interpreting quantum mechanics were then avoided by the Copenhagen interpretation, at the expense of introducing the quantum paradoxes. Due to the persuasiveness of Bohr, the Copenhagen interpretation was generally accepted, and is now accepted, and is found in most textbooks and popular literature; as a result it has been uncritically accepted by most physicists. It has, however, been strongly criticized by philosophers of science, and many books have been devoted to alternative deterministic interpretations (Bohm 1952, 1957, 1980; de Broglie 1954; Belinfante 1973; Bell 1987; Holland 1993). One of these could well have been accepted long ago and then no one would have claimed that quantum mechanics provides evidence for radical indeterminacy of the world (Cushing 1994, Ch. 10)

Chaos Theory

The uncertainty principle, as it is usually understood, sets very tight limits on the results of measurements, so we can ask whether such minute interventions are adequate to produce the macroscopic effects implied by God's action in the world. We could imagine

God making billions of such minute interventions so that eventually they produce macroscopic effects (Clayton 1997, 194), though whether this is consistent with the omnipotence and dignity of God is another question. This may, however, be unnecessary given the effects studied in chaos theory (Russell, Murphy, and Peacocke 1995). It is well known that even in classical systems very small changes in the initial conditions often produce very different subsequent behavior. For example, a minute change in the trajectory of a gas molecule greatly affects the dynamics of a collision, and this is magnified in subsequent collisions. More picturesquely, it is referred to as the "butterfly effect" in climate predictions. Such effects have been studied in recent years because computers provide the means to make the lengthy calculations that are required. If we assume that God could foresee the ultimate effects of divine intervention at the quantum level, then a minute intervention could indeed produce a macroscopic effect. Furthermore, in certain circumstances a single quantum event can produce a macroscopic effect, as in the case of Schrödinger's cat.

Quantum Mechanics and the Material World

Quantum mechanics is a very successful theory and describes a wide range of phenomena in great detail and to a high degree of accuracy. In many cases it gives us a good understanding of what is taking place. However, we may be so impressed by the success of quantum mechanics that we overlook its defects. Its results are expressed in terms of probabilities. Thus, we cannot calculate in which direction a particle will scatter or when a particular nucleus will decay. Quantum mechanics is therefore incomplete. The question is whether this incompleteness is irreducible or whether there will eventually be a more fundamental theory that gives a more detailed account of reality.

There is another sense in which most physical theories are incomplete, especially quantum mechanics. We can describe some aspects of a process very well, but do we really understand what is happening and why? Is it sufficient to be able to calculate the results of measurements, or do we seek something more? We can describe pair production, but we do not understand how or why it happens as it does. This remark applies also to classical mechanics; we can describe gravitational phenomena extremely well, but we do not really understand them.

The first question to be answered is therefore whether the incompleteness of our understanding is compatible with the conclusions that are drawn.

Whereas Bohr maintained that quantum mechanics is the final theory, Albert Einstein maintained that quantum mechanics is but one step on the road to a full understanding of the world. In this view, the wavefunction gives the average behavior of an ensemble of similar systems.

This is illustrated by some examples in the following sections.

The Heisenberg Uncertainty Principle

The Heisenberg uncertainty principle may be illustrated by considering the diffraction of a beam of electrons by a narrow slit. In this experiment, a collimated beam of monoenergetic electrons is directed toward a narrow slit. As they pass through the slit, the directions of motions of the electrons are changed so that they fan out over a certain angular range, just like the diffraction of light in optics. It is found that the narrower the slit, the wider the angular range of the fan, again just as in optics. Since the width of the slit determines the position of the electron and its subsequent direction determines its transverse momentum it was deduced that there are limits to the accuracy with which position and the momentum can be simultaneously ascribed to the electron, so both are "fuzzy and indeterminate" (Merzbacher 1961).

A closer analysis shows, however, that it is possible to measure the position and momentum of an electron to much greater accuracy than is allowed by the uncertainty principle. To see this, first consider the motion in a direction perpendicular to that of the incident beam: the uncertainty in position corresponds to the width of the slit, and the uncertainty in momentum is given by the angular spread of the electrons after passing through the slit. If we examine these uncertainties, we find that they indeed satisfy Heisenberg's Uncertainty Principle $\Delta x \Delta p = h/4p$. This relation is inherent in quantum mechanics and may easily be deduced by describing the electron beam by a wavepacket.

If, however, we consider a single electron emitted at a particular angle, we find a different result. We can allow this electron to hit a screen and thus determine its momentum in the direction perpendicular to that of the incident beam to a much higher accuracy than is allowed by the uncertainty principle. The technical details of this may be found in an article by Leslie Ballentine (1970; see Popper 1982, 62).

This illustrates the essential point that quantum mechanics describes the statistical behavior of a large number of particles, not the behavior of a single particle. Heisenberg's uncertainty principle thus gives the relation between the spreads in position and momenta of a large number of particles. It does not mean that we cannot measure the position and momentum of a single particle with higher accuracy. We cannot, however, predict which way an electron will go, although it is conceivable that a more developed theory will allow this to be done. At present this seems unlikely, but it has happened many times in the history of science that what seemed impossible at one time became a familiar achievement. Bohr's Copenhagen interpretation would prevent us from even trying to find a new theory, while that of Einstein leaves the door open to future advances. There are several possibilities, and the recent work on stochastic electrodynamics (de la Pena and Cetto 1996) is particularly promising.

Quantum mechanics is thus essentially a statistical theory that describes the average behavior of a large number of similar systems but not the behavior of each individual system. In some ways this is like the distinction between actuarial statements about populations, which are statistical, and the behavior of a particular individual, which is not.

Concerning our ability to calculate the position and momentum of an electron to an accuracy far greater than that implied by the uncertainty principle, Werner Heisenberg said that "this knowledge of the past is of a purely speculative character, since it can never be used as the initial condition in any calculation of the future progress of the electron." Thus "it is a matter of personal belief whether such a calculation concerning the past history of the electron can be assigned any physical reality or not" (quoted in Popper 1982, 62). Popper, however, denied that it is a matter of personal belief, because:

> to question whether the so ascertained "past history of the electron can be ascribed any physical reality or not" is to question the significance of an indispensable standard method of measurement (retrodictive, of course); indispensable, specially, for quantum physics. . . . But, once we ascribe physical reality to measurements for which, as Heisenberg admits, $\Delta x \Delta p \ll h$, the whole situation changes completely: for now there can be no question whether, according to the quantum theory, *an electron can "have" a precise position and momentum*. It can. (Popper 1982, 63)

This fact has been continually denied by the supporters of the Copenhagen interpretation.

Quite generally, our inability to measure any physical quantity with unlimited accuracy does not imply that it does not have a precise value, unless, of course, one believes that reality can be attached only to the results of a measurement. Such a positivistic view not only has been thoroughly discredited philosophically but also is inimical to science.

Thus physics gives us no grounds for saying that the position and momentum of a particle are unknowable within the limits of the uncertainty principle, and still less for saying that it does not have position and momentum. Indeed, the uncertainty principle is perfectly compatible with each electron moving along a definite trajectory determined by forces in the vicinity of the slit that we are as yet unable to calculate or measure. The same type of explanation applies to the other paradoxes connected with the interference at two slits and with the Bell inequalities.

Radioactive Decay

Radioactive decay is often cited as an example of the statistical nature of reality. We can calculate the probability of decay per unit time but not the actual instant of decay. If this is combined with the belief that quantum mechanics gives a complete account of reality, then we must conclude that radioactive decay provides an example of an uncaused event. If, however, we do not accept this view of quantum mechanics, then we can say that, indeed, each decay has a cause that we do not yet know. There are many possibilities: maybe the decay happens when the motions of the constituent nucleons reach a suitable configuration, or perhaps it is due to some external influence. These are possibilities that could provide a subject for future research. Certainly, radioactive decay cannot be proved to be uncaused.

The Double Slit Experiment
and Wave-Particle Duality

One of the most celebrated quantum paradoxes is that of the double slit. If a beam of electrons passes through a close pair of parallel slits, an interference pattern consisting of a series of alternating dark and light bands is obtained on a screen behind the slits. This again is exactly analogous to the corresponding situation in optics, where the interference pattern is interpreted by the wave theory. In the case of electrons it is surmised that the same intensity variations would be given by the corresponding quantum mechanical calculation, although this has not been verified.[2] As in the optical case, this gives us the behaviour of a large number of electrons.

The wave-particle duality of fundamental particles is often cited as an example of the mysterious and counterintuitive nature of the quantum world. In the double slit experiment the electrons seem to behave like waves when they pass through the slits and like particles when they impinge on the screen. The observation of an interference pattern raises the question, How can an interference pattern be formed if the

---

[2] A. Zeilinger (1986) has compared the interference pattern observed in the diffraction of a neutron beam by two slits with the predictions of the Fresnel-Kirchoff diffraction theory and finds excellent agreement.

electron is a particle that goes through only one slit? According to the Copenhagen interpretation this question is meaningless and so must not even be asked. Bransden and Joachain (1989) conclude that "the particle is not localised before it is detected, and hence must be considered as having passed through both slits" (53). And yet we know that an electron behaves like a point particle down to a very small distance. It must have passed through one slit or the other, and then why should there be an interference pattern and not the superposition of two diffraction patterns, each characteristic of one slit? There is, of course, no possibility of the electrons passing through one slit interfering with those passing through the other because we can still obtain the interference pattern when the intensity of the electron beam is so low that the electrons pass through the apparatus one by one.

The problem seems to be insuperable and, indeed, contrary to the laws of logic. A detailed analysis by Arthur Fine led him to the conclusion that it is necessary to abandon the distributive law of logic (Fine 1972, 3). If this were the case, it would indeed be an example of a philosophical implication of modern physics, but closer analysis shows that this argument is invalid (Brody 1993).

According to the Einstein interpretation, the electron, being a pointlike particle, goes through only one of the slits, and its trajectory is influenced, as in the single-slit case, by its incident direction and by where it passes through that slit. But how can we explain the observed interference? If the electron passes through one slit, how is its motion affected by whether the other slit is open or not? This is because the electron interacts with the whole system, and it is the field that tells it, while it is going through one slit, whether the other is open or not (Popper 1982, 59). It is then possible to give a consistent account of the observations.

The wave-particle duality is thus simply a category confusion. On the one hand we have particles moving along definite trajectories with definite momenta, and on the other we recognize that, due to their interactions with the slits and with other matter and radiation, these trajectories have a certain probability distribution calculable from Schrödinger's equation.

Theological Reflections

The foregoing has shown that the success of quantum mechanics does not imply that the world is indeterminate and so does not provide the means whereby God can intervene. Even if it did provide those means, they would not be able to account for all recorded interventions, since they violate other physical principles. For example, the feeding of the five thousand is contrary to the law of the conservation of matter, and so are several miracles of healing in recent times. It is an impoverished conception of God to suppose that he is bound by his own laws. God is the supreme lord of nature, who can make and unmake its laws and bring it into being, modify it, or extinguish it at will. It is unnecessary to think of God trying to change the course of events by keeping within the limits of quantum indeterminacy.[3]   ⚛

References

Ballentine, L. E. 1970. "The Statistical Interpretation of Quantum Mechanics." *Reviews of Modern Physics* 42: 358.

Belinfante, F. J. 1973. *A Survey of Hidden Variable Theories.* Oxford: Pergamon Press.

Bell, J. S. [1964] 1965. "On the Einstein-Podolsky-Rosen Paradox." *Physics* 1: 195.

———. 1966. "On the Problem of Hidden Variables in Quantum Mechanics." *Reviews of Modern Physics* 38: 447.

———. 1987. *Speakable and Unspeakable in Quantum Mechanics.* Cambridge: Cambridge University Press.

Bohm, D. 1952. "A Suggested Interpretation of Quantum Theory in Terms of 'Hidden' Variables." *Physical Review* 85: 166, 186.

———. 1957. *Causality and Chance in Modern Physics.* New York: Van Nostrand.

———. 1980. *Wholeness and the Implicate Order.* London: Routledge and Kegan Paul.

---

3 Polkinghorne (1988, 339) pertinently asks whether "God is the ultimate Hidden Variable, skillfully exercising his room to maneuver at the rickety constituent roots of the world, whilst cleverly respecting the statistical regularity which his faithfulness imposes?"

Bohm, D., and B. J. Hiley. 1993. *The Undivided Universe: An Ontological Interpretation of Quantum Theory.* London: Routledge, Chapman and Hall.

Born, M. 1926. "Quantenmechanik der Stossvorgänge." *Zeitschrift für Physik* 38: 803.

Bransden, B. H., and C. J. Joachain. 1989. *Introduction to Quantum Mechanics.* London: Longmans.

Brody, T. A. 1993. *The Philosophy Behind Physics.* Eds. L. de la Pena and P. E. Hodgson. Berlin: Springer-Verlag.

Clayton, P. 1997. *God and Contemporary Science.* Grand Rapids, MI: Eerdmans.

Cushing, J. T. 1994. *Quantum Mechanics: Historical Contingency and the Copenhagen Hegemony.* Chicago: University of Chicago Press.

de Broglie, L. 1928. *Conseil de Physique Solvay.* Paris: Gauthier-Villars.

———. 1954. *The Revolution in Physics.* London: Routledge and Kegan Paul.

———. 1993. *Heisenbergs Uncertainties and the Probabilistic Interpretation of Wave Mechanics.* Cambridge: Cambridge University Press.

de la Pena, L., and A. M. Cetto. 1996. *The Quantum Dice: An Introduction to Stochastic Electrodynamics.* Dordrecht: Kluwer.

Ellis, G. F. R. 1995. "Ordinary and Extraordinary Divine Action." In *Chaos and Complexity: Scientific Perspectives on Divine Action.* Eds. R. J. Russell, N. Murphy, and A. R. Peacocke. Vatican City State: Vatican Observatory; and Berkeley: Center for Theology and the Natural Sciences.

Fine, A. 1972. "Some Conceptual Problems of Quantum Theory." In *Paradigms and Paradoxes.* Ed. R. G. Colodney. Pittsburgh, PA: University of Pittsburgh Press.

Gleason, A. M. 1957. "Measures on the Cloised Subspaces of a Hilbert Space." *Journal of Mathematics and Mechanics* 6: 885.

Heisenberg, W. 1958. "The Representation of Nature in Contemporary Physics." *Daedalus* 87(Summer): 95.

Holland, P. R. 1993. *The Quantum Theory of Motion: An Account of the de Broglie-Bohm Causal Interpretation of Quantum Mechanics.* Cambridge: Cambridge University Press.

Jauch, J. M., and C. Pirion. 1963. "Can Hidden Variables be Excluded in Quantum Mechanics?" *Helvetica Physica Acta* 26: 827.

Merzbacher, E. 1961. *Quantum Mechancis.* New York: Wiley, 22.

Murphy, N. 1995. "Divine Action in the Natural Order." In *Chaos and Complexity: Scientific Perspectives on Divine Action*. Eds. R. J. Russell, N. Murphy, and A. R. Peacocke. Vatican City State: Vatican Observatory; and Berkeley: Center for Theology and the Natural Sciences.

Philippidis, C., C. Dewdney, and B. J. Hiley. 1979. "Quantum Interference and the Quantum Potential." *Nuovo Cimento* 52B.15.

Polkinghorne, J. 1988. "The Quantum World." In *Physics, Philosophy and Theology: A Common Quest for Understanding*. Eds. R. J. Russell, W. R. Stoeger, and G. V. Coyne. Vatican City State: Vatican Observatory.

Pollard, W. G. 1958. *Chance and Providence: God's Action in a World Governed by Scientific Thought*. New York: Charles Scribner's Sons.

Popper, K. R. 1959. *The Logic of Scientific Discovery*. London: Hutchinson.

———. 1982. *Quantum Theory and the Schism in Physics*. Ed. W. W. Barclay III. London: Hutchinson.

Russell, R. J. 1988. "Quantum Physics in Philosophical and Theological Perspective." In *Physics, Philosophy and Theology: A Common Quest for Understanding*. Eds. R. J. Russell, W. R. Stoeger, and G. V. Coyne. Vatican City State: Vatican Observatory.

———, N. Murphy, and A. R. Peacocke, eds. 1995. *Chaos and Complexity: Scientific Perspectives on Divine Action*. Vatican City State: Vatican Observatory; and Berkeley: Center for Theology and the Natural Sciences.

Tracy, T. F. 1995. "Particular Providence and the God of the Gaps." In *Chaos and Complexity: Scientific Perspectives on Divine Action*. Eds. R. J. Russell, N. Murphy, and A. R. Peacocke. Vatican City State: Vatican Observatory; and Berkeley: Center for Theology and the Natural Sciences.

von Neumann, J. 1955. *Mathematical Foundations of Quantum Mechanics*. Princeton, NJ: Princeton University Press.

Wilson, D. 1984. *Rutherford: Simple Genius*. London: Hodder and Stoughton.

Zeilinger, A. 1986. "Testing Quantum Superposition with Gold Neutrons." In *Quantum Concepts in Space and Time*, eds. R. Penrose and C. J. Isham. Oxford: Oxford University Press.

CHAPTER 19

Einstein's Religion*

THE PRE-EMINENCE of Einstein among twentieth-century physicists ensures that a book on his life and thought will be welcomed, especially as it comes from the pen of Professor Max Jammer, a distinguished philosopher of science who has written extensively on the development of our concepts of space and time, matter and energy, and on the conceptual development and philosophy of quantum mechanics. He has now chosen to describe a lesser-known aspect of Einstein's thought that is nevertheless closely related to his scientific creativity. He examines "not only how deeply religion affected Einstein and his work, but also conversely how deeply Einstein's work, and in particular his theory of relativity, affected theological thought, a problem that has not yet been explored systematically." This subject is of great interest not only to professional scientists but also to all those concerned with the relation between religion and science.

The book is divided into three sections: first on Einstein's religiosity and the role of religion in his private life; secondly on Einstein's philosophy of religion; and thirdly on the effects of Einstein's physics on theology. Professor Jammer emphasizes that his aim is simply to describe Einstein's views "in a completely unbiased way

---

* A review of *Einstein and Religion* by M. Jammer (Princeton: Princeton University Press, 2000), reprinted with permission from *Contemporary Physics* 42 (2001): 117.

and in a historical and philosophical perspective without judgment of any kind." Since Einstein never wrote a systematic account of his philosophy of religion, it is necessary to piece together his views from his occasional writings, public lectures, and replies to the many letters he received asking about his religious beliefs.

Einstein was born into a non-practising Jewish family that had not renounced their Jewish heritage but did not follow traditional rites or attend services in the synagogue. At the age of six Einstein entered a Catholic primary school and at the same time his parents arranged for a relative to give him instruction in the principles of Judaism. This latter teaching filled him with religious enthusiasm, and he fervently followed religious prescriptions. His love for music appeared at an early age, and "Music, Nature and God became intermingled in him in a complex of feeling." His schooling led him to respect both the Catholic and the Jewish religions and an attitude of toleration toward all sincerely held beliefs remained throughout his life, although he rejected any affiliation with organized religious bodies.

His religious phase came to an end at the age of about twelve as a result of reading some popular science books. These convinced him that many of the biblical stories cannot be true. As he recalls in his autobiography, "the consequence was a positive orgy of free-thinking coupled with the impression that youth is intentionally being deceived by the state through lies. . . . Suspicion against every kind of authority grew out of this experience," and as a result he refused to be bar-mitzvahed.

Later in life, Einstein wryly remarked that "to punish me for my contempt of authority, Fate made me an authority myself." It has been suggested that this "enabled him to develop the powerful independence of mind that gave him the courage to challenge established scientific beliefs and thereby revolutionize physics." However, in spite of this attitude to authority, Einstein always regarded science and religion as complementary to each other. In 1930 he declared emphatically that: "I am of the opinion that all the finer speculations in the realm of science spring from a deep religious feeling, and that without such feeling they would not be fruitful."

The contradiction between such remarks and his aversion to institutional religion is only apparent, and can be understood by recognizing that Einstein used the word "religion" in two senses: the recognition of a mind behind nature on the one hand, and institutional religion on the other.

When Einstein was asked whether he was deeply religious, he replied: "Yes, you can call it that. Try and penetrate with our limited means the secrets of nature and you will find that, behind all the discernable concatenations, there remains something subtle, intangible and inexplicable. Veneration for this force beyond anything we can comprehend is my religion. To that extent I am, in point of fact, religious." Concerned by accusations that Einstein was an atheist, Rabbi Goldstein asked him whether he believed in God. Einstein replied: "I believe in Spinoza's God who reveals himself in the orderly harmony of what exists, not in a God who concerns himself with fates and actions of human beings." When a secularist said that this was indistinguishable from atheism, Einstein replied that "we followers of Spinoza see our God in the wonderful order and lawfulness of all that exists and in its soul as it reveals itself in man and animal."

This belief in the lawfulness of nature is the basis of Einstein's epistemological realism: he regarded "physics as an attempt to grasp reality as it is thought, independently of its being observed." He believed in the mysterious comprehensibility of the world, that our equations accurately describe an objectively existing reality, and yet he was astonished that this is so.

Spinoza believed that all natural events follow immutable laws of cause and effect, and this led him to reject a theistic concept of God. This belief implies that the universe is like a giant machine following mathematical laws and so there is no place for purpose or morality. This denies human freedom and is quite contrary to the Judeo-Christian concept of a personal God. And yet Einstein was horrified by the brutalities of Nazi Germany and never forgave the Germans for voting for Hitler. He justified this apparent inconsistency by maintaining that although we are bound by determinism, we must conduct our moral lives as if we are free.

It is widely believed that the theory of relativity is a radical break with the past and that it implies that all beliefs, including religious beliefs, are not absolute but relative. Einstein rejected this view and saw his theory as a natural development of classical physics, remarking that "the men who have laid the foundations of physics on which I have been able to construct my theory are Galileo, Newton, Maxwell, and Lorentz."

It is instructive to ask to what extent Einstein's religion affected his scientific work. Religion can affect the attitude of the scientist to his work, and it could also give him new ideas. Einstein certainly believed that "ultimately the belief in the existence of fundamental all-embracing laws also rests on a sort of faith," so that religion provides psychological motivation for the scientists: "What a deep conviction of the rationality of the universe. . . . Kepler and Newton must have had to enable them to spend years of solitary labour in disentangling the principles of classical mechanics!" As Whitehead has remarked, it is the conviction that there is a rational order in nature and that it can be found that provides the strength to carry on in spite of the difficulties encountered, and this is essentially a religious conviction. It provided Einstein with the motivation to spend years in an ultimately unsuccessful attempt to formulate a unified theory of matter. He wanted to know "whether God could have created the world in a different way; in other words, whether the requirement of logical simplicity admits a margin of freedom."

His belief that the universe is ruled by strict deterministic laws lay behind his objection to the new quantum mechanics, expressed by the remark that "quantum mechanics is very worthy of regard; but an inner voice tells me that it is not the true Jacob. The theory yields much, but it hardly brings us close to the secrets of the Old One. In any case, I am convinced that He does not play dice." At this point it should have been made clear that Einstein had no objection to quantum mechanics as a scientific theory, but only to its most popular interpretation.

Einstein was concerned when he failed to find a way to overcome the apparent lack of precision implied by the Heisenberg uncertainty relations. According to a letter from Pauli to Born in 1954 he was at one time inclined to deny "that he uses as a criterion for the admissibility of a theory the question: 'Is it rigorously deterministic?'" However, as Ballentine has shown, the position and momentum of an electron can be measured to any accuracy and, as Popper has pointed out, the uncertainty relations can be understood as scatter diagrams if one accepts the statistical interpretation.

Einstein proposed another possible way of measuring to any degree of accuracy the values of conjugate variables (in this case the position and momentum of a particle) in a paper with Podolsky and Rosen. The argument assumes the locality or separability principle, namely that a measurement made on one physical system cannot be affected by the result of a simultaneous measurement on another spatially separated system. This is equivalent to the denial of the possibility of non-local interactions, which are also inconsistent with special relativity. Jammer remarks that the violation of the Bell inequalities implies that "the philosophical problem of whether local realism is maintainable has been settled in the laboratory, but alas with a negative result." However, all derivations of the Bell inequalities assume joint measurability and since this is inconsistent with quantum mechanics, the violation of the inequalities is to be expected. Other arguments against the locality principle assume that it is acceptable to introduce counterfactual conditionals in a physical argument.

In a contribution to a theological conference in 1939, Einstein began by emphasizing that science on its own cannot tell us the ultimate reason and purpose of our lives. Science cannot teach men to be moral and "every attempt to reduce ethics to scientific formulas must fail." The reason for this is that science tells us what is, whereas morality is concerned with what ought to be. He went on to deny that there is a personal God, and this provoked a strong adverse reaction.

The final section of the book is concerned with the effect that Einstein's work, especially his theory of relativity, has on theology. Einstein's work has influenced a wide range of theological discussions, such as the age-old question of God and time, and the implications of quantum mechanics. Traditional Christianity holds that God is timeless, and that matter and time were created together. And yet in the Bible God is referred to in anthropomorphic terms as if He is in time like us. If God is outside time, then past, present, and future are to Him an ever-present now; how then can we have free will if the future is already known to God and therefore determined? This is why the Heisenberg uncertainty principle was welcomed in some quarters as it seemed to provide an opportunity for God to act on the world without violating the laws of physics. This argument is fundamentally misconceived, as described above.

More recently, the process theology developed by Whitehead and Hartshorne has provided an alternative view, replacing "the mechanistic physical world picture of substances by an organic conception of reality as a network of events in space and time." According to this view, God is in time, participating in natural events. Discussions of these and other theories are being carried on at a high level of sophistication by theologians and philosophers, but as they are not of direct interest to physicists they will not be discussed further here. Professor Jammer's account will certainly be of great value to those concerned with such problems.

Throughout the book, Professor Jammer takes for granted the usual interpretations of the theory of relativity and of quantum mechanics. Consideration of other possible interpretations would have shown more clearly a key aspect of the development of Einstein's thought. Einstein's work involved him in two great debates: first that with Lorentz on space and time, and secondly that with Bohr on quantum mechanics. In the first, it was Lorentz who maintained the existence of absolute space and time, while Einstein said that we can only consider space and time from the point of view of the observer, and thus admit only measurable quantities. In the second, it was Einstein who held an objective deterministic view of the world, whereas Bohr held that we must only consider measurable quantities. Between the time of his formulation of the theory of relativity and the beginning of his work on quantum mechanics, however, Einstein's deeply held Judeo-Christian beliefs reasserted themselves and he came to believe that the aim of science is to find out about an objective external world. Einstein knew that his science and his philosophy were closely interrelated and when writing to Lanczos recalled: "I began with a sceptical empiricism more or less like that of Mach. But the problem of gravitation converted me into a believing rationalist, that is, into someone who searches for the only reliable source of Truth in mathematical simplicity." He was well aware that "there is, of course, no logical way leading to the establishment of a theory but only groping constructive attempts by careful considerations of factual knowledge." According to Einstein, "scientific concepts are freely created inventions of the human mind and no logical connection exists between our sense experience and our theoretical concepts of the Universe." He adopted a realist stance on the interpretation of quantum mechanics, and when Heisenberg asked him why he did not still adhere to the positivist approach underlying the theory of relativity he replied: "Maybe I did believe that, but it is nonsense all the same." ❋

PART IV
Nuclear Power

CHAPTER 20

Nuclear Power and the Pontifical Academy of Sciences[*]

IN NOVEMBER 1980 the Pontifical Academy of Sciences held a meeting to discuss world energy problems. The papers presented at this meeting and the conclusions were published in a volume of 776 pages.[1] Although these conclusions were of great importance and deserved wide publicity they remain almost entirely unknown. This shows a serious deficiency in communication that merits urgent attention.

The widespread applications of science frequently raise moral problems that are of great importance for the future of society. Such problems are often the subject of statements by bishops' conferences and other Church bodies. Among contemporary problems that have been treated in this way is the question of energy supplies in general and nuclear power in particular; by nuclear power is meant the generation of electrical power by nuclear reactors, not nuclear weapons. Many Church statements have been made on nuclear power, but most of them are unsatisfactory because they are based on an inadequate knowledge of the basic science and technology.[2] It

---

[*] Reprinted with permission from *Fellowship of Catholic Scholars Quarterly* (Summer 1999): 7.

[1] "Semaine D'Étude sur le thème Humanité et Énergie: Besoins–Ressources–Espoirs." November 10–15, 1980. Édite par André Blanc-Lapierre. Pontificiae Academiae Scientiarum Scripta Varia, No. 46, 1981.

[2] P. E. Hodgson. "The Churches and Nuclear Power." August 1984 (unpublished). Noteworthy among Church statements on nuclear power is that of the U.S.

is often not sufficiently well understood that it is only possible to reach a sound moral judgment on such questions by taking full and balanced account of a large number of connected scientific and technical problems, wherever possible expressed numerically.

One of the few such statements that satisfies these criteria is that published by the Pontifical Academy of Sciences in 1981. Realizing the importance and complexity of the problem, the Academy invited a group of 32 scientists from many countries worldwide to a meeting held in November 1980. They included experts in nuclear physics, the electrical industry, biophysics, plant science, chemistry, and medicine;[3] this ensured an authoritative study at the highest level.

The published proceedings of the meeting contains the full texts of the papers presented, together with the ensuing discussions, and ends with a four-page summary of the conclusions. This begins by emphasizing that "Energy plays an essential role in the material, social and cultural life of mankind. At the present stage of world development it is not possible without additional energy availability to cope with the population growth, increasing demand for food, and with the problem of unemployment: furthermore, a lack of energy can

---

Bishops, see "The Moral Dimensions of Energy Policy," Bishops' Committee for Social Development, *Origins*, NC Documentary Service, 23 April 1981, 10 (45): 706. This document was critically analyzed by P. E. Hodgson in "Reflections on the Energy Crisis," *The Month* (November 1982): 382.

[3] The participants included: Professor A. M. Angelini, Honorary President of the Ente Nazionale per l'Energia Elletrica, Rome; Professor C. Chagas, Institute of Biophysics, Rio de Janeiro; Professor U. Columbo, President of the Comitato Nazionale per l'Energia Nucleate; A. Danzin, President of the Comite Europeen de Recherche et de Developpment; P. Desprairies, President of the Institit Francais du Petrole; Professor L. Leprince-Ringuet, nuclear physicist and Member of the Academie Francaise; Professor G. B. Marini-Bettolo, Istituto di Chemica, Facolta di Medicina; Profesor L. Paris, Director of the Study and Research Department of the Ente Nazionale per l'Energia Elettrica; Dr. I. Pasztor. World Council of Churches; Professor G. Porter, Director and Fullerian Professor of Chemistry, The Royal Institution; Professor G. Puppi, Professor of Physics, University of Bologna; Professor C. Salvetti, Vice-President of the Comitato Nazionale per l'Energia Nucleate; C. Starr, Vice Chairman of the Electric Power Institute, California; Professor J. Teillac, Haut-Commissaire a l'Energie Atomique; Professor R. van Overstraeten, Catholic University of Louvain, Department of Electrotechnics; Professor C. Wilson, Director of the World Coal Study, and many others.

indeed menace world peace." The abundance and low price of oil has fueled rapid economic growth in recent decades, but without reducing the economic gap between industrialized and third world countries. The increasing dependence on oil "has contributed to the instability of the world economy." The world demand for energy will continue to increase due to population growth and to the increase in the energy consumption per capita. World oil production is unlikely to increase and so world energy needs cannot be satisfied. The steep rise in oil prices has destabilized world financial systems, contributing to inflation and unemployment. "This situation has placed non-industrialised countries in an extraordinarily vulnerable position."

As a result, "We have no time to waste. Energy policies are urgently needed, involving concerted action by the responsible bodies, and this requires the support of public opinion and energy users. Unfortunately, even in the industrialized countries, public consciousness of the problem is lacking." Thus "a joint effort by the industrialized countries and the oil-exporting countries is required to provide means—such as a joint fund—to help the poorest countries to develop their own energy resources. Only coal and nuclear power together with a strong energy conservation policy and continued gas and oil exploitation and exploration can allow us to effectively meet the additional needs for the next two decades. It is emphasized that the industrialized countries must reduce their oil consumption and leave it essentially for specific end uses (transportation, petrochemistry, etc.), and for the basic needs of the developing countries. No energy source should be neglected if we wish to resolve the energy crisis. A strong research effort must be made to develop renewable energy sources, which, among other things, can encourage decentralization of human settlements, thus reducing the disturbances of the excessive urbanization process that has occurred and is still occurring in the world. In particular, solar energy, under its various forms (thermal, thermodynamic, and photovoltaic energy, biomass, etc.), have demonstrated good potential especially for non-centralized energy supply." Wood is still extensively used as a fuel, and so increased attention must be paid to tropical forest management.

A mix of energy sources is desirable to deal with unexpected scarcities. Energy issues must be tackled at the national and regional, as well as the global, levels. Problems of energy management, storage, and transport require attention. "Electricity can be expected to play an increasingly important role in the life of mankind, in view of its convenience and flexibility."

Particular attention was paid to the possible effects of the increase in the carbon dioxide content of the atmosphere, and extensive research was advocated.

"As regards nuclear energy, some concern has been voiced as to the possible links between nuclear energy and the proliferation of nuclear weapons. In this field, however, it is recognized that, once a certain general level of knowledge and technical expertise has been acquired, a country's development of nuclear weapons is primarily determined by political considerations. Thus, with adequate precautions, there is no reason to bar the development of nuclear energy for civil uses." It is essential to take care of the health of those engaged in energy generation, and to respect the environment and the health of humanity.

The summary concludes that it should be possible "to assure adequate availability of energy before or about the turn of the century, provided necessary actions are taken now with sufficient vigor." The present growth of energy consumption cannot continue forever and so it is necessary to develop less energy-consuming ways of life. The developed countries should help the developing countries by promoting technology transfer, education, and training. Nations are increasingly interdependent so that new modes of cooperation should be developed.

Scientists have particular responsibilities to evaluate the data and advise political leaders so that they can make decisions that will satisfy the needs of present and future generations. Co-operation between scientists, engineers, sociologists, and churchmen "is highly desirable, on the national and even international level, especially in so far as it brings out the human and hence ethical dimension of energy issues."

This study by the Pontifical Academy was made the basis of the submission of the Holy See to the International Conference in Nuclear Power held in Vienna, September 13–17, 1982.[4] The leader of the Vatican Delegation, Msgr. Peressin, referred to the peaceful applications of atomic energy, including food conservation, new techniques of plant breeding, medicine, hydrology, and, most important of all, energy for industrial and private use. He reminded the Conference that many United Nations Agencies have stressed that the economic growth of the third world countries seems "to be impossible without some applications of nuclear energy." Therefore, Msgr. Peressin continued, "my Delegation believes that all possible efforts should be made to extend to all countries, especially the developing ones, the benefits contained in the peaceful uses of nuclear energy."

Although I try to keep myself informed about Church statements on nuclear power, I heard about the work of the Pontifical Academy quite by accident. I was unable to obtain a copy by writing to the Academy, and eventually succeeded through the personal efforts of one of my Oxford physics students, who was at that time studying for the priesthood in Rome. As soon as I read the document I realized its importance, and urged that it be reviewed in a prominent Catholic weekly, but without success. I therefore wrote an article on it that was published in the *Clergy Review*.[5]

A conference on the Christian Dimensions of Energy Problems was organized by the Catholic Union and the Commission for International Justice and Peace and held in England in April 1982. It is noteworthy that it took no notice of the work of the Pontifical Academy in 1980. This is unfortunately quite typical; studies are undertaken and conferences arranged by people without any knowledge of what has already been achieved. It is therefore impossible to make any progress; they are continually trying to invent the wheel. By contrast, in the scientific community, a prime requisite for serious

[4] Statement of the Holy See to the International Conference on Nuclear Power, Vienna, September 13–17, 1982, International Atomic Energy Agency. Paper CN–42/449.
[5] Peter Hodgson. "Nuclear Power: Rome Speaks," *The Clergy Review* LXXVIII (February 1983): 49.

research is a thorough knowledge of what is already known. There are scientists who are unfamiliar with the literature (often through no fault of their own) and write papers that might have been interesting two years ago, but are now quite useless. Such scientists are not taken seriously and their papers are rejected.

The result of all this is the production of statements that are frequently worse than useless, with a small number of very competent and valuable statements that are so poorly publicized that they have little effect.

There are several reasons for this unsatisfactory state of affairs. The first and fatal mistake of those responsible for many Church studies is to underestimate the magnitude of the scientific and technical work that must be undertaken before any realistic moral judgment can be made. In the case of nuclear power, it is essential to study in a quantitative way the world energy needs, the resources of raw materials, the economics of the different methods of energy generation, and their associated hazards and effects on the environment. This requires the co-operation of experts in many fields. Only when this is done is it possible to cut through the smoke-screen of politically motivated propaganda obscuring the whole subject and then go on to establish the true situation that must be taken as the basis of any realistic moral judgment on the best energy sources to choose. The report should be written up by the scientists and the moral theologians working together.

Without the participation of qualified scientists the report may well contain many wise and sensible thoughts, but the cumulative impression will inevitably be that it comprises well-meaning generalities that are unlikely to have any practical result at all.

This work need not be done in every country; indeed it is preferable that it be done on an international level. Nevertheless it is also desirable that there is in each country a group of qualified people who keep the subject constantly under review. If this is not done, then when the report comes from the international committee it will not be well understood and so its conclusions cannot be properly implemented.

The work of the Pontifical Academy was of the highest standard, and its conclusions have stood the test of time. It has had, however, very little effect because of a scandalous and disgraceful failure in communication. The Pontifical Academy apparently considered that its work was done when the volume was published, but apart from the submission to the IAEA Conference in Vienna it had very little additional publicity, so far as I am aware. In Britain, the Catholic press has adopted much the same anti-nuclear stance as the secular media. If it had been properly publicized, the Report of the Pontifical Academy would have enabled the Church to give a valuable lead in public discussions concerning the acceptance of nuclear power.

To ensure this, the summary of the Report should have been printed in large numbers and sent to a wide range of key people, from bishops to media leaders. A vital link in this process is the weekly press and also magazines dealing with world affairs. The editors need to be aware of the status of the international committee and the importance of giving wide publicity to their Report. They should also know some well-qualified scientists who can comment on the Report and answer questions.

This failure of communication in the Church is widespread: many valuable documents are produced in Rome, but their contents never reach the people for whom they are intended.

The chief merit of the work of the Pontifical Academy is that they got the facts right. There is little that is new in their Report; it simply presents in a balanced way material that is available elsewhere in much greater detail. The specifically Christian contribution is by comparison rather meager, and this is a real weakness of the work of the churches in such areas. There is little long-term scholarly commitment to the moral analysis of problems like global warming, the energy crisis, and nuclear power. Few moral theologians devote their lives to thinking about them. The authorities of most churches failed even to discover the essential facts and to put them into perspective, and this is no more than an essential preliminary to serious moral thinking. There is an urgent need for some moral theologians to spend years mastering the facts and thinking about them in the light of Christian principles. This very necessary theological work simply cannot be done by busy bishops on the evening before they are due to address some conference. There are some men in the Church who are potentially able to do such work, namely the young clergy who studied science to degree standard before ordination. They know enough to understand what is going on, but not enough to make weighty contributions to the debate. They see very clearly that vague and well-meaning platitudes are no substitute for a clear moral lead. Usually their scientific knowledge rusts as they are swamped by other duties. Yet if they were specifically assigned to theological studies where their scientific knowledge would be used, and given the opportunities to learn from experts, to take higher degrees, to devote most of their lives to study, then in a few decades we would be in a position to make a serious contribution to the debates on global warming, nuclear power, and similar problems that are of such vital importance for the future of humanity. Then, in the words of *Fides et Ratio*, "moral theology will be able to tackle the various problems in its competence such as peace, social justice, the family, the defense of life and the natural environment, in a more appropriate and effective way."

CHAPTER 21

Reflections at La Rabida: The Responsibilities of the Nuclear Physicist for Peace[*]

I BEGAN TO WRITE this lecture in the grounds of the Franciscan monastery of Santa Maria de la Rabida near Huelva in southern Spain. When you visit that monastery you are shown a small room where, nearly five hundred years ago, a man asked the Prior of the monastery, Fr. Antonio de Marchena, for help. He wanted the Prior to ask the Queen to support a certain project of his. The very experienced Portuguese navigators had already turned down his request pointing out, quite correctly, that he had made a mistake in his calculations. But still he persisted with his idea and, in that small room in La Rabida, he won over the Prior. The Prior in turn succeeded in convincing the Queen and some months later three ships sailed from the nearby port of Palos de la Frontiera, and after sailing for thirty-three days Columbus discovered the new world.

Four hundred and fifty years later, in another not-so-small room under the disused squash courts of the University of Chicago, another discoverer, Enrico Fermi, told his assistants to withdraw the control rods from a pile of graphite and uranium. The neutron counters clicked faster and faster. When he was satisfied that the neutron production was rising exponentially, just as he had predicted, Fermi told

---

[*] The text of this lecture has been revised to take account of developments in the nuclear debate since it was delivered on 20 November 1985. I am grateful to Professor B.L.Cohen for permitting me to quote from his book, *Before It's Too Late: A Scientist's Case for Nuclear Energy* (New York: Plenum Press, 1983).

the operators to replace the control rods, and the neutron counters fell silent. Later that day, the prearranged code message was sent out:"The Italian navigator has landed in the New World. The natives are friendly."

Five hundred years from now, an historian might have some difficulty in deciding which discovery was the more momentous for the subsequent history of mankind. The discovery of the nuclear chain reaction, which enables the energy of the atomic nucleus to be released on a large scale, has consequences that are familiar to us all. Fermi's pile was the direct ancestor of the nuclear power reactors that are now generating increasing amounts of electricity in many countries of the world. It was unfortunately not in this form that atomic energy first hit the headlines of the world. It was first applied not to peace, but to war on 8 August 1945 when Hiroshima was destroyed. Though it was first used in war, it must be added that it was used with the aim of bringing peace, and in that it was success-ful. Japan surrendered five days later and the otherwise almost inevitable prolongation of a bitter conflict was avoided. Since that time, the shadow of nuclear weapons has arguably prevented the outbreak of further world wars, although of course there have been numerous tragic conflicts on a smaller scale.

Nuclear physicists have been responsible as initiators for these momentous changes in the affairs of men. What are our continuing responsibilities? That is the question that I would like to address in this lecture. What I will maintain is that our principal responsibility is to see that the public debates on nuclear questions, both of war and of peace, are conducted with due regard for the essential scien-tific facts, so far as these are known. Certainly the physicist is fur-ther entitled to participate in the subsequent debate, but in political and other questions his views are hardly more worthy of attention than those of any other concerned member of the public. But as a source and guardian of balanced and accurate factual information he has a unique and irreplaceable role.

I will approach my task historically, recalling how the atomic scientists first faced up to their new responsibilities in the immediate postwar years. I will contrast this with the situation today and draw a number of disturbing conclusions. In particular, I want to highlight the growing unreality of what is called the nuclear debate, and the perils that this holds for us all. I will end by posing a question that I am not able to answer, namely what is to be done about this situation.

I would like at the outset to make quite clear the strict limits that I put on this lecture: I will discuss the responsibilities of nuclear physicists toward society as a whole, particularly in matters relating to peace. I will not however discuss any particular scientific matter except by way of illustration, nor am I concerned to put the case either for or against nuclear power. Most importantly, although I may have occasion to remark on the influence of political considerations on the nuclear debate, I will not make any political statements. I do of course have political views, but not as a consequence of my being a physicist, and in this lecture I want to speak primarily as a physicist.

Who are the nuclear physicists on whom the responsibilities fall? Three conditions are essential: they must have adequate knowledge; they must be able to speak freely, to say what they believe to be true; and they must enjoy public credibility. The first is obvious, although it must be remarked that it is not at all obvious who has the requisite knowledge. Very few people have encyclopaedic knowledge of the whole field of nuclear physics and its applications. Most nuclear physicists have expert knowledge of only a relatively narrow range of their subject, although if they undertake the necessary studies they can quickly become sufficiently familiar with a wider range, so that they can speak on it with some authority. Lack of freedom to speak openly unfortunately excludes some of the most knowledgeable physicists from the public debate. Physicists engaged in weapons research, and to a lesser extent those engaged in reactor design, may by their terms of employment be forbidden to speak publicly. Their knowledge is necessarily kept secret for defence or commercial reasons. The third requirement, of public credibility, also unfortunately tends to exclude at least some of the scientists employed by the nuclear industry. Many of them are free to write, and their articles are published in journals like *Atom*. However such journals are often seen as biased; it is thought that they are obliged to support nuclear power and so they are not given the weight they deserve. This leaves the academic nuclear physicists in universities, so on them falls the main responsibility. Even they are often dismissed from consideration by the argument that inevitably they support the applications of their own knowledge.

The atomic bomb was designed and built at Los Alamos during the years 1943 to 1945. It was a time of intense activity, because it was known that German scientists were also working on the bomb and it was essential to get there first. As it happened the Germans had not made much progress and in any case the war in Europe ended before the bomb was ready.

During those hectic years at Los Alamos attention was so concentrated on the prime task that there was virtually no discussion of its social implications. After Hiroshima, there was an outburst of words, feelings, emotions, and expressions of guilt. The scientists realized that they must educate the public about the new force that had entered world history through their hands. Why should they do this? The question is answered by Laura Fermi: "Unless the public come to understand some of the basic scientific, technological and political aspects of the bomb, the Americans will not be able to make well-reasoned decisions. Our husbands went ahead and gave lectures in Santa Fe and Albuquerque and they organized the Association of Los Alamos Scientists. They drafted statements, they wrote articles."[1]

In the late nineteen forties there was very little public understanding of nuclear power; everyone had heard about the atomic bombs that had brought the war with Japan to an abrupt end, but the basic physics, and especially the nature of nuclear radiations, was not understood. The scientists who had participated in the wartime developments, and others who had graduated since then,

---

[1] Laura Fermi, *Reminiscences of Los Alamos 1943–1945,* L. Badash, J. D. Hirschfelder, and H. R. Brioda, eds. (Dordrecht: Reidel, 1980).

realized that there was a great and urgent work of public education to be tackled. They formed the Atomic Scientists' Association in Britain, and the Federation of Atomic Scientists in the United States, both devoted to the task of educating the people for the nuclear age. They published periodicals, organized exhibitions, and lectured up and down the country. They were everywhere listened to with close attention, and soon more and more people began to understand the age they were about to enter.

Their main concern was to warn about the dangers of nuclear war, and to make it clear that the advent of nuclear weapons had completely changed the nature of war. Their second concern was to show how the same power could be used for peaceful purposes. This included not only nuclear power, but also a wide variety of medical applications of nuclear radiations, as well as the use of isotopes in industry and agriculture.

It is particularly notable that this work was strongly supported by the scientific community, particularly by nuclear physicists. In England the Atomic Scientists' Association had as its successive presidents Professor N. F. Mott, Professor R. E. Peierls and Professor H. S. W. Massey, with many vice-presidents of the highest distinction including Professor Lord Cherwell, Sir John Cockcroft, Professor P. M. S. Blackett, Professor Dame Kathleen Lonsdale, Professor Sir Francis Simon, and Professor Sir George Thomson. As will be noticed these include scientists in high public positions such as Sir John Cockcroft, Director of the Atomic Energy Research Establishment, Harwell, and embrace a considerable range of religious and political convictions.

Most of the work of the Association concerned the dissemination of factual information, but occasionally there were more sensitive decisions to take. One of these occurred in 1955, soon after the hydrogen bomb test at Bikini Atoll. The radioactive debris from this explosion fell over a wide area, and some of it on the Japanese fishing boat *Fukuryu Maru*. The crew noticed the whitish powder that fell on the boat, and about three days later they found that those parts of skin that had touched the powder became dark red and began to swell up like ordinary burns. Professor Yasushi Nishiwaki, a professor of radiation biophysics at Osaka City University School of Medicine, read a report of this in the newspaper and was then asked by the Public Health Department of Osaka to examine some of the tuna brought back by the *Fukuryu Maru*. He found that the fish were highly radioactive, and was able to establish the presence of a range of fission products in dust he found on the boat itself.

Professor Nishiwaki wrote a detailed article on his findings that was published in the *Atomic Scientists' Journal* for November 1954.[2] These were analyzed by Professor Rotblat, Professor of Physics at St. Bartholomew's Hospital in London. He concluded that "fission accounts for most of the energy released by the hydrogen bomb." This was contrary to the general belief at the time that a fission bomb simply served as a detonator to initiate the much more powerful hydrogen reaction. Professor Rotblat then realized that the mechanism of the bomb was rather more complicated; there was an additional third stage composed of a shell of uranium 238. This shell serves the double purpose of holding the reacting mass together for a short time longer, thus increasing the explosive power, and far more importantly boosting the power still further by the extra fissions caused in the uranium 238 by the fast neutrons from the hydrogen reaction. Since the energy per fission is about 200 MeV, and that from the three main fusion reactions 4.0, 3.3, and 17.7 MeV, it is easy to see that most of the explosive power from such a device comes from fission and not from fusion.[3]

This was a startling conclusion and shows how an academic scientist, by reasoning from published data, can reach conclusions about matters that are considered most secret by the authorities. Professor Rotblat wrote an article on his work and it was published in the *Atomic Scientists' Journal* of March 1955. I do not recall any hesitations about this; it seemed to us to be our duty to make this knowledge generally available.

---

[2] Yasushi Nishiwaki, "Bikini Ash," *Atomic Scientists' Journal* (4; 1954): 97.

[3] J. Rotblat, "The Hydrogen-Uranium Bomb," *Atomic Scientists' Journal* (3; 1955): 224.

The same issue of the *Atomic Scientists' Journal* contains a symposium of articles on "Science and the Press." The editorial of that number contains some reflections on this subject that are worth repeating now:

> It is one of the main aims of the Atomic Scientists' Association to disseminate reliable knowledge about atomic energy and its medical and industrial applications, so that the public may intelligently co-operate in assisting their realization. Since the *Journal* is not widely read by the public, we have to rely on those who write for newspapers to transmit the information we publish to their readers. In order that this shall be done with the maximum efficiency it is necessary that scientists and journalists should understand each others' difficulties and preoccupations so that they can co-operate effectively. The scientist is mainly concerned with presenting an accurate and balanced account of new discoveries with all the necessary qualifications and reservations concerning its possible future applications. The journalist, on the other hand, primarily wants an account that will be interesting and intelligible to his readers, and if he is to achieve this he cannot use the technical terminology of the scientist. This might make it appear that it is well-nigh impossible to satisfy both the scientist and the journalist and indeed this is the case for some scientific advances. But usually it is possible to explain the essentials of a discovery in everyday language without sacrificing accuracy providing that the scientist understands the needs of the journalist and the journalist respects the desire for accuracy of the scientist.
>
> This understanding is of course greatly facilitated if the journalist has some knowledge of science, and indeed all our contributors come into this category. But it is also desirable that the scientist should understand more of the difficulties of the journalist, and the chief value of this symposium will probably be to bring this about. He will then be better equipped to discharge one of the most important of his social responsibilities, that of keeping the public well informed of the implications of his work.[4]

---

[4] P. E. Hodgson, "Science and the Press," *Atomic Scientists' Journal* (4; 1955): 201.

If I were to rewrite that editorial today, I would not be so optimistic. This work continued for some years, and gradually the situation changed so that the scientists felt their responsibilities to be less pressing. In the first place there grew up a generation of science journalists, well-trained and articulate, who progressively took over the role of informing the public. Many books were published by those involved in the wartime project so that detailed and accurate information became readily available. Many scientists, with some reason, felt that their work was essentially done, and they could henceforward concentrate on their academic work. Others thought that scientists still had urgent responsibilities. The result in Britain was that the Atomic Scientists' Association was disbanded, and many of its members transferred their energies to the Pugwash movement, established as a result of the Russell-Einstein Manifesto.

The motivation behind the Pugwash Movement is that, in the words of a document issued on the occasion of its twenty-first anniversary, "An ever-growing number of scientists now realize that they have to share in the responsibility of governments to utilise knowledge for constructive purposes, so that beyond the interests of individual groups and countries the achievements of science and technology shall benefit the welfare of mankind as a whole and not contribute to its detriment."[5]

The Pugwash movement was originally concerned mainly with the problems of disarmament, but over the years its concern has widened to include the whole field of science and public affairs. At the same time its membership, originally mainly physicists, broadened to include chemists, biologists, sociologists, lawyers, historians, statesmen, and indeed all who were concerned at a professional level with scientific and technical subjects and their implications for human society.

Thus it was decided that "while arms control aiming at nuclear disarmament must continue as the priority objective, Pugwash

---

[5] J. Rotblat, *Pugwash: A History of the Conferences on Science and World Affairs* (London: Heinemann, 1967).

should concern itself with other questions closely related to world security and an enduring peace: sources of conflict and international tension, such as the technological development of new weapons of mass destruction; the enormous and increasing economic disparity between developed and developing countries; environmental deterioration; energy; depletion of natural resources; and problems of population growth."[6]

The first meeting was held in 1957 at the small fishing village of Pugwash in Nova Scotia, and was one of the first occasions when scientists from east and west met to discuss ways to avoid nuclear war. In the following years many such discussions were held, and they undoubtedly had a beneficial influence. Scientists usually have little difficulty in transcending national and ideological barriers and agreeing on factual matters. These in turn often affect political initiatives; for example, a particular proposal to monitor test explosions may be technically impossible. Scientists who recognize such facts can convey them to their governments after the meeting and this can lead to more realistic initiatives.

Pugwash has made many contributions toward the control and reduction of the number of nuclear weapons. An example is the suggestion made in 1962 for improving the detection of underground tests by "black-box" sealed seismic recording stations. The groundwork for the Non-Proliferation Treaty was prepared at a Pugwash meeting in 1958, and at later meetings the main provisions covering the obligations of both nuclear and non-nuclear nations were formulated. Pugwash meetings have been devoted to the limitation of ballistic missiles, anti-submarine warfare, and chemical and bacteriological weapons. Recognizing that the widening gap between living conditions in industrialised and developing countries is a major source of international tension, Pugwash has organized many symposia to promote the indigenous capacities of the developing countries and facilitate technology transfer. "The start of official negotiations between the U.S.A. and North Vietnam in the spring of 1968 was helped by a mission of French Pugwash scientists, sent

---

[6] Ibid.

from Paris in 1967, that conveyed to Hanoi the U.S.A. terms for terminating the war." Pugwash also provided an important channel of communication between the U.S.A. and the U.S.S.R. during the Cuban crisis in 1962. A cable was sent at the most critical stage from the American scientists to their colleagues in the Soviet Union asking them "to urge their government to re-route their ships so as to avoid a clash, pledging themselves at the same time to urge their own government to avoid any precipitate action."[7]

There are many facts that are quite obvious to scientists and yet come as a surprise to politicians. For example after the war it was hoped in some governmental circles that if only we could keep the "secret of the atomic bomb" from falling into Russian hands, then peace would be secured for decades. Scientists were quick to point out that any well-developed nation could make nuclear weapons starting from scratch in a very few years, and this was borne out by events when Russia exploded its first atomic bomb in 1949. This is worth remembering today.

Over the years there have been many other sensitive issues of great importance for world peace that are closely related to scientific and technical facts. To give just a few examples, there are the genetic hazards of nuclear radiations, the feasibility of diverting fissile material from civil reactors, the neutron bomb, the possibility of a nuclear winter following many nuclear explosions, and, of course, the practicability of detecting and destroying oncoming strategic missiles, the so-called Strategic Defence Initiative or "Star Wars" proposal. On all these and many similar problems it is essential to collect and master the relevant scientific and technical data before embarking on a discussion. The principal contribution of the nuclear physicist to peace is to provide the requisite data in terms that can be readily understood.

The problems of nuclear power must be discussed together with those of nuclear weapons because the two are closely related, although not in the ways generally thought. Both originated together; Fermi's atomic pile is the ancestor of our power reactors

---

[7] Ibid.

and of the reactors that produce weapons-grade plutonium. Some of the early power reactors were designed to produce plutonium as well. This is now unnecessary because the nuclear powers have more than enough plutonium for all conceivable military needs. This is why Sir John Hill said: "If we were to shut down and dismantle every nuclear power plant throughout the world, and every nuclear submarine, nuclear cruiser and nuclear aircraft carrier, the problem of proliferation would still be with us and we would hardly have reduced its dimension one inch."[8]

Nevertheless there are connections between nuclear power reactors and nuclear war, first at the industrial level and second through the energy crisis. The basic nuclear industry that is responsible for designing nuclear reactors, for providing and reprocessing the fuel, and for controlling the safety aspects, is the same for both power and weapons reactors. There are thus strong commercial, economic, and organizational links between the two. A country that develops a nuclear power programme possesses the capacity to manufacture nuclear weapons much more rapidly, should it decide to do so, than a country with no nuclear programme.

However it could be argued that the main threat to peace comes from the larger powers that already have well-developed nuclear capacities. Furthermore, the rising cost of energy in many countries is itself a serious source of international tensions. If nuclear power is not available, the scramble for the remaining oil reserves would be much more acute, and this is very likely to provoke conflict. The tension in the Middle East, for example, is largely due to the presence there of about 50% of the world's remaining oil. As oil becomes more scarce, the price will increase and production will decline. Nuclear power is thus a strong force for peace due to its massive contribution toward the alleviation of the energy crisis, which reduces the tensions induced by the competition for the remaining oil supplies.

Discussions on all these and many related questions have taken place continually over the past thirty years. In that time the situation

---

[8] Sir John Hill, "Energy Choices for the Future," *Atom* (January 1980).

has changed quite radically: the number of books on atomic matters has multiplied, news items are frequently published in daily papers, colour supplements, and magazines and broadcast by television. If however you were to ask a well-informed scientist to assess the total impact of this material he would be obliged to say that it presents a gravely distorted view of the reality.

The situation now is much more complicated than it was forty years ago. At that time, scientists usually had a rather receptive audience. Now, we are caught up in a maelstrom of politics and our task has become almost impossible.

Our main concern, as scientists, is to present the facts as clearly and accurately as possible, together with their implications. Unless the basic facts are reasonably well known there is no hope of making wise decisions. The scientist as such is therefore neither pronuclear nor anti-nuclear. We know that the facts are complicated, that our knowledge is always growing, and that new knowledge may oblige us to modify our conclusions. The only way to decide the best energy policy is to evaluate, as carefully and objectively as possible, the capacity, the cost, the safety, and the effects on the environment of each energy source and to compare the results. This must be done separately for each country or even part of a country; there are so many contributing factors that there is no single overall solution.

Even if we strive to be as objective as possible, scientists will still differ among themselves in their assessment of the situation. Some factors do not lend themselves to objective analysis, and personal judgment may affect the conclusion. How, for example, should one balance safety against cost? Even more difficult, what is the value of preserving some aspect of the environment? In addition there are political considerations such as the effect of energy policies on the likelihood of nuclear war.

However much a scientist tries to be objective and impartial, he will very easily be seen as partisan. As the views expressed in the media swing from one extreme to the other, the scientist, simply by striving to tell the truth, is at any one time almost always pulling one way, and that is against the media. In the days of uncritical enthusiasm for nuclear power, a scientist who ventured a word of caution would be branded as anti-nuclear. Now, with the media predominantly anti-nuclear, he inevitably appears to be pro-nuclear. Quite apart from this, there are indeed some scientists who are obviously partisan as a result of their employment by the nuclear industry or by some environmentalist group.

I want to make it quite clear that in this lecture I am not trying to argue the case for or against nuclear power; I have given my views on that question in other publications.[9] Here I am concerned with a different question, namely to what extent is it possible to discuss these matters at all in a reasonable and objective manner.

The reasons for the worsening of the nuclear debate are complicated, and include political and psychological considerations that I prefer to leave to others to consider in detail. I will concentrate on the factors more or less closely related to the scientific facts.

In the first place there has been in recent years a widespread reaction against the technological society. Many, while accepting its benefits, also see it as inhuman, ugly, and polluting; the mushroom cloud of the atomic bomb and the nuclear power station have been adopted as its symbols. Associated with this is the fear of the unknown that has hindered new developments throughout history. In some quarters there is a nostalgic yearning for the simple pastoral life, without much attempt to think out its implications.

Fear of the unknown particularly surrounds radioactivity. It is amusing to recall that soon after Madame Curie discovered radioactivity, the purveyors of mineral waters would proudly announce on the labels of their bottles that they contained radioactivity, a sure cure for numerous ills. You do not find such claims on bottles of mineral water today. The public image of radioactivity was decisively changed by Hiroshima and Nagasaki, when the horrified world first saw the hideous effects of high doses of nuclear radiation. The public reaction to radiation has gone from one extreme to the other. If there is a small leak of radioactivity from a nuclear

---

9 P. E. Hodgson, *Our Nuclear Future?* (London: Marshall Pickering, 1984).

reactor, alarmist stories are published. Such releases are followed by careful enquiry, and when it is subsequently explained that the radiation levels were never remotely harmful no one takes any notice. Radioactive releases are newsworthy; scientific explanations are not.

In this as in so many other matters the truth is only expressible numerically. The radiation dose must be measured, and only then can we know whether it is safe or not. Unfortunately most people are not familiar with numbers, and if you tell them they have just received a microsievert of nuclear radiation they don't know whether to laugh or scream. Here we encounter a basic obstacle to communication between scientists and the public. To the scientist the matter is extremely clear and simple; to the public it is impenetrably obscure.

The first observation to make is that nuclear radiations did not first enter our world as a result of the experiments of the nuclear physicists. Nuclear radiations are all around us, here and now. They are emitted from radioactive minerals in the earth and from radioactive materials in our bodies; we are subjected to a continuous bombardment of cosmic rays from outer space. This radiation has been present throughout the history of the earth, and there are speculations that it played an essential part in evolution.

Thus when we consider the extra radiation due to the nuclear industry we have first to ask ourselves how it compares with the radiation we receive already from natural sources. The answer is clear. Some recent figures for the United Kingdom are: from natural background radiation 186 millirem per year and from the nuclear industry 0.5 millirem per year. At this point it is frequently argued that since all nuclear radiations are harmful, any addition, however small, is wrong and must be avoided. In answer to this it must first be pointed out that it has never been proved that small doses of radiation are harmful; all we know for certain is that very large doses are harmful. Nevertheless, to be on the safe side, it is assumed in establishing radiation limits that the danger is proportional to the dose. This incidentally ignores another effect that is certainly present, namely the ability of an organism to repair the damage when the doses are small. Since it is known that the background radiation of 186 millirem per year is apparently harmless, it may be reasonably concluded that an extra dose of less than 1% is not any cause for concern.[10]

Any further doubts may be met by pointing out that the background radiation itself varies from one place to another, often by large amounts. In granite areas such as Cornwall the natural background may be twice the average. No one to my knowledge has ever cancelled a holiday in Cornwall on this account. In other parts of the world, in Brazil and on the monazite sands of Travancore, the natural background may be ten times normal, and even this has no detectable effects on the inhabitants.

One can point all this out a thousand times, and yet the next day another radiation scare story will appear and cause widespread dismay. This is not to say, of course, that we can afford to be complacent about radiation damage. It remains essential to take the greatest care of radioactive wastes so that they do not cause appreciable hazard.

A consequence of this reluctance to treat risks quantitatively is that people in general have very little appreciation of the relative importance of the risks they run each day. This was tested recently by presenting several people with a list of activities involving risk and asking them to rank them in order of seriousness. The risks were then ranked by experts and it was found that there was almost no similarity between the two lists. On the whole people worried about very small risks while ignoring serious ones. Risk assessment has now been developed to a reliable discipline, and yet its results are very poorly known.[11]

A notable example of this concerns the risks of generating electric power in various ways. It is possible to estimate the number of deaths and man-hours lost through injury associated with the main ways of generating electricity. The generation of a gigawatt year of energy claims on the average forty deaths for coal and ten for oil. By contrast, nuclear claims about one death (not from nuclear radiation) and

---

[10] Sir Walter Bodmer, *Science and Public Affairs* (2; 1987): 69.

[11] E. E. Pochin, "The Need to Estimate Risks," *Physics in Medicine and Biology* 25 (1; 1981). H. Inhaber, *Risk of Energy Production* (Ottawa: Atomic Energy Control Board, 1981).

wind and solar five each. Thus the so-called "benign renewables" are far more dangerous than nuclear, though less than coal and oil.

What is the nuclear physicist to do when confronted with this deluge of misinformation? He can try to make his voice heard amid the clamour, but it is not easy. Sensational articles and books proliferate and find a ready sale while factual information is largely ignored. The situation is made worse by a disinclination to listen to anything that goes against the popular misconceptions.

As an illustration of this I recall an attempt to discuss the effects of nuclear radiations with a well-known politician. In a public speech, he said that if there were an accident at a proposed nuclear power station in Britain similar to that at Three Mile Island there would be some thousands of deaths from cancer. This figure seemed rather high to me, so I wrote to him asking if he would kindly tell me how these figures were obtained. I added that I would be grateful to him for his permission to quote his reply.

He answered saying that he regretted that he could not find the documents that he had used to obtain these figures, but he assured me that at the time he made the statement he had the authority on which he could have relied if his statement had been questioned.

Meanwhile, I found that Dr. Martin Goldman of the Energy-Related Health Research Laboratory of the University of California had obtained a figure of 0.4 extra cases of cancer in the surrounding area due to the Three Mile Island accident. I quoted this to him, and added that this figure is inconsistent with the ones he had quoted, so that his statement could give rise to unnecessary public anxiety. I expressed my regret that he had been unable to justify his figures, and asked if he had any further comments to make.

In his reply he began by saying that he regarded my letter as impertinent, adding that he was quite certain that he would be able to find the source of his figures. He went on to say that if I had done a little more research I would have found the source myself. He recommended that I seek out a certain doctor, whose name he was unfortunately not able to recall, who had been making many public statements on the public hazards of radiation. He added that if I was not too lazy I could easily do this, but concluded that he doubted if I would take the trouble to do so.

I therefore decided to repeat the calculations for myself. Published figures show that the accident at Three Mile Island increased the average radiation dose to the people in the surrounding area by about one millirem. Reviews by the National Academy of Sciences and the United Nations give an estimate of the cancer risk as about 100 cases per million person-rem. Thus for every million people we expect an additional 100/1,000 or one-tenth of a case. This figure is quite similar to that of Dr. Goldman. I wrote a further letter saying this, but received no reply.

About a week later, I read an article in *Atom* that refers to some writing of a scientist in the United States who obtained figures for the number of extra deaths from the Three Mile Accident that are very similar to those originally quoted. It was further explained how these figures were obtained from the published data by an elementary statistical error. The actual figures showed no evidence of any effect attributable to the accident. I therefore sent a copy of this article to the politician, but received no reply.

Subsequently I found many more articles containing detailed estimates of the number of casualties attributable to the accident. All were consistent with a small number, probably less than one. I sent copies of these articles to the politician, requesting his comments, but again received no reply.[12]

It is of course true that politicians are very busy people, and it is always tiresome to have one's views challenged. But the scientist knows very well that it is always important to listen to adverse criticism because he might be wrong. Indeed we should welcome it, because who in their senses wants to go on saying things that are not true? And yet it is undoubtedly the case that there are many people, including some in high places, whose minds are so firmly closed that they are unable to entertain the possibility that they are wrong, or to listen to

---

[12] I have not named the politician concerned, partly because I have no wish to criticize personalities as such, and partly because he indignantly refused my request for permission to quote from his letters.

•

any counterarguments. This makes it quite impossible to carry out the reasoned dialogue that is the only way of reaching the truth.

No physicist would want his views to be accepted without critical discussion; indeed he welcomes it because he knows only too well from his own experiences in physics that this is the only way to truth. But after a few experiences of the type related he is inclined to decide that his time may be more profitably spent, and concentrate on his academic work.

The present situation concerning the public debate on nuclear matters is quite unlike the research and teaching situation with which the scientist is familiar. In scientific research, the results are published in scientific journals, and great efforts are made to ensure that they are clear and accurate. Other scientists read them, and it is taken for granted that scientists working in a particular field are familiar with the papers that have been published. Subsequent research and the papers describing it take account of previous work and refer to it. In this way a coherent body of knowledge is gradually built up. In teaching science, lecturers try to be as clear as possible and to present a balanced and accurate account. The students listen, ask questions if they do not understand, and study the answers. This is how they learn.

The public debate on nuclear matters is completely different from this. The aim of most writing is to scare, to create a sensation, or to promote a politically orientated conclusion. Articles and letters are frequently one-sided or erroneous. People write with great confidence, but they frequently know very little about the subject. There is no accepted accurate body of knowledge that is taken as the basis of discussion.

Scientists who feel that it is their duty to provide some factual information thus encounter an unfamiliar situation. It is in the first place very difficult to get factual articles published; editors want sensational stories, and frequently they have been influenced by antinuclear activists who see to it that the factual articles are rejected. If the scientist persists, he may eventually get it published; frequently he finds that it has been altered and even rewritten without his knowledge, and in the next issue there is a barrage of ill-informed criticism. If he finds time to answer this, his letters are cut or ignored. If he points out to the editor that this is really not a good way to promote public understanding of grave issues, and that it would be better not to publish those ill-informed letters, he is liable to be told that such discussion is healthy and democratic. It is no wonder that most scientists soon abandon the task as a waste of time. I could give very many examples of this, but here one must suffice.

Soon after the Chernobyl accident there was a leading article in a prominent daily newspaper reporting a large increase in the death rate in the United States due to the dust from Chernobyl, complete with a large picture of Death the Reaper. It was obvious that this was extremely unlikely because such no effects had been reported from Europe, where the amount of dust deposited was much larger, though still far below that likely to cause any detectable effects. The article was however supported by statistical data apparently showing a strong correlation between the amount of dust deposited and the death rate in several areas.

Since the story seemed to be unlikely, I contacted the Atomic Energy Research Establishment at Harwell, and asked them to obtain the detailed figures for me. This took some time, and when they arrived it was clear that the figures had been obtained by statistical fudging, and that they showed no effect whatsoever. I wrote to the newspaper, but was told that it was now so long ago that everyone would have forgotten all about it and so no action could be taken to correct the story. It is, however, more than likely that they remember the association between nuclear power and Death the Reaper.

My experiences with the Church have been somewhat mixed. The editor of the *Fact and Faith* books, Lancelot Sheppard, invited me to contribute to the series, and I wrote a book titled *Nuclear Physics in Peace and War*.[13] Subsequently, Professor Torrance invited me to contribute to the series of books, *Theology and Scientific Culture*, and I wrote *Our Nuclear Future*.[14] Several monthly journals

---

[13] P. E. Hodgson, *Nuclear Physics in Peace and War* (London: Burns and Oates, Hawthorn Books, 1961).

[14] P. E. Hodgson, *Our Nuclear Future?* (Belfast: Christian Journals, 1983).

such as *The Month, New Blackfriars,* and *The Clergy Review* have published articles on nuclear power and the environment.

Other experiences have not been so good. The Catholic newspapers tend to accept the misconceptions of the secular media, and it is often impossible to present a balanced view without it being contradicted in a subsequent issue, with no opportunity for reply.

I once wrote a booklet, *World Energy Needs and Resources,* and sent it to a leading Catholic publisher. Subsequently, I was told that it could not be accepted because it was contrary to the statement of the English and Welsh bishops. I asked for a copy of this statement, and was told that it was to be found in a periodical called *Briefings,* which however was confidential. I therefore wrote to a few bishops known personally to me, asking about their teaching on nuclear power. Many of them thought that I was asking about nuclear weapons, but those who read my letter all said that they knew nothing about this statement, even the bishop who lectured on energy affairs. After some detective work I found out that my booklet had been sent for refereeing to a Jesuit scientist, a distinguished Catholic nuclear physicist, and a lawyer. The Jesuit and the physicist recommended publication but the lawyer made the objection already mentioned. Eventually I obtained a copy of the issue of *Briefings* that contained the statement in question, and found that it was brief, trivial, unbalanced, and innumerate. Who then wrote it? Not one of our bishops, or a committee appointed by them to examine the problem, but the aforesaid lawyer, a member of an anti-nuclear group. Meanwhile I had sent my booklet to a non-Catholic Christian publisher, and it was published without any difficulties.[15] This shows how simple-minded scientists are easily outmanoeuvered by clever lawyers.

From such experiences one learns that it is difficult for scientists to contribute to the public debate on matters related to our specialised knowledge. It is a great mistake to assume that our contributions will be welcomed. If what we say is contrary to the agenda of some pressure group, we will have great difficulty in even obtaining a

---

15 P. E. Hodgson, *World Energy Needs and Resources,* Grove Booklet on Ethics, vol. 44 (Bramcote: Grove Books, 1981).

hearing. No sensible scientist would want his views to be taken on trust, but he does expect them to be given a hearing. He is familiar with what happens within scientific research: new ideas are put forward and subjected to rigorous criticism and testing until eventually the truth becomes clear. No one stands on ceremony or defers to authority: the sole object is to find out the truth. The public debate on scientific questions should also be like this. However, this sort of debate very rarely happens; usually one realizes that one is dealing with people who do not know, who do not know that they do not know, and who do not even know what knowing means.

It is however important to ask why such a situation has arisen. Why is there this widespread distrust of anything connected with nuclear physics? One of the most potent causes of the general aversion to nuclear activities is undoubtedly the regrettable circumstance that it was the atomic bomb that first brought the word "nuclear" into general circulation. There was thus established in people's minds an unbreakable link between violent explosions and nuclear power stations. There was indeed a time in the nineteen fifties, particularly after the Atoms for Peace Conference in Geneva, when there was great public euphoria about nuclear power, but this has now faded. The link with bombs is still strong in the public imagination, and it is thought that nuclear power stations can explode just like nuclear bombs, which is physically impossible.

Then there is the associated fear of nuclear radiations, which has already been mentioned. If this were all, we could derive some comfort from the history of similar protest movements in the past. They are present in every generation. They opposed gaslight, they opposed vaccination, they drove Semmelweiss insane, they opposed steam trains, they opposed airplanes, and now they oppose nuclear power. While they were shouting and protesting, the future was being built by quiet and determined men. The railways, as George Stephenson foretold, became the "great highway of the world," and electric light soon became generally accepted. The same is happening with nuclear power; last year it overtook coal as the major generator of electricity in the EEC.

This success is not however sufficient to carry general conviction. The opposition to nuclear power has behind it powerful political forces, who do their best to discredit the scientist. They know that he has access to the factual knowledge that provides the most cogent arguments against their propaganda, so if he can be discredited they will be able to spread their views unchecked. The most basic of these attempts is the attack on the objectivity of science. I am occasionally informed, after one of my attempts to convey a few facts about nuclear energy, that my views are "value-laden." This means, I discovered, that our views on the optimum energy sources derive from our political convictions. We may, for example, dislike nuclear power because it has been instrumental in reducing the influence of the coal miners or because it is part of the capitalist economy. We may prefer wind and solar power because they are homely, small-scale, and familiar, and seem to be clean and safe. These are the considerations that must decide our energy policy; the rest concerns technical details that must be worked out by those who know about such things. And indeed there are people who appear to think along these lines.

Many participants in the nuclear debate are often very assiduous in collecting arguments against this or that method of energy generation, but neglect to discuss it in the wider context of energy needs and the available alternatives. In this country the CEGB has the statutory obligation to provide electricity economically and safely, and if it fails the lights will go out. If anyone objects, then the onus is on them to explain exactly how the demand can be met in other ways; to fail to do this is to act irresponsibly.

One of the most important values associated with this debate is the right of everyone to sufficient energy to maintain their dignity as human beings. Electricity has already lifted many of the burdens of life, especially for women. Without energy, we would not be able to heat our homes or cook our food. Long distance travel and communication would be drastically changed, and our factories could no longer produce the goods that we need. The world demand for energy has increased rapidly due to the population increase and the overall rise in living standards. Globally the world population is doubling every thirty-five years and energy use every fourteen years. Furthermore, energy use differs from energy need: much energy is wasted in the richer countries, while the poorer ones lack the minimum needed for an acceptable lifestyle. It is not surprising that people in the poorer countries want the same benefits, and do not appreciate lectures on the virtues of the simple life from people in affluent countries.

There remains the problem of finding out what is the truth. Attempts are often made by well-meaning bodies to contribute to the public debate on scientific questions by organizing conferences to which the advocates of various views are invited. The lectures are then printed as a contribution to the debate. But as all views are presented, what is needed is an objective analysis of the debate, followed by the drawing of conclusions that can be the basis of action. This essential final step is usually lacking. Who is to draw the conclusions? Presumably a scientist of great distinction. I recall a well-organized conference at which two very distinguished physicists, Hans Bethe and Hannes Alfven, both Nobel prizewinners, gave the arguments for and against nuclear power. There was no attempt to weigh these lectures against each other. Yet every nuclear physicist is well aware that one of these men has made most distinguished and weighty contributions to nuclear physics for the last fifty years, while the other has made distinguished contributions to magneto-hydrodynamics, but not to nuclear physics. Thus one spoke with immense authority whereas the other did not. This was not of course clear to those attending the conference who concluded that since such distinguished experts disagreed there was much uncertainty on the whole subject.[16]

Another source of confusion is the anti-expert, that is a scientist, who, for various reasons, does all he can to discredit the general expert consensus. He knows enough of the terminology to impress those unfamiliar with the subject, and is adept at gathering data that suit his case and presenting it in a one-sided way that supports

---

[16] *Anticipation* (24; 1977).

his views. This further muddies the waters and makes it very difficult for the non-expert to arrive at the truth.

In some countries a misguided form of democracy has led to the appointment of equal numbers of experts and anti-experts on committees formed to decide some matter of public interest. Professor Maier-Leibnitz has described what happened in Germany, where parliament established a commission of enquiry for the future of atomic energy with an equal number of experts and anti-experts.

> The result was a great mass of paper, minutes of meetings, opinions, counter-opinions, responses and counter-responses. Everything was discussed and nothing became clear. And what is worse, the experts were the best experts that could be found, so there was nobody left who could have given a final opinion. Is this the end of technical advice to a parliament?[17]

Another obstacle to the spread of truth is the apparently insatiable public appetite for the bizarre and the sensational. A recent article by Mr. Adrian Berry reveals what he calls the modern law of publishing: that there can be a direct link between the sales of a book and the enormity of the falsehood that it contains. Why do publishers accept what they know to be false? Mr. Berry asked one of them and he replied, "It was a commercial decision." That describes the present situation in publishing ethics: if you write a book packed with sensational lies you will sell by the million, if you stick closely to the facts you will sell a few thousand if you are lucky. Gardner has recounted the occasion when he protested against the broadcasting of outrageous pseudo-documentaries. He recalls that "one official shouted in anger, 'I'll produce anything that gets high ratings.'"[18] It is just the same in the nuclear field: write a sensational book about the horrors of nuclear radiations and the devastation of nuclear war and your paperback will be on the bookstalls; write an accurate factual survey and your work will remain completely unknown.

---

[17] See P. E. Hodgson, "The Objectivity of Science," *Month* 18 (1985): 256; *Our Nuclear Future* (London: Marshall Pickering, 1984), 122.

[18] Martin Gardner, *Science: Good, Bad and Bogus* (Buffalo, NY: Prometheus, 1981).

The result of all this is that the scientists have lost the battle to convey the facts about nuclear physics to the society in which they live. The way this happened in the United States has been well described by Professor Bernard Cohen in a recent book that deserves to be widely read:

First let's consider the cast of characters in the battle. The two sides are of an entirely different ilk. One of the main interests in life for a typical anti-nuclear activist is political battling, while the vast majority of nuclear scientists have no inclination or interests in political battling, and even if they did they have little native ability or educational preparation for it. . . . While the former was making political contacts and developing know-how in securing media co-operation, the latter was absorbed in labora-tory or field problems with no thought of politics or media involvement. At this juncture the former went out looking for a new battle to fight and decided to attack the latter; it was like a lion attacking a lamb.

Nuclear scientists had long agonised over such questions as what safety measures were needed in power plants, and what health impacts their radioactivity releases might cause. All the arguments were published for anyone to see. It took little effort for the anti-nuclear activists to collect, organize selectively, and distort this information into ammunition for their battle. Anyone experienced in debate and political battles is well prepared to do that. When they charged into the battle wildly firing this ammu-nition, the nuclear scientists first laughed at the *naiveté* of the charges, but they didn't laugh for long. They could easily explain the invalidity of the attacks by scientific and technical arguments, but no one would listen to them. The phony charges of the attackers dressed up with their considerable skills in presentation sounded much better to the media and others with no scientific knowledge or experience. When people wanted to hear from sci-entists, the attackers supplied their own—there are always a few available to present any point of view, and who was to know that they represented only a very tiny minority of the scientific com-munity. The anti-nuclear activists never even let it be made clear who they were and whom they were attacking. The battle was *not* billed as a bunch of scientifically illiterate political activists attacking the community of nuclear scientists, which is the true situation. It was rather represented as "environmentalists"—what a good, sweet, and pure connotation that name carries—attacking big business interests (the nuclear industry) that were trying to make money at the expense of the public's health and safety.

The rout was rapid and complete. In fact the nuclear scientists were never even allowed on the battlefield. The battlefield here was the media, which alone have the power to influence public opinion. The media establishment swallowed the attackers' story, hook, line, and sinker, becoming their allies. They freely and continually gave exposure to the anti-nuclear activists but never gave the nuclear scientists a chance. With constant exposure to this one-sided propaganda, the public was slowly but surely won over. The public was driven insane over fear of radiation; it became convinced of the utterly and demonstrably false notion that nuclear power was more likely to kill them than such well-known killers as motor vehicle accidents, cigarette smoking, and alcohol; that burying nuclear waste, actually a very simple operation, was one of the world's great unsolved problems; that, contrary to all informed sources, the Three Mile Island accident was a close call to a disaster and so on. Fears of everything connected with nuclear power were blown completely out of perspective with other risks. Hitler's man, Goebbels, had shown what propaganda can do, but the nuclear scientists never believed that it could succeed against the rationalism of science; yet succeed it did. The victory of the anti-nuclear activists was complete.

The anti-nuclear activists have won their battle, and to the victors belong the spoils—the failure of nuclear science to provide the cheap and abundant energy we sorely need. That is the goal they cherished and they have achieved it. Our children and grandchildren will be the victims of their heartless tactics. When Shakespeare said, "The truth will out," he didn't reckon with the power of the modern media.[19]

---

[19] Bernard Cohen, *Before It's Too Late: A Scientist's Case for Nuclear Energy* (New York: Plenum Press, 1983).

This extract captures very well the exasperation of the nuclear scientist at the present situation concerning the public discussion of nuclear power. Anti-nuclear activists see the situation in an entirely different light. They also are exasperated because in spite of all their protests nuclear power stations are still being built in many countries. The establishment seems to be impervious to their arguments, secretive about its activities, and inclined to publish only a whitewashed version of what is going on.

The tragedy is that these two groups rarely listen to each other. The scientists have a massive body of facts that must be taken seriously. The activists have genuine fears that deserve objective and sympathetic analysis. Attempts by scientists to establish a useful dialogue almost always fail.

This can be illustrated by some recent events in Britain, in particular the Sizewell enquiry, the reactions to the Chernobyl accident, and the nuclear policies presented to the electorate at the recent election.

After reviewing the likely energy needs over the next decade, the Central Electricity Generating Board applied for permission to build a nuclear power station at Sizewell. In response to public pressure, the government of the day set up an exceedingly thorough and lengthy public enquiry. Every possible argument for and against was discussed, and the final transcript ran to over sixteen million words. The assessor, Sir Frank Layfield, took a long time to draft his report but when he had considered all the evidence he recommended that permission to build the reactor be granted. This was not to the liking of the anti-nuclear lobby, who immediately rejected his report, without detailed discussion of his reasons.

The case for rejection was strengthened by the Chernobyl accident, which occurred while Sir Frank was drafting his report. The accident was a serious blow to the supporters of nuclear power. It exposed the overoptimism of their statements to the effect that a major reactor disaster was almost impossible, and showed once again the importance of the human factor. The reactor briefly went critical, the power level surged upward, the graphite moderator caught fire, and a plume of radioactive smoke went high into the atmosphere and spread over all Europe. The important point for us, however, is whether such an accident could happen to any existing nuclear power station. As the facts became known, it was realized that the design of the reactor was inherently unsatisfactory, and would never have been accepted in the West. Furthermore, the reactor operators had flagrantly disobeyed their operating instructions. On the fatal night the operators wanted to make an experiment on the reactor and to prevent the reactor from automatically shutting down they switched off the safety circuits. Inevitably disaster followed. To oppose nuclear power because of Chernobyl is like opposing modern cruise liners because of the Titanic.

It is now clear that the design of the reactor should never have been adopted, and that its safety should have been ensured not by instructions to fallible operators but by fail-safe design.[20]

Heroic efforts were made to control the reactor, and many of the firefighters received lethal doses of radioactivity. A total of thirty-three deaths resulted, and since then another twelve have died from delayed effects. The radioactivity spread over Europe was at such a low intensity that it caused little damage. The area around the reactor remains quite highly radioactive, and many people who were evacuated from their homes are still not allowed to return. There are still many stories in the press about the damage due to the radioactivity, and many detailed studies have been made.

During the period from 1969 to 1986, there were over 6,000 deaths due to oil-related accidents; over 5,000 from hydropower; nearly 4,000 from coal; and over 3,000 from gas. These figures are to be compared with the 45 from Chernobyl.[21]

Another current cause of concern is the clusters of cases of leukaemia around nuclear centres. On general grounds it is difficult to understand how there could be any causal connection because the additional irradiation attributable to the nuclear centres is a very small addition to the natural background that is there all the time. Statistical analyses provide no firm ground for believing that the

---

[20] *Nuclear Issues* 22:12 (December 2000).
[21] Ibid., 6 (4; June 1985).

numbers of extra cases are significant. Extensive studies over the whole country have now shown that there are even larger clusters of cases in areas where there are no nuclear centres. This suggests that their causes are non-nuclear, and a chemical agent or a virus have been suggested as possibilities to be investigated. An alternative explanation, due to Kinlen, is that the excess leukaemia cases, where they occur, are due to viral effects connected with the movement of populations, and have been supported by studies of similar effects in regions not associated with nuclear installations. These possibilities are seldom mentioned by the media, and it has been suggested that by concentrating on nuclear radiation the opponents of nuclear power have hampered the search for the real cause.

An example of how the media campaigns have led to decisions being taken on political rather than on scientific grounds is provided by the story of the ocean disposal of radioactive waste. Two years ago the London Dumping Convention voted for a moratorium "to allow time for the completion of scientific studies of the suitability of carefully selected and controlled ocean dumping sites for the acceptance of low level wastes." Now the work has been completed, it is clear that the "risks associated with the continued dumping at the previous levels, and even at a level ten times higher, are vanishingly small and quite trivial compared with other natural and man-made risks." In spite of this the LDC voted recently to extend its moratorium on dumping, showing that it is impervious to scientific arguments. Meanwhile huge quantities of poisonous chemicals and untreated sewage are dumped in the sea with hardly any protest.[22]

These debates formed the background to the General Election in 1987. It was clear that the general public was deeply worried about nuclear power, so this was one of the issues that was prominent in the manifestos of the contending parties.[23] One might have hoped that they would be based on established facts, and then go on to describe

---

[22] Ibid.

[23] *Civil Nuclear: Statement adopted by the Labour Party Conference,* 1986. *Politics Today No 8. Energy: Developing Britain's Resources,* Conservative Research Department.

their parties' energy policy in the light of perceived needs over the next few years. Examination of the published documents shows however that this is not the case, and that the parties were influenced by purely political considerations.

The Labour Party document was based on resolutions passed at the last Party Conference, which called for a halt to the nuclear power programme and the phasing out of all existing plants. It promises to stop the new Advanced Gas-Cooled Reactors at Torness and Heysham if they are not already operating, to cancel the Sizewell contract, and not to buy electricity generated by French nuclear power stations. Instead, it promises to develop coal, to promote energy efficiency, and to develop alternative energy sources. Given public apprehension about nuclear power, this is clearly a programme likely to appeal to the electorate.

What was lacking, unfortunately, was any attempt to show that such a programme is practicable, and to spell out the consequences. No attempt was made to put numbers to the capacities and costs and safety of the possible power sources, or to evaluate the social consequences of the programme. The alternative energy sources make an insignificant contribution to our present energy needs, and there is no hope of any substantial improvement in the forseeable future. They are also uneconomic, much more hazardous than is commonly realized, and damaging to the environment. Combined with the refusal to buy French nuclear electricity, this programme seems very likely to increase the cost of our power, thus handicapping our industry and leading to increased unemployment. It is astonishing that a party that aspires to govern the country should seriously advocate such policies. Yet presumably it does so because it is a popular policy, showing once again the power of the media and how it has become saturated by unbalanced information.

The Conservative Party documents are packed with facts and figures and on the whole give a much clearer assessment of our future energy needs and the pros and cons of the various possible energy sources. Safety is considered in detail, and it is recognized that every form of energy has its hazards. The energy policies of

Britain are considered, as they should be, in the context of world energy needs, bearing in mind the needs of the third world countries. All these considerations tend to support the continuation of the present energy policies.

To some extent these party documents reflect the preoccupations of the two parties, the one to obtain power, and the other to defend its record. Nevertheless there is a startling difference between them, and careful study would repay any student of the political scene. It should be added that the government, just before the election, decided to shelve its plans for the burial of radioactive waste, which had caused bitter controversy in several constituencies. This was, perhaps unjustly, seen as a purely political decision, quite contrary to the scientific evidence about the safety of underground disposal.

These and many other examples show that vital decisions concerning our future are being taken not as a result of careful analysis of the facts but in response to media pressure. This means in practical terms that dangerous and uneconomic policies are being adopted, that people are being killed and injured unnecessarily, in order to satisfy a gravely ill-informed public opinion.

If you are shocked by this you may ask what can be done about it. I am sorry to say that I do not have any solution to offer. My aim in this lecture is to draw attention to the unreality of the nuclear debate. I am sure that much of what is said is gravely misleading; I am much less sure what can be done about it. It is not an easy problem and I have no easy answers.

It is now time to draw these reflections to a close.

There is a certain irreversibility in human affairs. You may regret that Columbus discovered America, or you may not. It makes no difference; America is there, an inevitable part of our lives. It is the same with the intellectual discoveries of man, from the wheel to nuclear fission. You may regret the coming of the railways, or of electricity. Very well, if you are rich enough you may indulge your nostalgia by traveling on horseback and illuminating your home with candles. But for the great majority of men there is no practicable option. A leaf has been turned in the book of history. Such a leaf was turned in 1942 when the potentialities of nuclear fission were realized.

The turning of such a leaf means no more, but also no less, than the presence of a new power in our lives. We cannot banish it without further consideration, neither must it be used with uncritical enthusiasm. It must be considered along with the existing powers and evaluated by the same criteria. We must ask how it compares for practicability, for economy, for safety, for adverse environmental effects. Such comparisons require the services of many experts, and among these the nuclear physicist must be included.

What I have tried to say in this lecture is extremely simple:

1. We cannot hope to make wise decisions about peace, or indeed about anything else, unless we first know the facts.

2. The media, and hence the public consciousness, is now saturated with false information about nuclear physics and related questions.

3. Those who know the facts find it almost impossible to make their voices heard.

4. This is exceedingly dangerous for our society.

In this situation the responsibility of the nuclear physicist for peace remains, in the words of Hans Morgenthau, to speak truth to power: "For those who have made it their business to speak truth to power, there is nothing left but to continue so to speak, less frequently perhaps than they used to and certainly with less confidence that it will in the short run make much of a difference in the affairs of men."[24]

Perhaps we should not be too surprised that the clear voice of reason is so difficult to hear among the clamour of ideologies, that it is almost drowned by the flood of emotive propaganda. In the words of a son of our university, John Henry Newman: "Quarry the

---

[24] Hans J. Morgenthau, *Truth and Power* (London: Pall Mall Press, 1970).

granite rock with razors, moor the vessel with a thread of silk, and then you may hope with such keen and delicate instruments as human knowledge and human reason to contend against those giants, the passion and the pride of man."[25] ⚛

---

[25] J. H. Newman, "The Idea of a University" (1854). In *Essays, English and American,* Harvard Classics, no. XXVI (New York: P. F. Collier & Son, ca. 1910).

CHAPTER 22

The First Nuclear Era[*]

FROM THE EARLIEST DAYS of the Oak Ridge National Laboratory, Alvin Weinberg was one of the pioneers of nuclear reactor development. He was one of the designers of early reactors and proposed the pressurized-water reactor. Together with Wigner, he wrote the classic book *The Physical Theory of Nuclear Chain Reactors.* He directed Oak Ridge from 1955 to 1973 and later on the Institute for Energy Analysis. Few, if any, are as well qualified as he to tell the story of the development of nuclear reactors, with all its hopes and disappointments, successes and failures.

The early research at the Metallurgial Laboratory of the University of Chicago was directed to the construction of nuclear reactors to make plutonium for the bomb. There were many difficult engineering problems to solve. What form should the uranium take, and how should the moderator be placed? What degree of purity is needed, and how should the reactor be cooled? These and many other problems were solved largely empirically, relying particularly on Wigner's deep physical insight and engineering skill. There was no time for pilot plant studies; full-scale reactors were built immediately, at Hanford on the Columbia River, to provide the necessary cooling water, and these provided the plutonium for the second atomic bomb.

---

[*] A review of *The First Nuclear Era: The Life and Times of a Technological Fixer* by Alvin M. Weinberg (College Park, MD: American Institute of Physics, 1995), reprinted with permission from *Contemporary Physics* (36; 1995): 197.

It had been obvious, from Fermi's first achievement of a self-sustaining chain reaction in his experimental reactor at Chicago in 1942, that here was potentially a great source of power for the future. Weinberg was filled with enthusiasm at the prospect of providing unlimited power for the world's needs, and thus removing one of the principal causes of conflict. It was a supreme example of what he called a technological fix.

There are very many different types of reactor, depending on the fissile material, the coolant, and the moderator. The fissile material can be uranium 233 or 235 or plutonium 239; the coolant may be water, heavy water, gas, or liquid metal; and the moderator may be water, heavy water, beryllium, or graphite. Weinberg estimates that there are about one thousand different possibilities. It is not easy to decide which one to build. Once the choice is made, a huge engineering effort is needed to bring the idea to fruition and to make it economically viable. It is impracticable to try out a large number of possibilities so the initial choice determines the whole future of the enterprise. The more effort devoted to a particular type, the more attractive it becomes; this is essentially the reason for the present dominance of the light-water reactors.

At that time it was believed that the reserves of uranium were rather small, certainly insufficient to support a large worldwide nuclear programme. Weinberg therefore believed that the future of nuclear power depended on the development of breeder reactors, and indeed the first civil reactor in November 1968 was a fast-neutron breeder. Subsequently, however, it was realized that the uranium reserves are much greater than previously thought; they are limited only by the price that one is prepared to pay. Thus the technically more difficult breeder reactors were given a lower priority, although they remain the reactors of the future when eventually the price of uranium makes thermal reactors less economic.

Much of the early work at Oak Ridge was devoted to the development of reactors for submarines and for airplanes. Admiral Rickover energetically pushed the submarine programme and chose the pressurized-water reactor as the best option. This was successfully developed and powered the first nuclear submarine and also served as the prototype for the most popular type of civil reactor.

A reactor-powered plane was quite a different matter. Instinctively Weinberg, together with the other reactor designers, balked at the idea, but it was strongly pushed by the very powerful U.S. Air Force. The need for the reactor to be compact led to the choice of a high-temperature reactor with liquid-metal cooling and the uranium dissolved in molten alkali fluorides. While this design was not quite impracticable, the difficulties were so great that the project was eventually abandoned. Nevertheless it did have some useful spin-offs; the extensive work on molten fluoride and high-temperature alloys was one of Oak Ridge's most outstanding achievements.

At that time there was enormous enthusiasm for nuclear reactors. They were going to solve the world's energy problems. The early estimates of construction costs by the U.S. utilities were very optimistic, and there was talk of electricity too cheap to monitor. At a very early stage, Fermi sounded a warning note, when he asked whether society would be willing to accept the price, in particular the production of unprecedentedly large amounts of highly radioactive material and also the possibility of diversion of plutonium for bombs. In the prevailing euphoria he was not heeded, but subsequent developments showed how prescient he was.

It was indeed realized from the first that the disposal of radioactive wastes is a serious problem, but Weinberg admits that it was always treated as a side issue that did not merit the attention of the most sophisticated people. The waste disposal methods seemed good enough at the time; storage in concrete tanks for the highly radioactive effluents and shallow burial for the slightly radioactive waste. The radiation levels were carefully monitored, but the allowable levels were much higher than those in force today. Weinberg speculates that if they had paid more attention to waste disposal in the early days that issue would not loom so large today.

The practicability of commercial nuclear power depended on economics: How does the cost compare with that of fossil fuels? Even today the answer is not clear in the U.S., but the situation is quite different in Europe, particularly in countries such as France where there is no practicable alternative. Early estimates of the cost of reactors in the U.S. were very encouraging, and many reactors were built. The 515-MW boiling-water reactor built by General Electric in 1964 was priced at US$129 per KW, US$20 less than a contemporary 900-MW coal-fired plant. Similarly low prices were quoted by Westinghouse and by Babcock and Wilcox. Experience showed, however, that environmental concerns and the need for precision engineering pushed the costs up to an uneconomic level, and so fewer and fewer reactors were built

The success of nuclear-powered submarines, for which economic considerations were not critical, encouraged the construction of nuclear-powered surface ships. The *N. S. Savannah* was launched in 1959 and operated as a container ship for a few years but was eventually found to be uneconomic. Nuclear-powered ships built in Germany and in Japan were also unsuccessful.

If indeed nuclear reactors are a source of cheap power, there are several other applications worth considering, the first being the desalination of sea water. Very large plants were envisaged to take advantage of the economies of scale, and they would generate electricity as well as evaporate sea water. Once again, practicability depends on economics, and which looked very promising at the earlier optimistic price levels. This was in 1967, after the Six-Day War, and the idea was to build several large reactors in Egypt, Israel, and Jordan to make the deserts bloom and thus remove many of the causes of conflict in the Middle East. These plans came to naught; the political will was lacking and the rising costs made nuclear desalting plants uneconomic compared with those using gas and oil. In the nuclear euphoria of the 1960s, many other possible applications of nuclear reactors to industrial processes were considered, such as the production of ammonia, iron, aluminum, and steel, and also gasoline from coal. All in the end proved uneconomic.

Weinberg, fired with the vision of unlimited cheap energy, played a major role in pushing these projects. He regarded nuclear energy "as a symbol of a new, technologically orientated civilization—the ultimate technological fix that would forever eliminate quarrels over scarce raw materials." The basic idea of a technological fix is the use of technological means to solve social problems. He saw nuclear desalting as solving the problems of the Middle East, and the hydrogen bomb as stabilizing the relations between the U.S. and the U.S.S.R. He proposed television and air conditioning to reduce ghetto riots and was criticized for tackling symptoms but not root causes, often also incurring unwanted side effects. The dream faded as the costs of building reactors escalated.

He now wonders why he ever accepted those overoptimistic costs estimates: "I suppose it was because we wanted to believe. We were the tiny group who started nuclear energy; it was only human for us to view nuclear energy as a great technical boon for humanity. Eliminating the Malthusian crises, making deserts bloom, burning the rocks—all these seemed to be within our grasp." Harsh reality destroyed this dream; it was what he called the end of the first nuclear era.

His intense disappointment is very understandable, but he could well reflect that without burning enthusiasm nothing ever gets done, and all new ideas deserve to be pushed to the limit and beyond to find out what is practicable and what is not. It may well be that nuclear power is still doubtfully economic in the U.S., but its prospects are far more favourable in other countries. Furthermore, nuclear plants are almost non-polluting, and this is likely to be counted increasingly in their favour as anxiety rises concerning acid rain and the greenhouse effect.

During the late 1950s and 1960s, as many as thirty countries established their own nuclear power programmes, so that there are now over 400 power reactors worldwide. The international enthusiasm for nuclear power was greatly encouraged by the four International Conferences on the Peaceful Uses of Atomic Energy that were held in Geneva in 1955, 1958, 1963, and 1971. The first conference took place just after President Eisenhower had met Bulganin and Khruschev in Geneva. The superpower summit and the conference on atoms for peace were universally seen as part of the spirit of detente. Oak Ridge built a reactor in Geneva that was the highlight of the conference. Nuclear power was presented as a panacea for an energy-hungry world. Extensive discussions took place on uranium resources, the nuclear properties of fissile isotopes, power reactors, research reactors, waste disposal, chemical reprocessing, metallurgy, applications of isotopes, and radiobiology. The fifteen volumes of the conference proceedings still constitute a comprehensive hand-book of nuclear science and engineering. However, as Weinberg remarks, there was hardly any discussion of the possibility that the problems mentioned by Fermi in 1951, the disposal of the immense amounts of radioactivity and the dangers of nuclear proliferation, might ultimately prove intractable.

The mood of optimism persisted through the second and third Geneva conferences, but by the fourth there had accumulated more experience of building and operating reactors. Although the mood was still generally optimistic, there was more realism about nuclear costs and the problems of waste disposal.

Weinberg believes that nuclear wastes are far less hazardous than the reactors themselves. Reactors contain huge amounts of radioactivity and heat energy. If a reactor is badly designed and treated irresponsibly, the radioactivity can be spread widely and cause immense damage.

The biological effects of extremely small amounts of radiation is a continuing source of controversy. Whether they can cause harm is what Weinberg calls a trans-scientific question. This is a question that has the same structure as a genuine scientific question but can-not be answered scientifically. Thus, for example, the question what the effect is on a human population of a dose of 400 rems has a def-inite answer: about half will die. However, the question what is the effect of 400 microrems cannot be answered because, if it exists, it is so small that it is undetectable. Similar questions could be asked for any poisonous substance. It is sometimes argued that we cannot prove that there are no deleterious effects but, as Weinberg remarks, thousands of women were burnt as witches because they could not prove that they had not caused harm.

Reliance on proportionality leads to the large numbers that are sometimes quoted as the result of radioactive releases. Thus the BBC has claimed that thousands of people have died as a result of the Chernobyl accident, whereas the real figure is 45. A complaint was made to the BBC, and they accepted that they had made a serious error, and the BBC news editor was told the true state of affairs.[1] This is an example of the frequent distortion of the news even by the BBC, to say nothing of the press and other media.

The United Nations Scientific Committee on the Effects of Atomic Radiations has estimated the average radiation doses in the year 2000 from various sources (expressed in millisieverts): natural background 2.4; diagnostic medical examination 0.4; Chernobyl accident 0.002; nuclear power production 0.002.[2] In spite of such figures, people worry about the radiation from nuclear power stations, but not about taking a holiday in a place where the natural background is several times the figure given above.[3]

The initial work at Oak Ridge was largely devoted to assessing the optimum design of reactors, but during the 1960s the problems of safety became increasingly important. In any industrial process, there is a tension between the requirements of economy, speed, and efficiency on the one hand, and of safety on the other hand. It is very rarely possible to ensure that a process is absolutely safe, and yet this is demanded of nuclear reactors. In the pursuit of safety, extensive studies were made of all conceivable accidents. Inevitably this remains probabilistic, and it is difficult to take full account of the human factor. Is it possible to design a reactor that is inherently safe so that whatever the operator does it is impossible for an accident to occur? There is little doubt that this is indeed possible, but such reactors are inevitably more expensive and may not be economically viable. But why should absolute safety be demanded only of nuclear reactors? In a modern technological society we continually strive to

---

[1] *Supporters of Nuclear Energy* (August 2000).
[2] *Nuclear Issues* (June 2000).
[3] Ibid. (May 2000).

improve the designs and operation of trains, ships, and airplanes, but accept the possibility of rare accidents.

Weinberg's concern with reactor safety led him to be increasingly critical of some of the new designs being studied in the early 1970s. He tried to steer between the enthusiasms of the engineers and the pessimism of the critics of nuclear power. Eventually he found himself in an impossible position and was fired from his position as Director of Oak Ridge. This gave him the opportunity to reflect, write, and advise on all aspects of nuclear energy. He was invited to direct the Institute of Energy Analysis that was influential during subsequent years.

Freed from the day-to-day problems of reactor development, he could take a longer view of world energy needs. Eventually all the fossil fuels will be exhausted, and there will remain only solar and nuclear. Is it possible to envisage our energy needs being provided by the sun? He was instrumental in founding the Solar Energy Institute devoted to these problems. Studies showed that it is likely that solar power will be several times as costly, and it is doubtful whether it could ever sustain a technological society and whether it could provide the needs of the poorer countries of the world.

On a shorter term, the choice is between coal and nuclear. As Weinberg remarks, radical environmentalists are faced with a dilemma. How can they advocate the reduction of carbon dioxide emissions and then argue against nuclear power when they know that nuclear is the only large-scale power source that emits no carbon dioxide? Their reply that solar is the answer is totally impracticable, and they have no answer to the question about the provision of energy for India and China.

Ultimately, it will be realized that nuclear power has a major role to play in providing world power needs, and Weinberg looks forward to the dawn of the second nuclear era. He lists six measures that should be taken to hasten the day. First, reactors should be built in groups in remote sites. Second, new inherently safe reactors should be developed. Third, nuclear power generation and distribution should be separated. Fourth, a high degree of professionalism, comparable with airplane pilots, should be required of the operators of nuclear plants. Fifth, nuclear plants demand high security. Finally there should be a programme of public education, particularly concerning the biological effects of low levels of radiation. It is essential for the future of nuclear energy that the public fear of radiation should be overcome.

Like any great human enterprise, the development of nuclear energy has its share of unjustified enthusiasms, inexcusable blunders, political interference, triumphs, and failures. We can now see more clearly, thanks in no small part to people such as Alvin Weinberg, what it can do and what it cannot do. We have the choice; if we accept nuclear power, it can provide the energy we need relatively cheaply, reliably, with almost no environmental effects, and with a degree of safety that compares favourably with other technologies. Acceptance does, however, require a high degree of stability in our society and responsibility in the construction and operation of reactors. It also requires a degree of public maturity that can assess at their true worth the arguments that are made both for and against nuclear reactors.

CHAPTER 23

A Sense of Proportion*

An academic without mathematics is the same as an earth without a sun, or a body without a soul. For just as the sun lights up our whole universe . . . and as the soul gives movement to an otherwise lifeless body so does our nourishing mathematics extend its certainty and clarity to the other sciences intelligible ideas which . . . are eternally with God and not created.

—Johann Bernouilli

MANY CONTEMPORARY QUESTIONS that exercise moral theologians, excite journalists, fill the columns of newspapers, and are the subject of dramatic television programmes can only be answered by paying attention to numbers, but this is seldom realized. The age-old Aristotelian indifference to numerical precision, regarding mathematics as a *terra incognita*, and disdaining scientists as a species of low artisans, is still with us. Serious moral judgments are then made without any rational justification.

Some familiar examples are the current scares about radiation from mobile phones, mad cow disease, genetically modified (GM) crops, global warming, and of course the perennial problems of energy and nuclear radiations. We are urged to be careful about using mobile phones, to avoid beef and GM foods, and to support the abolition of nuclear power. These discussions take place on an

---

* Reprinted with permission from *The Month* (November 2000): 445.

emotional level, without any attempt to analyze the dangers numerically and to compare them with other dangers.

When we are faced with any of these problems, the first step is to try to evaluate the hazards numerically or, if that is not possible, to compare them quantitatively with other similar dangers. Unless this is done almost *nothing* useful is known about the problem, and any pronouncement is likely to be worthless.

Consider first mobile phones. The hazard presumably comes from the electromagnetic field they generate. There is no doubt that electromagnetic radiation can be dangerous; it is not advisable, for example, to put one's head in a microwave oven. I am not aware of any direct evidence of physical harm resulting from the use of mobile phones. To see if this is likely, one can measure the electromagnetic field around a phone and then compare it with other fields, such as those from electrical appliances in our homes—for example, electric kettles and television sets—and also the fields due to the sun and to nearby transmission lines. If we find that the field of the mobile phone is small compared with those due to the other sources, then we may reasonably consider them to be safe. It is the proportion that is decisive.

The scare about mad cow disease has caused immense damage to the British beef industry. A small number of people were affected by eating contaminated beef, and it is certainly necessary to identify the cause and to eliminate the factors responsible for it. It is necessary to establish the probability of contracting the disease, and to compare it with that of contracting other diseases. A table of such probabilities would put the scare in its proper proportion. The fatal mistake in such cases is to demand perfect safety. When questioned, a scientist will almost always refuse to say that a particular course of action is perfectly safe, and the politician will then say that he will not permit the process until it is shown to be perfectly safe, and the remainder of the story then unfolds with inexorable logic. What the politician should do is to tell people the probability of harm, and leave it to them to decide.

Such scares illustrate the familiar and depressing truth that people worry themselves sick about negligible dangers and ignore serious ones. If you compare the above examples with the dangers of smoking tobacco, or driving a car, or even crossing a road, all things we do frequently, we find that they are very much more serious. A little care and thought spent reducing really serious dangers is of far more value than going to great lengths to remove minuscule ones. It is only by expressing the dangers numerically that we can decide on a sensible course of action.

The Fear of Nuclear Radiations

Nuclear power and nuclear radiations provide further examples of fears that can only be laid to rest by looking at the numbers. Remembering Hiroshima and Nagasaki, Three Mile Island and Chernobyl, people understandably fear nuclear radiations. "Nuclear" has become a politically incorrect word; so much so that the medical diagnostic technique known as nuclear magnetic resonance (which has nothing to do with nuclear radiations) is now called magnetic resonance, so as not to alarm patients.

A striking example is provided by a recent review of a book about Chernobyl, placed at the head of the review section of a well-known Catholic weekly. The review reproduces in graphic detail some of the stories in the book of the horrible deaths of people who lived near Chernobyl. There is not a single number in the review to indicate the radiation level to which the victims were exposed, nor any proof that the deaths were indeed due to radiation from Chernobyl. The review also mentioned that "Chernobyl cancer was something new, unheard of, and its victims were buried in more than one coffin, a lead one on the outside, far from home to avoid contamination." It is remarked that "food was imported from clean areas because food near Chernobyl—especially anything that grew in the polluted soil—was radioactive," without mentioning that everything is radioactive to some extent, even our own bodies (because of the potassium they contain). What is important is not that the food is radioactive, but the amount of radioactivity, which must be measured and expressed in numbers.

To put all this in perspective, one may recall that Swedish scientists who visited the area in September 1990 recorded radiation levels of 30 to 50 near the reactor (all numbers in microsieverts per hour), 0.5 to 0.9 in Pripyat, and 0.2 in a building 18 km from the reactor. For comparison the average British exposure from natural radiation is 0.25, and 0.85 in Cornwall, due to the granitic rocks. In other words, the radioactive contaminations around Chernobyl, except in the immediate vicinity of the reactor, were similar or less than that in Cornwall. Even in the zones of high contamination, the radiation level is less than the natural background radiation in France, Spain, and Finland. Furthermore, the radiations from the fission fragments from the reactor are essentially the same as those from the natural background, so there is no reason to suppose that the cancers due to Chernobyl, if any, are any different from usual cancers.

The health of the million or so people still living in 2,700 settlements in the contaminated area was studied by 200 international experts from 22 countries coordinated by the International Energy Agency, and the results were published in 1991 in an 800-page technical report. The project was led by the Director of the Hiroshima Radiation Effects Foundation and included members of the World Health Organisation, the International Labour Organisation, the UN Scientific Committee on the Effects of Atomic Radiation, and three other independent organizations. They found no health disorders directly attributable to radiation exposure, and in particular no indications of increased mortality rates, still births, and incidence of cancers, with the single exception of thyroid leukaemia, which is easily curable. Studies have continued since that time, and the final draft of the UNSCEAR 200 Report submitted to the General Assembly of the United Nations states that:

> Apart from the substantial increase in thyroid cancer after childhood exposure, there is no evidence of a major public health impact related to the ionizing radiation 13 years after the Chernobyl incident. No increase in overall cancer incidence or mortality that could be associated with radiation exposure have been observed. Risk of leukaemia, one of the most sensitive indicators of radiation exposure, is not elevated, even among accident-recovery workers or in children. There is no scientific proof of an

increase in other non-malignant disorders, somatic or mental, that are related to ionizing radiation.

This statement was reiterated at an international conference sponsored by the Russian Academy of Sciences and the Ministry concerned with environmental monitoring in Moscow in May 2000. It should be added that the thyroid cancer mentioned above is readily curable.[1]

It is unhappily true that there was much suffering and ill-health in the Chernobyl area, not induced by radiation but to the widespread fears due to misinformation. Thousands of people were uprooted from their homes and told to avoid certain foods. Every sufferer from leukaemia is officially classified as a "Victim of Chernobyl," and is entitled to compensation, although there is no evidence that the illness is actually due to Chernobyl. Groups of children who have been sent to recuperate in other countries have been found to suffer from malnutrition, but not from the effects of radiation. The international report commented that "a large proportion of the population have serious concerns. The vast majority of adults examined in both contaminated and control settlements either believed or suspected that they had illness due to radiation." Scientists who visited the area believed that "many people are exploiting the biggest consequence of the Chernobyl accident—the radiophobia—to further their own aims." They interviewed Professor Guskowa, a member of the Soviet Academy of Sciences, and noted that she was a woman:

> who all her professional life has been engaged in work at home and abroad to cure people suffering from the effects of radiation, to spread information about these effects, and who has endeavoured to estimate the risks of radiation. It was obvious that she was disappointed in how the egoistical interests of politicians and such like who, totally without support for such a claim, pose as experts, have managed to sabotage everything she has worked for.[2]

---

[1] P. E. Hodgson, *After Chernobyl*. Occasional paper obtainable from the Farmington Institute, Harris-Manchester College, Oxford.

[2] A more detailed account of the accident at Chernobyl and its consequences may be found in *Nuclear Power, Energy and the Environment* by P. E. Hodgson (London: Imperial College Press, 1999).

It may indeed also be asked why the above-mentioned review was published, and so prominently, whereas the many sober and well-informed books on the same subject receive no mention. Furthermore, a letter that I sent to the editor, commenting on the review and reproducing the conclusions of the UN report, was not published. In addition, the Catholic newspaper that published the picture of the "doomed" children of Chernobyl also declined to publish my letter observing that they were suffering from malnutrition and not radiation sickness.

Global Warming

Another problem of great contemporary interest is the effects of global warming. While the rise in greenhouse gasses in the atmosphere has been well-established, and it has been conjectured reasonably that these toxins are responsible for global warming, there is still no excuse for the proliferation of sensational writings that make little or no attempt to establish the scientific facts or to propose realistic remedies.

An example of this is provided by an article by a well-known theologian and historian published last January in the same Catholic weekly. This article states that:

> babies born at the start of the new millennium will be faced in their sixties, if not before, with a crisis in human history so unprecedented that it is hard even now to imagine it. . . . The most uncontrollable factor will be global warming, working more rapidly than anyone thought possible until very recently. The rise in sea level may already have wiped out the Maldives, most of Bangladesh, the Netherlands, the Mississippi delta, Florida, the English fens and much else, generating a frantic exercise in rehousing tens of millions. . . . Millions of houses will have been lost on every coast. . . . The whole balance of the world will have changed and the weather everywhere will become increasingly erratic and violent with a great increase in wind force. . . .

and so on for several paragraphs.

Throughout the article, no evidence was given that showed just how the global warming, if it occurs, can cause a rise in the sea level that will have such dramatic effects or cause such catastrophic climate changes. Arguments supporting global warming indeed exist, together with estimates of the probable rise in the sea level, but these are still controversial in several respects and deserve careful study. I therefore wrote to the author and asked him for the data on which he based his article, and received the reply that he was speaking prophetically, not scientifically. I replied that if one speaks prophetically it is preferable to base one's prophecies on established facts, for otherwise one is spreading ungrounded fears. In addition, I pointed out that while castigating the government for their inaction, he made no attempt to propose any solutions to the problem. It is ironic that one who blames science for letting "a genie out of the bottle" shows so little interest in what scientists have to say. I also submitted an article to the periodical on "Global Warming and the Rise in Sea Level," in an attempt to inject some reality into the debate, but it was not published.

So far this discussion of the importance of making numerical estimates of the dangers has avoided giving any numbers, except in the case of Chernobyl. This was done to emphasize the main arguments, without turning off all readers who dislike numbers. It may however be useful to give just another specific example.

Sellafield has been strongly criticized by the Danish Minister of the Environment for releasing radioactivity into the sea. In particular, he is concerned about the level of the radioactive isotope technetium-99 in the sea around Denmark. Measurements have shown that the radiation due to this isotope is around two or three becquerels (Bq) per cubic metre of sea water. Levels of 0.1 Bq per kg are found in fish and 20–25 Bq/kg in lobsters. A fish-lover who eats 50 kg of fish and 20 kg of shellfish per year would receive a dose of about 0.14 microsievert (ms).

This may be put into proportion by comparing it with the dose of 0.3 ms per hour received inside a typical Danish house due to inhaling radon from radioactive rocks. Thus during the year a Dane receives about two thousand times more radiation from radon than from the fish. The variations in the radiation exposure due to radon thus varies from house to house by far greater amounts than the total radiation from the fish. It is thus ridiculous to worry about such a minuscule hazard. The figures in the example are taken from a statement from a group of Danish health physicists and radioecologists and reprinted in *Nuclear Issues*, May 2000. In addition to the minuscule radiation from technetium, there are far greater, but still minuscule, radiation levels due to many other radioactive isotopes in sea water.

Such examples could easily be multiplied many times. The message is that if we read some sensational story about some new hazard of life, our reaction must be to insist on seeing the numbers before we draw any conclusions about the best course of action. If no numbers are forthcoming, the story can be dismissed as worthless and probably also misleading.

CHAPTER 24

Nuclear Power, Energy, and the Environment*

Introduction

NUCLEAR PHYSICS has affected human society in many ways. The first dramatic effect was the devastation of Hiroshima and Nagasaki. Subsequently it became clear that nuclear physics provides a source of plentiful energy. In addition, radioactive isotopes found many beneficial applications in medicine, agriculture, and industry. As the memory of the atomic bombs receded, it was gradually replaced by optimistic expectations of the coming nuclear age. Now that dream has faded, and there is great controversy about the future of nuclear power and its place in society.

In order to determine the optimum energy policy it is absolutely necessary to establish the objective facts, expressed numerically whenever possible. Only then is it possible to see what is important and what is not. Even when we know the facts, it is difficult enough to get people to take the decisions they demand; without the facts there is no possibility of useful progress. Reality can be avoided for a while by political expediency, but the longer this goes on the more terrible will be the ultimate reckoning.

---

* Extended version of a lecture given at a meeting on "Carbon-Free Energy: Nuclear Power and Renewables," Institute of Mechanical Engineers, London, 12 September 2002.

295

The Energy Crisis

The world at present is faced with the problem of increasing demands for energy at a time when the known sources are drying up. Unless something is done about this, the world will face ever increasing difficulties over the coming decades.

Our very existence and our standard of living depend on an adequate supply of energy. Without energy, we would not be able to heat our homes or cook our food. Long distance travel and communication would be drastically changed, and our factories could no longer produce the goods that we need. The world demand for energy has increased rapidly due to the population increase and the overall rise in living standards. Globally the world population is doubling every thirty-five years and energy use every fourteen years. Furthermore, energy use differs from the energy need: much energy is wasted in the richer countries, while the poorer ones lack the minimum energy needed for an acceptable lifestyle.

A century ago the world's energy came almost wholly from coal and age-old sources such as wood, crop residues, and animal dung. These are indeed still widely used in the poorer, developing countries. Then, in the late nineteenth-century, oil and its associated natural gas became an important energy source. It has several advantages over coal: it has a higher calorific value and is more easily transported across large distance by tanker and pipeline. The use of oil and gas grew steadily through the twentieth century and is now globally more important than coal.

At present we are highly dependent on oil, particularly for transport. As we know from recent events, road transport is brought to a standstill in a few days if the supply is cut off. Agriculture is also heavily dependent on oil for fertilisers and machines. Planes are completely dependent on oil.

The vital question is how long will there be enough oil and the other fossil fuels, gas and coal, to supply our needs? The current estimates are that at the present rate of use there is enough oil to last 40 years; natural gas, 60 years; and coal, 230 years. These figures are not so alarming as they appear, because they are obtained by dividing the known reserves by the annual consumption and this does not imply that after these times the reserves will be exhausted. Indeed, continuing studies reveal the surprising fact that these figures remain almost constant from decade to decade. The explanation is that as the existing reserves are used up the price rises and this stimulates searches for new oilfields and the development of new techniques for extracting more oil from existing ones. This produces more oil, so the price falls again. This in turn increases consumption, so that more oil is used and the price rises again. The overall result of this feedback mechanism is that the oil price remains fairly steady in the range $15 to $30 per barrel. Of course this cannot go on forever, and then it will become economic to use other sources such as tar sands and oil shale. Already the cost of oil from tar sands has dropped from $28 to $11 per barrel. So, contrary to the general belief, there is no immediate danger of an oil shortage. Similar remarks apply to gas ands coal.[1]

In addition to these economic considerations, oil prices are subject to political decisions by the OPEC countries. This was the reason for the sharp rise in oil prices in 1973.

These remarks refer to the world as a whole. The changes are more rapid in individual countries. Thus, for example, in Britain oil will be exhausted in about five years, and gas in about seven. After that, without a new energy source, we will have to rely on gas imported from Libya and Russia.

Thus while there is no reason to expect an imminent shortage of fossil fuels, there is continuing need for flexible planning and the search for new sources. Already two of the best analyses[2,3] of energy needs written over twenty years ago emphasized that there is no time to lose. Those twenty years have been largely wasted in futile

---

[1] Bjorn Lomborg. 2001. The Skeptical Environmentalist. Cambridge: Cambridge University Press.

[2] Edgar Boyes, ed., *Shaping Tomorrow* (London: Home Mission Division of the Methodist Church, 1981).

[3] André Blanc-Lapierre (ed.). Semaine d'étude sur le thème humanité et energie: Besoins-Ressources-Espoirs. November 10–15, 1980. Academiae Scientiarum Scripts Varia, No. 46, 1981.

and ill-informed controversies, and already we are seeing some of the effects: power blackouts even in highly developed countries, persisting energy shortages in poorer countries, and mounting evidence of pollution and climate change.

Climate Change

Over the past few years there has been increasing realization that our present energy policies are probably having a potentially disastrous effect on world climate. The burning of fossil fuels inevitably releases large amounts of carbon dioxide into the atmosphere. There is no way to avoid this because the chemical reaction that releases heat is the combination of carbon and oxygen to produce carbon dioxide. In addition fossil fuel power stations also release into the atmosphere substantial quantities of poisonous gases such as sulphur dioxide and the nitrous oxides, as well as a whole range of poisons such as arsenic. These eventually fall to the earth as acid rain, killing trees and rendering lakes and rivers sterile.

The result of burning fossil fuels is that the proportion of carbon dioxide in the atmosphere is steadily increasing. This is an established fact. It is then very plausibly suggested that through a mechanism known as the greenhouse effect world temperature will steadily rise. The latest report of the Intergovernmental Panel for Climate Change indicates that world temperature will increase by between 1.4° C and 5.8° C over the present century. This may not seem much, and some of us would welcome warmer weather. Furthermore, there is a wide range of uncertainty. It is supported by observations such as that the 1990s were the hottest decade, snow cover has declined by 10% in the last 40 years, and since the 1950s Arctic sea ice has declined by 10 to 15% in area and up to 40% in thickness. It could, however, be argued that temperatures fluctuate from year to year, and it is notoriously difficult to detect a long-term trend in a fluctuating quantity. This is particularly the case if short-scale and long-scale fluctuations are superimposed, as is indeed the case for world temperature. We know that over long timescales there have been very large fluctuations causing a succession of ice ages. How can we be sure that another is not just around the corner?

Another consequence of the greenhouse effect is a worldwide rise in sea level, by up to 88 cm in the present century. This is due to a complicated series of causes. It is not due, as is sometimes said, to the melting of the polar ice caps. The Arctic ice is floating and so, as Archimedes knew, melting does not affect the sea level, though there is a minuscule effect due to differences in salinity. The Antarctic ice is either on floating ice shelves, to which the same arguments apply, or to ice on the continent itself. There the temperatures range from $-20°$ C to $-60°$ C, so a temperature rise of a few degrees has no effect. A rise in sea level of the amount predicted will have devastating effects on low-lying countries, such as parts of Holland and Bangladesh, and the Maldives and some of the Pacific islands.

In addition to these effects that can be expressed numerically, though with a considerable range of uncertainty, there are other effects that may prove equally devastating. In the past few years there have been widespread floods in Mozambique and Venezuela, and hurricanes in the United States, causing billions in damage. In Europe there have been floods in some areas and droughts in others. Such natural events are not new, but they seem to be becoming more frequent.

There are already noticeable biological effects of climate change. In his book *The Earth Under Threat*, Sir Ghillean Prance, former Director of the Royal Botanical Gardens at Kew, describes in graphic detail the devastating effects on animal and plant life attributable to climate change.[4] Many species have become extinct and any reduction in the number of plant and animal species is an irreplaceable loss.

Although it cannot be reasonably maintained that all these results of the greenhouse effect are established beyond doubt, the evidence is steadily increasing and it is prudent to take it seriously. Very often important decisions have to be taken on the basis of

---

[4] Sir Ghillean Prance, *The Earth Under Threat* (Edinburgh: Wild Goose Publications, Saint Andrews Press, 1996)

incomplete knowledge, and it is exceedingly dangerous to postpone taking decisions until perfect knowledge is available. In the present case, whatever the strength of the case for the greenhouse effect, there is the undeniable fact of the pollution of the atmosphere and the earth due to the impurities in all fossil fuels.

It is therefore imperative to reduce our dependence on fossil fuels as rapidly as possible. It is unacceptable to say that we can continue to use them at the present rate and hope that something new will turn up before they are gone. The poisoning of the earth is taking place now, and unless we take urgent action we run the risk of irreversibly polluting the earth.

Many international conferences have been held to address the problem of climate change, the more important being at Rio in 1992 and Kyoto in 1997. At Rio there was general agreement on the need to stabilise greenhouse gas emissions, and at Kyoto it was agreed to reduce them by an average of 5.2%. This would reduce global warming by 4%, but it is now doubtful if even this modest target can be met. In the United Kingdom, fossil fuel dependence was reduced from 91% to 87% during the 1990s, mainly by increasing the efficiency of the nuclear power stations, but is likely to rise again during the next decade as the older nuclear power stations retire. The U.S., the largest emitter, has withdrawn from the agreement because of the likely effects on its economy.

Energy Conservation

At present we are using energy very wastefully. It is therefore argued that if we were to adopt more efficient ways of using energy so much could be saved that our problems would be solved. A recent book, *Factor Four: Doubling Wealth Halving Resource Use* by Ernst von Weizacker, Amory B. Lovins, and L. Hunter Lovins,[5] shows in detail how the adoption of increased energy efficiency and energy-saving lifestyles can reduce our energy consumption by a factor of about four without affecting our standard of living. It is clear that

---

[5] Ernst Von Weizacker, Amory B. Lovins, and L. Hunter Lovins (1998); *Factor Four: Doubleday Wealth, Halving Resource Use* (London: Earthscan Publishers).

all this is most valuable and needs to be strongly supported. It is intolerable and immoral for people in the more developed countries to use more than a hundred times as much energy per capita as billions of people in the poorer countries. As this becomes widely known to people in the poorer countries they will be filled with righteous anger at this scandalous situation. It is vitally important not only as a matter of justice but also of self-interest to tackle this problem urgently.

Urgent and necessary though this is, energy-saving policies are not the whole solution to the energy problem. First of all, even if we save three-quarters of our energy, we still have to produce the remaining quarter, to say nothing of the huge amounts of energy we need to satisfy the billions of people in the poorer countries. So at best we only postpone the ultimate reckoning. Second, the energy-saving measures themselves often use energy, so that there is a payback time before there is a net energy gain. Third, energy-saving measures take time to implement. It is, for example, relatively easy to design an energy-saving house, but much more difficult and expensive to convert an existing house. With the best will in the world, it will be many decades before most houses can be converted. Similar remarks can be made for energy-saving transport.

All this refers to what could be done. By far the most serious difficulty is the psychological one of persuading people to put this into practice. Energy saving is quite expensive, even if it can be shown that there will ultimately be a cost saving. People are extremely reluctant to spend money in ways that are not to their immediate advantage. Attempts to enforce energy saving by legislation would be bitterly opposed, so that it would be politically unacceptable for any party to adopt it as their policy. We have seen this recently in the U.K. when increased fuel prices were proposed. Furthermore, such price increases bear heavily on the poor and those living in rural areas, and would make our industries uncompetitive compared with other countries with cheap power.

This is not to say that energy efficiency is not extremely important. Continuing efforts should be made to implement energy savings wherever practicable. Energy is a precious resource, particularly when it is derived from limited amounts of coal, oil, or gas in the earth. The imperative to save energy in this way should not, however, delay efforts to find new energy sources.

Alternative Energy Sources

The pressing need for energy imposes on us an obligation to examine possible substitutes for fossil fuels. There is one general consideration that provides a useful guide, though of course it has to be followed up by detailed examination. What we need is not just energy but concentrated energy. If we want to boil a kettle, we need energy that can be concentrated on the kettle. There are large amounts of energy in the air and materials in the kitchen, but this is useless for our purpose. It is therefore instructive to grade possible energy sources by their degrees of concentration. The more concentrated the source, the easier it is to use; if it is not concentrated we have to go to much trouble to concentrate it.

Energy sources fall into three categories: diffuse, intermediate, and concentrated. The diffuse sources are the energy in the wind and the waves, the tides and the sunlight. There are enormous amounts of energy in these sources, enough to satisfy our needs a thousand times. Unfortunately their energy is thinly spread, so we have to use much energy to put it into concentrated form.

Hydroelectric power is in an intermediate position. The gravitational energy in raindrops is indeed thinly spread, but the valleys do much of the work of concentrating it for us. By the time the rain has been collected to form rivers it is fairly well concentrated. Hydropower is, however, limited by the number of suitable rivers, so that it accounts for less than 3% of world energy. Even if many other rivers are used, it is unlikely to provide more than at most 5% of the energy we need. Furthermore, it takes up large areas of valuable land and is highly dangerous due to the possibility of dam collapse. For these reasons it will not be considered further.

The energy in wood, coal, oil, and gas is so highly concentrated that it can be used immediately, and so these were the first energy sources to be used. Nuclear energy is even more concentrated: there is as much useable energy in a ton of uranium as in a million tons of coal.

These are useful guidelines, but need to be supplemented by a detailed comparison between the various possible energy sources. The following criteria are proposed: capacity, reliability, cost, safety, and effects on the environment, expressed numerically as far as possible. Here we are primarily concerned with large-scale energy sources that are able to power industries and cities.

The Diffuse Energy Sources

Usually the diffuse sources are called the renewable sources, but this is misleading as it applies also to hydroelectric, wood, and biomass, which need to be distinguished from each other. Renewable by itself is not a virtue; what matters is whether the supplies are unlimited for all practicable purposes, or whether the reserves will run out in the foreseeable future.

For example, water on earth is not renewable because there is only a finite amount, but we are never likely to exhaust the supplies. Eventually, even the so-called renewables are limited by the life of the sun.

The diffuse energy sources are wind, solar, wave, tidal, and geothermal. The amounts of energy in these sources is enormous, as already mentioned. There is no doubt about their capacity; it is the other criteria that pose serious problems.

Wind and solar are unreliable. We need an energy source that is always available. This would not be much of a problem for unreliable sources if there were a way of storing energy cheaply in large amounts, but there is not. For small-scale applications, such as providing water to irrigate a farm, unreliability is not a problem since wind can be used to raise water to an elevated tank, whence it can be used as required.

Such a solution is not available for the large amounts of energy needed to power industries or cities. Even when the wind is blowing the available energy changes, particularly as it varies as the cube of the wind velocity. When velocity is small, little energy is produced, and when it is very large the blades have to be feathered to prevent catastrophic damage.

Solar energy is limited by the intensity of the sun's rays. On the average, the sun gives about 200 watts per square metre at the earth's surface, with maximum values of up to 1,000 watts per square metre in desert areas. There is no way to increase this, so large amounts of energy require large collectors. There are two ways of tapping this energy: by photoelectric cells and by direct heating. The former has useful small-scale applications such as powering satellites and lights on ocean buoys, where batteries can be used for storage. Direct sunlight can be used for domestic water heating.

Wave and tidal are reliable, although waves vary in intensity and tidal is available only intermittently but predictably. Geothermal is reliable but uneconomic.

Evaluation of the costs of the diffuse sources poses several problems. Many of them have hardly passed the experimental stage when a variety of devices are being tried. To determine the cost it is necessary to run a device for several years, and such experience is often lacking. Of all the diffuse sources, wind seems to be the most promising. There is now considerable experience with a variety of wind turbines. Recent studies indicate that the present cost is about twice that of coal or nuclear. In spite of strenuous efforts over the years, the contribution of wind power to our energy needs remains minuscule; in the U.K. its contribution amounts to around 0.16%. The contributions of the other diffuse sources are essentially zero.

The cost of electricity from photovoltaic cells has fallen over the years, but it is still several times that of coal or nuclear. Great hopes are placed on these diffuse sources, and it is quite possible that further research will improve their performance. Until this is demonstrated, it is premature to deploy them on a large scale. To give some idea of when this is likely to happen, it would be very useful to have reliable figures for the cost of electricity produced by wind and solar as a function of time.

Of the remaining diffuse sources, there have been several experimental wave devices that have produced small amounts of power.

They have obviously to be sited in regions of the coastline where the waves are large, and then it is very likely that they will be destroyed by the first storm.

Tidal power is practicable only where there is a suitable estuary. A tidal power station has been operating at La Rance in France for many years. It has an average energy output of 65 MW, but is not economic. The only practical possibility in the U.K. is the Severn estuary between England and Wales. A detailed study has been made of the feasibility of using this estuary, which is much larger than that of La Rance and could produce up to 7 GW. It is estimated that the cost of the energy would be about twice that of coal or nuclear. An initial investment of about £15 billion spread over ten years would be needed before any power is produced, and the environmental effects are likely to be severe.

Geothermal power can be derived either from hot springs or by boring deep holes into the earth's crust. Hot springs are useful renewable sources on a small scale, but the number of suitable sites is rather small. The heat deep in the earth can be extracted by boring two shafts, pulverising the rock between their ends and pumping cold water down one and using the hot water that emerges from the other. The difficulty is that it is very expensive to bore the shafts, and when the rock near their ends has been cooled there is no more heat to be obtained from them. The result is that the whole process is uneconomic.

The diffuse sources are widely believed to be particularly safe; they are indeed often referred to as the "benign renewables." Several studies show that they are safer than coal and oil, but more dangerous than gas and nuclear. The reason for this is that the energy output of each device is quite small, so that large numbers have to be manufactured to equal the power output of a coal or nuclear power station, and all manufacturing activities involve risks. In addition there are the construction hazards.

The effects on the environment of the diffuse sources are increasingly recognized. Wind turbines cannot be hidden; to be effective they have to be on high ground, and can be seen for miles.

In addition, they emit a persistent humming noise that is found very obnoxious by people living nearby. Finally, each windmill requires an access road. There are proposals for offshore wind farms, but these are more expensive to build and pose a danger to shipping. Solar panels for direct heating can be inconspicuously sited on roofs, while photovoltaics are best sited in desert areas. In neither case is there much effect on the environment.

It is sometimes said that if enough research is done these energy sources could be made economic. It is, however, a fallacy to suppose that enough money will solve every problem because the laws of physics cannot be circumvented. Nevertheless we may hope that eventually some of them will be improved sufficiently to contribute effectively to our energy supplies. Until this is shown by extensive trials, it is premature to deploy these energy sources on a large scale.

The Concentrated Energy Sources

The familiar concentrated energy sources—wood, biomass, coal, oil, and natural gas—have already been discussed, and it has been shown that for the future of the earth they must be phased out as soon as possible. This leaves only nuclear to be considered in this section.

Nuclear has the capacity to provide a large fraction of our energy needs. It supplies about 80% of the electricity generated in France, and about 50% in Western Europe as a whole. At present nuclear supplies 17% of world electrical energy, and this could easily be increased.

Nuclear is very reliable, and the best reactors operate over 90% of the time, the remainder being nearly all for planned maintenance. They are thus highly suitable for base load operation. Other power plants that can be switched on and off more rapidly are more suited to cope with the hourly fluctuations of energy needs.

The cost of nuclear power is generally comparable to that of coal or oil. It is not easy to make precise estimates because nuclear power stations are much more costly to build than coal power stations, but much cheaper to run. The amount of fuel that has to be brought to nuclear power stations is very small, compared with the thousand tons per day needed by coal power stations. The relative cost therefore depends on the working life of the power station, which can be about sixty years, and in that time the value of money can undergo substantial changes. The cost comparison also depends on the rate of interest required by the shareholders. Nuclear power stations are more costly to decommission, but these costs can easily be covered by investing a small amount during each year of a reactor's life. On the whole it seems that the costs of nuclear and coal power are quite similar.

Nuclear reactors have few adverse effects on the environment. Most important, they emit no greenhouse gases and so do not contribute to global warming. In 1996, 2,312 TWh of electricity was generated by nuclear power. The same amount would be produced by burning 900 million tons of coal or 600 million tons of oil. Thus the emission of 3,000 million tons of carbon dioxide has been saved per year by using nuclear power rather than coal. They also emit none of the poisonous gases that come from coal power stations. When nuclear power stations are built, the emissions of these gases is strikingly reduced. France is about 80% nuclear and has halved its carbon dioxide emissions; Japan (32% nuclear) has achieved a reduction of 20%, while the U.S. (20% nuclear) has reduced them by 6%. The emission of sulphur dioxide is also drastically reduced by replacing coal power stations by nuclear ones. The British government has set a target of a 10% cut in carbon emissions in the period from 1990 to 2010. By 1995, a cut of about 6% had been achieved, but this is due to the increase in nuclear output by 39% from 1990 to 1994. In the next few years, however, emissions are set to rise as the older nuclear power stations reach the end of their lives, and no new ones are being built. There is thus no hope that the targets will be met, and the situation is similar the U.S.

Many new gas power stations are now being built, and these emit only half the amount of carbon dioxide as coal power stations. However, this is offset by the leakage of methane, which has a global warming potential about sixty times that of carbon dioxide. The net effects of these two by-products are about the same, and so no reduction in global warming is to be expected from the switch to gas power stations. Even if this effect is neglected, if gas increases to 43.5% while coal declines to 2.5% we can expect a 10% reduction in carbon dioxide emissions, while if nuclear rises to 43.5% at the expense of coal there will be a reduction by 20%. Some recent estimates of the emission of carbon dioxide (in tons per gigawatt hour) from various power sources are: coal, 870; oil, 750; gas, 500; nuclear, 8; wind, 7; and hydro, 4.

There are several reasons for the widespread opposition to nuclear power. First, there is fear of nuclear radiation, which is deadly and invisible to the senses. We can receive a fatal dose of radiation and feel nothing. However nuclear radiation can easily be detected in exceedingly small amounts by instruments.

Such installations do emit minuscule amounts of radiation—far less than the natural background to which we are exposed all the time. Indeed, coal power stations emit more radioactivity than nuclear power stations due to small amounts of uranium in coal.

Another reason for opposition is a fear of the buildup of hazardous nuclear waste. However, the way to deal with nuclear waste has been well understood for years. First it is allowed to stand in secure tanks for about forty years to allow the short-lived radioactive isotopes to decay, and then the residue is concentrated and fused into an insoluble ceramic and encased in stainless steel cylinders. It is then buried deep in the earth in a stable geological formation where there is no chance that it will ever come into contact with people. Eventually the radioactivity will decay to a level comparable with that of the surrounding rocks. Even if small amounts of radioactivity are leached out by ground water, it is very unlikely to reach the human food chain, and then only in the minutest amounts to very few people. The amount of high level radioactive waste produced by a reactor each year is quite small; it could be loaded into a minibus. For comparison, coal power stations produce millions of tons of waste each year.

A more serious problem is the very large amount of radioactivity in the reactor core. If a terrorist group were able to blow up a reactor, certainly a very difficult task, this radioactivity would be spread over a wide area. In the developed countries nuclear reactors are now very safe, but the same cannot be said for all countries, and some governments may even use radioactivity for warlike purposes.

Nuclear reactors are continually being improved, and new types studied. Among the new fission reactors the pebble-bed reactor seems promising. Fast reactors, which burn uranium 238, which comprises 99.3% of natural uranium, have been studied for many years and pilot plants have operated successfully. At present they are not economic compared with the present reactors, but are available to take over from thermal reactors if uranium becomes scarce. This seems unlikely to happen for many decades because the cost of the fuel is a small fraction of the total cost of running a reactor, and so any increase is unimportant unless it becomes large. In addition, uranium is very widespread, though in small concentrations, and it may even be economic to extract it from sea water.

In progress are studies of accelerator-driven reactors, which consist of a subcritical uranium core irradiated by intense beams of neutron produced by spallation of high energy protons incident on a heavy metal target. This increases the fission rate, without the reactor becoming critical. Such reactors are very safe, as they shut down as soon as the proton beam is switched off, and in addition they can be run at such high flux densities that the fissile material is consumed inside the reactor.

Experiments have been in progress for over fifty years to utilise the fusion reaction to produce energy. Nuclear reactions between deuterium nuclei and between deuterium and tritium nuclei produce energy. This only happens when they are in the form of plasma at a very high energy, and the difficulty is to keep the plasma stable while the reaction takes place. Successive devices have come nearer to this goal, but it is not yet achieved. If it is, unlimited energy would be available using deuterium—this is a component of ordinary water, and tritium, which is radioactive, and can be made when needed. As the feasibility of fusion reactors has not yet been demonstrated, they should not be considered in the present context, although they are a bright hope for the future.

Comparison of Energy Sources

In order to provide the very large amounts of energy we need to sustain our living standards, and to raise those of people in poorer countries, we need energy sources of high capacity. The only sources in this category are the fossil fuels, coal, oil and natural gas, and nuclear. The fossil fuels are unacceptable because of the pollution they produce, and the likelihood that they are responsible for global warming. In addition, they will be exhausted in a few centuries. It is imperative to reduce our reliance on them before the earth is polluted beyond repair.

Renewable energy sources are all either of limited capacity, or too expensive to provide useful amounts of power. This is shown by the recently published plans of the European Union to spend £110 billion to double the contribution of renewables to 12% by 2010. Nearly all of this (96%) is hydropower and the burning of wood and farm wastes. In 1995 the contribution of wind power was 4 TWh, 0.2% of the EU total, and by 2010 it is proposed that this be increased to 80 TWh, or 2.8% of the total. Solar power is to be increased to 0.35%, and geothermal to 0.2% of the total. Overall, it is proposed to spend £43 billion on wind, solar, and geothermal to obtain an extra 82.5 TWh, just 3% of the EU total. It is difficult to avoid the conclusion that a totally disproportionate expenditure is being proposed for a very meagre return.

The diffuse energy sources, though very large, cannot at present produce amounts remotely approaching our energy needs. Continuing research is of course desirable, and if their disadvantages can be overcome they should certainly be deployed on a large scale. The British government aims to increase the contribution of renewables to 1.7% by 2010. Recent research by the LJI Group in Mannheim in 1998 concluded that a sustained effort could bring it to 35% in 50 years. This is simply too little and too late.

Even to stabilise the level of carbon dioxide by the middle of this century, we need to replace 2,000 fossil fuel power stations in the next 40 years, equivalent to a rate of one per week. Can we find 500 km^2 each week to install 4,000 windmills? Or perhaps we could cover 10 km^2 of desert each week with solar panels, together with the means to keep them clean? Tidal power can produce large amounts of energy, but can we find a new Severn estuary and build a barrage costing £9 billion every five weeks? What about nuclear? At the height of new nuclear construction in the 1980s, an average of 23 new nuclear reactors were being built each year, with a peak of 43 in 1983. A construction rate of one per week is therefore quite practicable.

The Belgian government recently set up a commission to examine the options for electricity generation. Taking into account fuel costs, non-fuel costs (investment, operation and maintenance), external costs (air pollution, noise, and greenhouse gases) as well as the costs of construction, grid connection, and decommissioning, the commission estimated that it will cost BFr. 2.34 to generate every kilowatt-hour of electricity from coal in 2010. The equivalent figures were 1.74 for gas, wind as 1.85 (seashore), 2.39 (off-shore) and 3.26 (inland), but just 1.22 to 1.28 for nuclear power.

Over twenty years ago, two detailed studies of the energy crisis by well-qualified experts[6,7] concluded that there is no time to lose. They examined nuclear power, and one of them drew the following conclusions:

> Nuclear energy is an integral part of nature, just as much God's creation as sunshine and rain. It offers mankind a new energy source which is very large, convenient and not very costly. Around the world the most important energy sources, oil in the rich world and wood in the poor, are becoming scarce, so that we cannot afford to set aside any energy technology with large potential which is cost effective, provided it is reasonably safe. There are risks associated with the use of nuclear power, as with everything else, but these have been very carefully evaluated, and are not very big and are not at all out of scale compared with risks of other energy sources and with other ordinary hazards.

---

[6] Semaine D'Etude sur le theme Humanite et Energie: Besoins–Resources–Espoirs. November 10-15, 1980. Edite par André Blanc-Lapierre. *Pontificiae Academiae Scientiarum Scripta Varia* No. 46, 1.

[7] Edgar Boyes, ed., *Shaping Tomorrow* (London: Home Mission Division of the Methodist Church, 1981).

During the next few decades most of our energy will have to be obtained from proven sources. If our dependence on coal and oil is reduced, the main burden falls on gas and nuclear. Gas power stations produce less, though still substantial, amounts of greenhouse gases, and future supplies are politically unreliable. Nuclear power stations produce essentially no greenhouse gases, but also have political difficulties.

In the longer term we may hope that the diffuse sources will be able to provide progressively more of our energy. To do this they will have to prove themselves, and will be in competition with new and safer nuclear reactors, and it is possible that fusion power will become viable in about fifty years. Research into these possibilities must continue, and time will tell which provide the most acceptable sources.

Political Considerations

The British Minister for the Environment, Michael Meacher, has recently stated that: "The Government recognizes that nuclear power assists the U.K. in limiting emissions of greenhouse gases, and provided that high standards of safety and environmental protection can be maintained and that decommissioning liabilities are fully funded, we believe that it will continue to be so."[8]

In spite, however, of the seriousness of the problem and the recognition of the contribution made by nuclear power in reducing carbon dioxide emission the public debate on the means to combat global warming is very different.

Sir John Houghton recently wrote an article on global warming in *Physics World*.[9] After describing the methods used to study global warming, he summarizes the ways to reduce carbon dioxide emission. "The key," he says, "lies in the rapid development and growth of renewable energy," and by this he means wind, biomass, solar, wave, and tidal. He gives no figures for the energy produced in this way, although as mentioned above the contribution of the most

[8] Letter from Michael Meacher to the British Nuclear Industry Forum (18 January 1988).
[9] John Houghton, "Climate Change: The Challenges," *Physics World* (February 1998): 17.

promising of the renewables, namely wind, is still extremely small. He simply expresses the hope that the renewable energy sources will make up 12% of total energy production by the year 2020.

He also mentions increasing the energy efficiency of coal power stations, improving the insulation of buildings; using cheap, long-life light sources; and making more efficient vehicles. All this is of course desirable, and improvements are being made continuously. All these measure are inherently costly and will take a long time to implement on a large scale. What is remarkable about the article is that there is no mention whatsoever of nuclear power. He certainly knows about it because in his book, *Global Warming*,[10] he remarks that "it has considerable attractiveness from the point of view of sustainable development because it does not produce greenhouse gas emissions." Furthermore, although "it is not strictly a renewable source, . . . the rate at which it uses up resources of radioactive material is small compared with the total resource available. . . . A further advantage of nuclear energy installations is that the technology is known: they can be built now and therefore contribute to the reduction of carbon dioxide emissions in the short term. The continued importance of nuclear energy is recognized in the WEC energy scenarios, which all assume growth in this energy source next century." He also wrote a similar article in the *Times Higher*,[11] again ignoring nuclear power.

The parliamentary Select Committee on Trade and Industry recently published a report on future energy policy. Presenting this to the press, the chairman Martin O'Neill said:

> We feel that while a major effort would have to be made to turn around public opinion, and despite the currently unfavourable economic case for new nuclear plant, the question as to eventual new nuclear build cannot and must not be ducked any longer. We recommend that a formal presumption be made now for the

---

[10] John Houghton, *Global Warming: The Complete Briefing* (Oxford: Lion Publishing, 1994).

[11] John Houghton, "The Two and a Half Degrees to Doomsday," *Times Higher* (3 December 1997): 21.

purposes of long-term planning that new nuclear plant may be required in the course of the next two decades.

The report further admits that

without a significant component of nuclear power generation in the plant mix, achievement—or maintenance—of [the Government commitment to] a 20% carbon dioxide reduction on the 1990 level in the period after 2010 appears doubtful.

These are significant admissions, bearing in mind that it is part of the policy of the Labour Party to phase out nuclear power.

The government plan to reduce fossil fuel emissions relies heavily on energy taxes, but also recommends extending the life of elderly nuclear power stations to 2011. Such an extension is justified only if the cost of upgrading to maintain safe operation is less than the value of the electricity produced. Ultimately it is better to build new, more efficient nuclear power stations, but this possibility is not even mentioned.

Politicians, ever sensitive to public opinion, are therefore in a difficult situation. The public is so scared of nuclear that even a proposal to make a test drilling to see if a possible site is suitable for the safe deposit of nuclear wastes evokes fierce opposition, and the proposal is rejected. Proposals to operate a newly built reprocessing plant that could earn the county billions of pounds were subject to interminable delays. The construction of new nuclear power stations are subjected to lengthy public enquiries, where every conceivable objection is given detailed examination. Rather than take a decision, it is always easier, and indeed appears statesmanlike, to propose yet another enquiry. Matters that have already been settled beyond any reasonable doubt are reopened and questioned again and again. As a result, the construction of new nuclear power stations has remained almost at a standstill for over ten years. Meanwhile the earth continues to be polluted, the greenhouse gases build up, and billions of the poorest people are deprived of the necessities of life.

By contrast, new schemes to build huge wind farms are readily approved, although a critical examination shows that they cannot satisfy our needs. Conferences are held to discuss ways to tackle the greenhouse effect, and detailed consideration is given to fiscal constraints, wind and solar power, wave and tidal power, but nuclear is not even mentioned.

Over the years, nuclear scientists and engineers have devoted their lives to developing the new energy source that has providentially become available just when it is desperately needed. We have made great efforts to publicise the potentialities of nuclear energy for mankind. These efforts have been wasted and ignored for purely political reasons.

When will governments find the will to take the right decisions before they are forced to do so by events? Will this happen before it is too late to avoid catastrophe?

Church Action

The Pope has frequently emphasized the need to care for the environment and has encouraged scientific study of this and related problems. Decisions vital for the future of humanity are being taken on political grounds, ignoring the long-term consequences. The Church is, or should be, above short-term political pressures, and is therefore in a strong position to speak out. As far as I know, there have not yet been any Church statements on global warming, but many Bishops' Conferences and other Church bodies have indeed spoken out on the question of nuclear power. These serve to illustrate some of the difficulties that are encountered.

The first requirement for such statements is that they should be based on a thorough knowledge of the scientific and technological facts. A survey[12] of Church statements on nuclear power shows, however, that in most cases they are gravely deficient; no one with any knowledge of the situation could take them seriously. They are worse than useless.

---

[12] P. E. Hodgson, "The Churches and Nuclear Power" (unpublished 1984); Friedhelm Solms, ed., *European Churches and the Energy Issue*, Forschungsstatte der Evangelischen Studiengemeinschaft, series A, vol. 11 (October 1980).

There are three exceptions to this that deserve more detailed comment. The first is the comprehensive statement made by the U.S. bishops in 1981.[13] This was based on good general knowledge, but nevertheless had several serious flaws. I published an analysis of that document,[14] but so far as I know it has had no effect.

The second statement was made by the Home Mission Division of the Methodist Church in Britain in 1981.[15] They assembled a group of about sixty scientists, technologists, and engineers, and for several years they studied the problems not only of nuclear power, but also of many other technological developments including electronic computers and genetic engineering. Their report is a very valuable survey of modern problems. Their conclusions concerning nuclear power are:

1. Nuclear energy is an integral part of nature, just as much God's creation as sunshine and rain.

2. It does offer mankind a new energy source that is very large, convenient, and not very costly.

3. Around the world the most important energy sources, oil in the rich world and wood in the poor, are becoming scarce, so that we cannot afford to set aside any energy technology with large potential that is cost effective, provided it is reasonably safe.

4. There are risks associated with the use of nuclear power, as with everything else, but these have been very carefully evaluated, are not very big, and are not at all out of scale compared with risks of other energy sources and other ordinary hazards.

The third Church document on nuclear power was produced by the Pontifical Academy of Science, the substance of which has

---

13 "The Moral Dimensions of Energy Policy," Bishops' Committee for Social Development, *Origins,* NC Documentary Service (23 April 1981), 10 (45): 706.
14 P. E. Hodgson, "Reflections on the Energy Crisis," *The Month* (November 1982): 382.
15 Boyes, *Shaping Tomorrow,* loc cit.

already been discussed in an earlier essay in this book "Nuclear Power and the Pontifical Academy of Sciences," p. 235.

It is recognized that it is desirable that: "The Church must draw into the work of evangelisation those Catholics who have a acknowledged competence in contemporary scientific disciplines."[16] Unfortunately these fine sentiments are seldom put into practice.

There is a fundamental and essential difference between the two acceptable statements on nuclear power and the remainder. Both groups of statements are written from inside Christianity, but the former are written from within science as well, while the latter by and large are not. The view from inside is always different from the view from outside. Those within science have much more chance of seeing technical matters in their true perspective, with the potentialities and dangers in proportion. In the words of C. P. Snow, we have the future in our bones, and we look forward to it with hope and confidence. So, of course, should Christians.

Viewed from outside, science apparently appears to many to be a fearful monster, giving birth to unimaginable evils that we will somehow have to fight and control. They do not understand science, so they fear science. Such people fall easy prey to every wild tale of the mass media, and lend their support to campaigns to slay the dragon.

Churchmen sometimes talk about the need for dialogue with scientists as if we were an alien species.[17] When will they realize that there are scientists actually inside the Church, kneeling in the pews, and sharing with them the Body and Blood of Christ? Why not listen to them for a change, instead of running after the first rabid journalist and swallowing his wild stories about the strange and menacing land of science?

---

[16] Submission of the Bishop's Conference of England and Wales to the Extraordinary Synod of Bishops held in Rome (November 1985).

[17] Until recently the relations with the scientific community were the responsibility of the Pontifical Consilium for Non-Believers. Now, more sensibly, it is included in the Pontifical Consilium for Culture.

PART V
Science and Society

CHAPTER 25

Science in the Service
of Mankind*

Introduction

THE SCIENTIFIC ADVANCES in our knowledge of the
natural world made during the last three hundred years,
and the associated technological applications, have changed
all our lives. There are, however, several disquieting features of the
present interactions between science and human society that deserve
some comments. These are based on various experiences around the
world and may not be found everywhere.

I propose to begin by considering the progress of science itself,
and what it needs to ensure its continuing growth. Most scientific
research is carried out in universities, and so the current situation in
universities is the next area to consider. Finally there is the contribution that can be made by science to the national welfare. There
areas overlap and interact, so no sharp separation is possible.

Scientific Research

Until about a century ago, most scientific research could be carried
out with very simple apparatus, often made by the scientist himself.
Scientists were supported by their universities, or by the patronage
of a prince, as Galileo was by the Duke Cosimo de Medici. The situation is now quite different. Most scientific research requires

---

* Lecture given at the University of Milan, 7 May 2002.

expensive apparatus, far beyond the resources of the individual scientist. Universities can provide some support, but as this is seldom sufficient governmental funds are necessary.

During the last century, governments learned that scientists can often provide effective solutions to pressing problems, and so they became increasingly willing to give the necessary support. Since governments are interested in practical results there is an increasing tendency to require that any new research should be directed toward solving some practical problem. Thus when scientists submit a research proposal they are now required to specify the expected benefits to mankind. All research must satisfy the criterion of social relevance. At first sight this seems very reasonable: scientific research is very expensive, and if society pays (and this means taking a portion of everyone's taxes), then surely society has the right to expect some return. In these times of financial stringency—when there are so many urgent problems in health care, relieving poverty, and providing education—scientists cannot expect to be given large sums just to satisfy their curiosity.

This view of the relation of science to human society has a long history. It was vigorously propagated about sixty years ago by the Marxist physicist J. D. Bernal. According to Bernal, the State must set the priorities for scientific research, and the whole scientific establishment must be organized to maximise the benefit to society. All research should be directed toward that end. The most important social problems must be identified, and teams of scientists given the task of solving them.

These ideas were vigorously opposed by Polanyi, Thomson, and many other scientists, who founded the Society for the Freedom of Science. The debate took place in Britain during the immediate postwar years. During the war, the whole scientific establishment had been harnessed to the war effort. When the war was over, the question was whether these controls should be kept on, with the object of serving society, or should they be relaxed or abolished, so that the prewar situation would be re-established?

In his many writings on the subject, Polanyi distinguished between pure and applied research. It must be emphasized at once that there is no implication whatever that one is in any sense better than the other, but rather that they are different. Pure research aims solely to increase our understanding of some aspect of the world without any thought of applications. Applied research is the development of existing knowledge to produce some device or product that is useful.

For example, Fermi was interested to know what would happen when he bombarded a series of elements with neutrons, and eventually this led in 1939 to the discovery of nuclear fission. It was then realized that this provided a way to release the energy inside the nucleus, and an immense industrial effort was organized to do this. Fermi's initial work was pure research and the rest was applied research.

Polanyi pointed out the fatal flaw in the argument that science should be organized for its social benefits, namely that it is impossible to foresee the results of any particular piece of pure research. For example, Rutherford, who discovered the nucleus and led the early research in nuclear physics, said as late as 1936 that he could foresee no more than small-scale applications of nuclear physics.

As a result, it is not possible to foresee the best way to solve a particular social problem. Polanyi took the development of domestic lighting as a example: first candles, then gas, electric light, and fluorescent tubes. There are no logical steps from one to the next, and they come from different areas of pure research. Thus, if a scientist had been given the task of improving domestic lighting, he might well have developed an improved type of candle, but he would never have discovered electricity. The advances in pure science are made by those who are filled with curiosity to find out about the world. They notice a strange phenomenon, such as thunderstorms or the behaviour of lodestone, and try to understand it. Now and then they make a breakthrough, and then there may be totally unexpected benefits that affect the lives of millions of people.

History provides numerous examples. The historian Frederick Artz recalls that Cicero praised the Romans because, unlike the Greeks, they were able "to confine the study of mathematics to the domain of useful applications." As a result, the growth of science stopped short in the second century. Nearer the present time, if Roentgen had been told to improve medical diagnosis, he would never have discovered X-rays. If Madame Curie had been told to find a cure for cancer, she would never have discovered radium. Michael Faraday was investigating the effects of an electric current and found that it would made a wheel turn. A lady who watched his demonstration asked what use it was. "What, madam, is the use of a baby," replied Faraday. In 1932 the Moscow Polytechnic Museum arranged a special exhibition showing the disintegration of 7Li into two alpha-particles by proton bombardment. Stalin came and asked "What is the use of splitting the nucleus?"

The lesson is clear. Truth must be sought for its own sake, not for any utilitarian ends, however praiseworthy they may be. Christ told us to "Seek first the kingdom of God and the rest will be added to you." Thus, if we set out to solve a particular social problem, applied science will produce an improvement. Without any planning, pure science, in a completely unexpected way, can produce a revolution.

It is thus impossible, and potentially disastrous, to try to direct pure scientific research for the good of mankind. It is essential to allow scientific research to develop in accord with its own internal criteria. It is only the actively working scientist, immersed in the present state of knowledge in a particular field, who knows what is worth doing next. He or she may be wrong, of course. The proposed experiment may not work, and the bright idea may turn out to be a blind alley. But gradually, through discussion, trial and error, the work of many scientists eventually leads to an increase in knowledge and understanding. The true scientist has a passion to know more about nature, and an insatiable curiosity to find our about the world. No other motive is acceptable: work undertaken for any other reason will almost certainly come to nothing.

This does not imply that every scientist should be given all the resources he asks for. That is quite impracticable. A wise government realizes that scientific research is not only valuable in itself, but leads to valuable practicable applications. But it has every right to insist, and indeed it must ensure, that the scientists it supports have adequate training, proved ability, and a project approved by peer review. It is prudent to insist on high standards, and every research proposal deserves careful scrutiny by independent experts before it is eligible for state funds. It is also desirable that there are two or more independent sources of support, so that a scientist whose application has been turned down by one source, perhaps unreasonably, can then apply to another. Scientists are fallible, have their likes and dislikes, and may be unable to perceive the merits of a proposal. It must be accepted that some experiments have a high chance of failing, but still deserve support if success would be very important. Other proposals may be sure to give some results, though they may not be sensational. There is a place for both types of research.

Scientists engaged in pure research can also, by their teaching and example, inspire the next generation of scientists. It has been well said that:

> He who learns from one engaged in learning
> Drinks the clear water of the running stream.
> But he who learns from one who has learned all he will ever know
> Drinks the green mantle of the stagnant pool.

The students who are taught by research scientists are the teachers and university lecturers of the future. This is indeed "social relevance." If scientists are prevented from doing scientific research in the only way that scientific research can be done, that is by giving them the freedom to choose their line of work, they will simply shake the dust of that country off their feet, and leave for a land where research is understood and respected.

To avoid this outcome, what must absolutely be avoided is to ask the scientist to show that his proposed research is socially relevant in some way. This is simply absurd, and if it is taken seriously is the sure road to mediocrity. This has not been understood by those responsible for public spending, and scientists are becoming, in self-defence, adept in finding ways to show that their proposed research, in fact designed to answer a fundamental question about nature, is also socially relevant. This is simply ridiculous, and those who impose such a requirement show that they have not understood the first thing about scientific research and the way to enable it to contribute to the welfare of mankind.

Universities

Most scientific research takes place in universities, and so it is important that they provide the conditions that enable it to flourish. It is notable that there has been a marked deterioration in those conditions in recent years.

As in the case of research itself, this stems from a good motive, vitiated by lack of understanding of the true situation. The admirable motive is to ensure that all the teaching and research is done well. To ensure this the authorities launch assessment exercises, so that every teacher and researcher is periodically sent detailed questionnaires asking a series of questions about their activities. Their replies are evaluated, and suitable remedial action is taken to correct any defects. In theory this sounds fine, but in practice it is a disaster. It is but one facet of a disease that increasingly paralyses our society.[1]

There are many chilling examples of this. Thus in Britain there is a growing shortage of competent science and mathematics teachers in schools, and we all know how important they are to inspire their students with a love of the subject. Most of us can trace our own interests to an inspired teacher. One reason for the shortage is not so much the financial rewards, which of course could be improved to good effect, but the cascade of instructions and questions and regulations and changes in the syllabus to be taught that descend on them from above. To deal with all this takes up so much time that teachers hardly have time or energy left to teach, and their family life suffers. Many regretfully decide to leave the profession, thus exacerbating the shortage.

Much the same is happening in the medical profession. The backbone of the medical profession, the family doctor, is feeling disillusioned and burnt out, and is opting for early retirement. The

[1] J. Magueijo, *Faster than the Speed of Light* (Cambridge, MA: Perseus Publishing, 2002), 204–5.

basic trouble is that politicians increased the number of National Health Service (NHS) managers from 500 to 24,000 in order, so they thought, to increase efficiency by running an internal market. Of course this failed to work, so the politicians abolished the internal market, but the managers remained, who thereupon looked for something to do. So they started to tell family doctors how to do their jobs. As Dr. Le Fanu remarks, "No words can describe the incomprehensible verbiage about standards, targets and protocols that showers down daily from on high."[2] The only result is the virtual destruction of doctors' morale.

Recently the new national budget increased the allocation for health care by billions of pounds. The newspapers were then filled with advertisements for more "liaison officers, regional development co-ordinators, race awareness counsellors, community outreach workers and the like." Huge salaries are paid to the highest managers of the Health Service, while the waiting list for people urgently requiring operations grows ever longer.

All this happens through the neglect of a very simple principle, one that is so blindingly obvious to everyone engaged in actually doing something constructive that it is not necessary to articulate it. By the same token, it is completely unknown to the bureaucrats who have never in their lives done anything constructive.

That principle was articulated with great clarity by an Oxford philosopher[3] who was employed by the Treasury before he was appointed to Oxford. His office in the Treasury was responsible for an organization in charge of the geological survey of East Africa. He had to check the accounts, and one day he received an "Application to Destroy Stores." Reading the document carefully, he realized that the stores in question had already been destroyed. "Ah ha," he said to himself "something is very wrong here." So he sent off a letter drawing their attention to the grave lapse of proper procedure. A few days later he received a telephone call from a man who said that he would

---

[2] Dr. James Le Fanu, "Farewell to the Wise Ones of the Family." *Daily Telegraph*, (23 October 2001): 23.

[3] David Wiggins, "Valediction for a Sub-Faculty." *Oxford Magazine*, (Fourth Week, Trinity Term, 2001): 8.

like to explain how things worked in East Africa. They take their equipment by jeep as far as they can go, and then use mules or carry it themselves through rough country for the rest of the journey. When they have finished their work, they collect the equipment that is still in good order and carry it back. However, some things by then are wrecked or useless. Were they really expected to carry useless equipment all the way back to the camp? At this point the future philosopher suddenly saw the light, and immediately promised the caller never ever to write such a letter again. He had learned in an instant something that current theories and practices of administration make almost unlearnable: "Those who do the work, once it is entrusted to them, must do it in accord with criteria internal to the work, which are implicit in the work." This principle should be engraved in letters of stone on all schools and universities.

He could have learned the same principle from the Papal Encyclical *Quadragesimo Anno* of Pius XI published in 1931 as a response to fascism and communism. There he enunciated the principle of subsidiarity, namely that a higher level of an organization should never arrogate to itself what a lower level can perfectly well carry out on its own. Individuals and intermediate institutions should have the freedom to exercise their proper responsibilities: "Just as it is wrong to take away from individuals what they can accomplish by their own ability and effort and entrust it to a community, so it is an injury and at the same time both a serious evil and a disturbance of right order to assign to a larger and higher society what can be performed successfully by smaller and lower communities." This was the basis of his teaching on social structure.

Another great Victorian, the Duke of Wellington, experienced intolerable interference from bureaucrats in London when he was in the midst of fighting Napoleon in the Peninsular War. He was driven to write to Secretary of State: "My Lord, if I attempted to answer the mass of futile correspondence that surrounds me, I should be debarred from all serious business of campaigning. . . . I shall see no officer under my command is debarred by attending to the futile driveling of mere quill driving from attending his first duty, which is and always has been so to train the private men under his command that they may without question beat any force opposed to them in the field."

The simple principle of non-interference is forgotten by every generation. A few years ago the universities in Britain were subjected to a research assessment exercise. We each received a thick wad of forms, with four pages of questions to be answered for each piece of research we had undertaken during the last two years. The amount of time that was wasted by completing such questionnaires is appalling, and one may well ask who are the mighty intellects able to read and assess the information provided by the hundred or so physicists at Oxford, experienced as they are in a wide range of specialities across the whole of physics? A colleague was so incensed that he wrote a letter to the *University Magazine*: "When I and my friends read these forms, we all fell about laughing. We asked ourselves whatever could be the purpose of these forms? Then we understood; obviously the university wanted to find out which members of its academic staff were mentally deficient, because obviously you were if you answered all these questions. Well, mine's in the bin, and if they want it they will find it there." He was rather unpopular with the university administration after that.

Rutherford was characteristically outspoken about the dangers of interference. He "foresaw that it was essential for men of science to take an interest in the administration of their own affairs or else the professional civil servants would step in—and then, the Lord help you!"

The lesson to be learned by universities is that scientists must be free to decide not only their field of research but the subjects they teach and how they should teach them. With freedom comes responsibility. It is inevitable that some scientists are more conscientious than others, but it is far better to put up with the occasional failure than to waste everyone's time with interminable questionnaires and assessment exercises that rarely have any good results. This also has a very important effect on morale. If people are trusted, most will do the best they can, well beyond the call of duty.

But if they are continually subject to assessments and interference they will not feel trusted, and will react by doing only what they are legally required to do, and no more. Since universities, and indeed all complex organizations, depend on people doing far more than their specified duties, this leads to a general breakdown of trust and efficiency.

Many universities wisely arrange tuition for newly appointed lecturers in the art of lecturing. After lecturing for about fifty years I went to one such course, and was required to give part of a sample lecture to some students and staff. I spoke about Rutherford's discovery of the nucleus, and learned some useful techniques from their comments. However, I mentioned that Rutherford remarked that his result was as surprising as the recoil of a 15-inch shell from a piece of tissue paper and was criticized for using the military metaphor!

National Politics

In the past, there have been several examples of governments that have presumed to direct science according to some ideological beliefs. There are several examples of this in rather recent history.

Thus the theoreticians of the Nazi Party in Germany developed the concept of "Ayran Science" distinct from the "Jewish Science" of Einstein, and Hitler declared that the idea of a free and unfettered science is absurd. This Ayran science was supported by a few well-known scientists like Stark and Lenard, who thereby rose to high positions in the academic establishment. Not a few scientists firmly opposed them, with great courage, and were exiled or removed from office. As a result, science in Germany was gravely hampered for a generation, and took twenty years to recover.

Much more pervasive and at times crude restrictions on the freedom of science occurred in countries where Marx–Leninism is imposed as the state orthodoxy. At the beginning of the revolution it was proclaimed that science is based on the iron rock of materialist dialectical thought and notices to that effect appeared in the scientific journals. Some scientists in Germany wrote saying that they were very interested to hear about this new scientific method, and would they please send them someone to tell them about it. The

Russian scientists, who did not believe it themselves, were much embarrassed by this invitation.

In the following years there were many clashes between the party theoreticians and the scientists that led at various times to the condemnation of the theory of relativity and also that of molecular bonding, and the virtual destruction of the science of genetics by Lysenko. Most scientists however managed to continue their work in spite of many restrictions, giving lip-service to the prevailing ideology as the price of survival.

These oppressive regimes no longer exist, and in their place we have democratic governments. One might have imagined that, knowing very well the potentialities of science and technology, such governments would welcome the advice of scientists concerning the best policies to adopt. Most politicians, however, are far more concerned with maintaining public support, even if that means enacting laws that hamper scientific advancement. As a result there are not only the pressures on scientific research already mentioned, but in addition the whole development of technology is governed by political considerations.

One obnoxious feature of contemporary public discussions is that they are often dominated by hidden motives, so much so that they are allowed to dominate the debate. Instead of listening to one's arguments, they are dismissed by alleging hidden motives. If I talk about nuclear power, this is attributed to my support of the global capitalist–militarist complex. Similarly I could say that those who argue against nuclear power are simply repeating Soviet propaganda designed to weaken the West. Another example is provided by the popularity of campaigns against global warming. This popularity is attributed to the belief that industrialisation and globalisation are enemies of humanity. This is a wonderful stick with which the weaker Western economies can beat up America and clothe anti-Western self-hatred in ostensibly scientific respectability. Whether all these allegations are true or not, they are irrelevant. Indeed they constitute an obstacle to the aim of the debate, which is to find the truth, which can be found only by examining the arguments as carefully and objectively as possible.

The result of all this is that decisions vitally important for our future are made on political grounds, often ignoring the scientific realities. Postponing decisions may not matter on the short term, but the longer they are delayed the greater will be the price that eventually we will all have to pay.

Conclusion

These examples of current policies and their effects show that scientific research is being hindered and is being prevented from making its full contribution to the welfare of mankind. This is being done by people who do not understand scientific research or the conditions for its growth, and by politicians and journalists who are more concerned with their own survival than with establishing the truth and acting upon it, however unpopular it may be. Scientists should not stand aside and let this happen.

CHAPTER 26

Science in the Life of the Church[*]

THE CHURCH is on the threshold of a new millennium, so it is an appropriate time to assess the present situation and to articulate our hopes for the future. It is always hazardous to look into the seeds of time, but hope is not prophecy and so we cannot be faulted if our hopes are unrealized. Nevertheless, if hope is to be realistic it must be based on solid fact and, whatever may happen in the next millennium, it seems almost certain that science and technology will play an even more important part than they did in the millennium just ending.

It is therefore vital that in all its activities the Church takes full account of the opportunities and dangers of science and technology. This is not only in the superficial sense of making use of technology in its work of spreading the Gospel, but in the more fundamental sense of being fully aware of the ideas and methodologies of science itself, and being alert to the likely effects of new technological developments on our lives and activities.

Many of the questions that need to be considered were discussed in a meeting of the Science Secretariat on "The Place of the Scientist in the Life of the Church" held in St. Albans in September

---

[*] Reprinted with permission from *Convergence.* 11 (2000): 32.

1998.[1] These discussions need to be continued and the conclusions implemented.

Science has profoundly altered the way we think about the world, and this affects our actions in many ways. We now know that we live on a relatively small blue ball orbiting the sun, itself a rather ordinary star on one of the spiral arms of a vast galaxy of stars, and that this galaxy is but one of many billions of such galaxies. The traditional teaching about heaven and hell, the Ascension and the Assumption, were easy to interpret in terms of a fixed earth at the centre of the world, but how should we think about them now?

The Galileo affair still casts a long shadow, despite his recent rehabilitation, and inclines theologians to be wary of science. They are not reassured by the secularist and anti-theological tone of many popular scientific writers. We may indeed be confident that the Church will not make the same mistake again.

One of the most pervasive impressions that we need to dispel is that there is a natural opposition between religion in general, and theology in particular, and modern science. Religion is often seen as a primitive irrational belief system, now replaced by the rational certainties of science. We no longer pray for health; we go to the doctor. Such views are very widespread and influential, and can only be dispelled by the writings and example of Catholic and other believing scientists. Within the Church these beliefs take a somewhat different form. It is, one hopes, recognized that science is the study of the world made by God and so must be good in itself. Very often, however, the exponents of science adopt a markedly hostile attitude to religion, and so science comes to be seen not as a friend to be welcomed but as an enemy to be repulsed. Many Catholics, recognizing the harm done by scientism, and lacking the specialised knowledge to analyze the roots of the difficulties, react by disparaging science, thus widening the gap. As Professor Tanzella-Nitti pointed out in his lecture at St. Albans,[2] many theologians feel uncomfortable when speaking of science, as if they

---

[1] *The Place of the Scientist in the Life of the Church,* papers presented at the meeting of the Secretariat for Scientific Questions, Pax Romana. Edited by P. E. Hodgson (St. Albans: Science Secretariat of Pax Romana, 1998).

[2] Ibid.

were in a foreign land. As a result, the reference to natural science in the major encyclicals on Sacred Scripture, for example, was primarily intended to reaffirm the absence of contradictions between the results of science and the word of God and prevent theologians from unnecessary changes in the exegesis of the biblical texts.

Providentissims Deus (1893) by Leo XIII is an example of a document written in an age of conflict. In a certain sense, this document considers science more as an invader needing to be driven back into its methodological domain rather than an ally from whom something can be learned. There has been some improvement since those days, but the tendency to see science as an entity outside the Church with whom we somehow have to come to terms is still widespread. Thus until recently it was the Pontifical Consilium for Non-believers that dealt with scientific matters; now, more happily, it is renamed the Pontifical Consilium for Culture. As Professor Tanzella-Nitti reminds us, "the way to overcome the present situation is that claimed by John Paul II when he asked for intellectuals trained in both theological and scientific disciplines.[3]

The greater part of our task is convey our understanding of the relation between theology and science to all members of the Church, and this is done through the educational system at all levels and through the media. Starting at the beginning, the first exposure to these problems occurs in schools, then in universities, and finally in seminaries for those called to the priesthood.

There is much work to be done on these problems. Catholic teachers at all levels need to be well informed on the relation between science and their faith, and they can be helped in this respect by suitable publications. The same applies to university chaplains.

It is not possible to devote much time in seminaries to scientific questions, but this is vitally important. Our culture is pervaded by science, and priests must be able to deal with questions from parishioners, either by answering them directly or by referring the questioner to some person or book for an answer. People, especially young people, are always asking questions, and this keeps us on our

---

[3] Ibid.

toes. It is not satisfactory to brush questions aside with cheerful *bonhomie*: the questions themselves may be silly or ignorant, but they deserve to be taken seriously and answered respectfully and honestly. If the priest or teacher does not know the answer this must be admitted. Some teachers make the fatal mistake of believing that they would lose face if they do not have the answer to every question, so when they do not know the answer they guess it or make a few dismissive and superficial remarks that are immediately seen through by the questioner, who never bothers to ask any more questions. Students respect someone who admits that he does not know the answer, but promises to find out and talk about it later.

It hardly practicable to teach much science directly in seminaries. A brilliant approach using the story of Galileo has been developed by Fr. Sharratt of Ushaw, and is described in a paper presented at the St. Albans meeting. It would be useful to make a survey of the books on theology and science in seminary libraries. Those that I have seen are generally weak and contain books by well-known atheists and enemies of religion, but very rarely any books by writers like Duhem, Crombie, and Jaki who provide a sound and acceptable account. This could be remedied relatively easily, given the cooperation of the librarians, but needs to be backed up by lectures outlining the essentials of the subject. Another curious habit of seminaries is to invite atheist scientists to give lectures to them when they want to learn something about science. It seems to be assumed that all scientists are atheists; are they not aware that there are also some Catholic scientists who might be better equipped to lecture on the relation of theology to science? These activities, of course, strengthen the belief that science and the faith are inimical to each other.

The bishops have the heavy task of showing how the Christian faith can be applied to contemporary problems, and this often requires the cooperation of scientists. It is for them to decide what problems need to be addressed at a particular time; if they seldom do this they easily give the impression that the Church has nothing to say to the modern world. Politicians notoriously have their eye on the next election, if not the next cabinet reshuffle, whereas bishops can take a longer view in the light of moral principles. It follows that very often what they have to say will be against the prevailing view, particularly of those influenced by the mass media and their party's political opinions. It is very likely that they will be embroiled in fierce controversy, but if they explain clearly the ground for their intervention, and show a sure grasp of the relevant technicalities, they will in the long run gain respect. Many of the most urgent moral problems such as those concerned with population and energy are related to scientific or technological questions, and require expert knowledge. All too frequently the depth of knowledge required for an effective statement is seriously underestimated, and the resulting statement is superficial or even wrong. A close cooperation between the bishops and carefully chosen experts is essential if this is to be avoided. That is why the English and Welsh bishops declared that "the Church must draw into the work of evangelisation those Catholics who have an acknowledged competence in contemporary scientific disciplines.[4] Unfortunately little has been done to implement this fine statement.

We can well ask what the bishops might be expected to do in order to put their statement into practice, and then we realize that it is a complicated and difficult task. They might well appoint a panel of Catholic scientists to advise them on scientific matters, but it is not easy to say who are suitable candidates; indeed in this respect the situation is much worse than it was a few decades ago. It is not enough for them to be a well-qualified as scientists; it is also highly desirable that they are philosophically and theologically literate, and that is a much more difficult criterion to satisfy. In most cases, only those scientists who have been working in a particular field for years are able to evaluate the problems accurately and objectively. It is always flattering to be treated as an authority, and the temptation to pronounce on matters far beyond one's specialty is not always resisted. A smattering of knowledge, such as may be obtained by taking a

4 Submission of the English and Welsh bishops to the Extraordinary Synod of Bishops held in Rome in November 1985.

degree in science followed after a few years research by a half-baked doctoral thesis, is not enough. As Duhem once remarked, "in order to speak of questions where science and Catholic theology touch one another, one must have done ten or fifteen years of study of the pure sciences."[5]

In the above remarks the Church is identified with the bishops, but of course the Church is really the whole body of the faithful. It is not realistic or sensible for the laity to sit back and expect the bishops to do everything and then complain that they do not do it very well. So what should priests and laypeople be doing to implement the statement? They can ensure that problems related to science are discussed properly, with the full involvement of qualified Catholic scientists. This means arranging meetings, asking them to give lectures and to write books and articles, and then listening to what they have to say. In that way it would be possible to build up a body of informed knowledge that can be drawn upon whenever the need arises. What actually happens is quite different. There seems to be no realization of the contribution that can be made by qualified scientists to the life of the Church. They are seldom invited to give lectures to Catholic audiences, are generally not able to publish their work in Catholic newspapers and magazines, and their books receive no publicity. The result of this neglect is that Catholic scientists soon find other outlets for their energies, and their unique contribution to the life of the Church is lost.

---

5 S. L. Jaki. *Uneasy Genius: The Life and Work of Pierre Duhem* (The Hague: Martinus Nijhoff Publisher, 1984), 114.

Index

Name Index

Subject Index

N

O